Remembering Spain

*Essays, Memoirs and Poems on the
International Brigades and the Spanish Civil War*

From the pages of the magazine of
the International Brigade Memorial Trust

Edited by Joshua Newmark

Preface by Peter Anderson

The Clapton Press

© 2023 IBMT, Joshua Newmark and contributors

All rights reserved

ISBN 978-1-913693-24-4

Published by the International Brigade Memorial Trust in conjunction with The Clapton Press Limited

www.international-brigades.org.uk

The Clapton Press Limited
38 Thistlewaite Road
London E5 0QQ

www.theclaptonpress.com

Manchester volunteer Victor Shammah (left, with pipe) of the British Battalion poses with unknown individuals thought to be fellow members of the XV Brigade. Courtesy of the IBMT.

Contents

Preface
- *Peter Anderson* 11

Introduction
- *Joshua Newmark* 14

The Volunteers

Were the 'Britons' British?
- *Richard Baxell* 23

Rambling to Spain
- *Mike Wild* 30

Volunteers from the valleys
- *Graham Davies* 33

The Connolly Column
- *Manus O'Riordan* 38

The legacy of the Scottish volunteers
- *Mike Arnott* 43

From an English Guest
- *Christopher Caudwell* 46

Inspired by the struggle for national independence
- *Paul Philippou* 47

Cloudless Day in Spain
- *Jimmy Moon* 50

The War

Not such a quiet front
- *Marshall Mateer* 57

Death and confusion among the olives groves
- *Sam Lesser* 61

Madrid lived!
- *Ajmal Waqif* 65

Panic at Brunete
- *Cyril Sexton* 67

There's Wally
- *Bob Beagrie* 69

4am: the great advance begins
- *Nathan Clark* 72

Across the river and into the fire
- *Bob Cooney* 74

You fool, you fool, why did you have to shoot me?
- *Steve Fullarton* 77

The experience of imprisonment
- *Jerry Harris* 79

A revolution in battlefield surgery
  Mark Derby and David Lowe 82
A nurse's notes from the Aragón front
  Margaret Powell 86
La Rioja 1936
  David Merino 88
The lessons of Spain
  Frank Farr 90

Solidarity

The women who helped rescue Basque children
  Sarah Lonsdale 95
The seafarers who went on strike against Franco
  Jim Jump 98
Red Ellen in Spain
  Paula Bartley 101
Minor role, massive effort: the Independent Labour Party
  Christopher Hall 104
Artists for Spain
  Christine Lindey 107
Spain in the heart
  Sheena Evans 111
Forgotten plays about the civil war
  Simon Breden 114
For the happiness of the children of Spain
  Ajmal Waqif 117

Aftermath

The struggle never stopped
  Bill Alexander 121
From the Ebro to the Battle of Britain
  Geoff Cowling 125
Forgotten heroine of Spain and France
  Angela Jackson 127
Reluctantly finding a home in Britain
  Herminio Martínez 129
Dad's Army: the Spanish connection
  Peter Frost 132
Ramona: the militiawoman who settled in England
  Marshall Mateer 135
Shunned for their politics?
  Fraser Raeburn 138

From refugee boys to professional players
Daniel Gray 141

I was spied on for being an anti-fascist
Chris Birch 147

The publisher who took on Franco
Adrian Pole 149

Brigaders' Reunion
Connie Fraser 155

Reflections

An inspiring spirt of humanity
President Michael D. Higgins 159

New perspectives on Orwell's memoir
Jim Jump 165

Blinded by anti-communism?
Helen Graham 167

A sketch and a song return from the past
Jim Jump 170

Fighting fascism then and now
John Pilger 172

Little resemblance to history — or my own experience
John Dunlop 175

Necessary lessons for the left
Ken Loach 178

My friend, the Scottish anarchist who wanted to kill Franco
Paul Preston 181

Saluting the Brigaders' internationalism
Ronan Burtenshaw 183

The Brigades in theatre
Marlene Sidaway 186

Making history: an interview with Paul Preston
Paul Preston and Jim Jump 190

My Pyrenees crossing inspired by Nat Cohen and Laurie Lee
Dan Carrier 201

We must remember them by building a better world
Owen Jones 203

Witness as Hero
Francesca Beard 205

Index of Contributors 208

Select Index 209

List of Illustrations

British volunteer Victor Shammah with other International Brigaders . . 4

Sam Lesser and Margaret Powell among a group of volunteer fighters and nurses in Spain 21

Walter Levine in Spain 32

Glasgow statue of Dolores 'La Pasionaria' Ibárruri 45

Veterans Jimmy Moon and Dr Reginald Saxton raise the British Battalion banner in Reading 53

Thomas Chilvers's painting of the XV Brigade's Anti-Tank Battery . . . 55

Members of the Tom Mann Centuria at the Karl Marx Barracks in Barcelona 58

The original British Battalion memorial on the Jarama battlefield . . . 64

Members of the British Workers' Sports Federation at Moscow Station in July 1928 71

Painting by Pere Piquer of International Brigaders crossing the Ebro . . 78

Medical personnel Dr Doug Jolly and Anna-Marie Basch visiting the Catalan countryside 85

Frank Farr with the first British ambulance unit in Spain 90

Activists with a van from the 'Milk for Spain' campaign 93

Basque refugee children at a camp shortly after their arrival in England . 97

All London Friends of Spain Week poster designed by Priscilla Thornycroft 108

Portait of Dame Janet Maria Vaughan by Victoria Crowe 113

Syd Harris at an anti-fascist rally in Chicago after the war 119

Luftwaffe warplanes with Spanish Civil War markings during the Battle of Britain 126

Herminio Martínez with a photo of the *Habana* 131

Militiawoman Ramona Siles García in a cutting from a Catalan women's magazine 137

Chris and Betty Birch and Alec Digges protesting at the Spanish Embassy 146

David Lomon unveiling the plaque on London's Jubilee Gardens International Brigades memorial 155

Stained-glass window tribute to the International Brigades in Belfast City Hall 157

Long-lost sketch of Brigader David Lomon by fellow POW Clive Branson 171

Ken Loach on the set of *Land and Freedom* 180

Poster from Teatre del Raval performance of *Goodbye Barcelona* . . 185

Actor David Heywood as Clem 'Dare Devil' Beckett in *Dare Devil Rides to Barcelona* 188

Paul Preston book launch in 1978 with Felipe González 191

Paul Preston addresses the 2016 International Brigade annual commemoration in London 198

Preface

Peter Anderson

On 28 August 1933, the *New York Times* correspondent in Berlin sent news of 65 concentration camps dotted across Germany. Hitler had not yet begun his full-scale onslaught against the Jews but Frederick T. Birchall reported that the Nazis had detained up to 45,000 prisoners in the camps 'on account of their political views.' The concentration camp at Dachau stood out as one of the largest with 3,500 political prisoners. Birchall carefully recorded that a further 45,000 political prisoners languished in police detention. He grimly observed too that walls, barbed wire and electric fences all encircled the camps while rifle-wielding guards patrolled the grounds. Among those incarcerated behind the wires stood a former member of the German parliament, the *Reichstag*; others interned included students, professors, businessmen and a large number of ordinary workers. Birchall also knew of several prisoners with scars on their backs from the floggings they had received. The report's message burned brightly and if anyone had harboured doubts about what fascism meant, those watching events unfold in Germany since Hitler's arrival in power on 30 January 1933 could only conclude that it signified terror, the destruction of democracy and the crushing of political freedom.

Despite the brutality of Hitler's actions, many appeared unwilling to stare reality in the face. The debate over Hitler's *Mein Kampf* helps tell this story. An English-language edition of the Nazi leader's notorious book appeared in abridged form in London in October 1933 to disquiet but not to consternation for the safety of world. E.C. Bentley in the *Daily Telegraph* certainly denounced Hitler's fanaticism, his delusions and his violent, unintelligent antisemitism. Hitler's lust for war and expansion, however, went unremarked. In other circles, more forgiving interpretations flourished, and the *Anglo-German Review* judged *My Struggle* 'innocuous' and 'a work of amazing moderation.' One of the reasons for this blind spot comes across in the *Manchester Guardian* on 13 October 1933 in an article on the English edition of Hitler's book. The article pointed out that while the German original stacked up over 225,000 words, the translation ran to just 100,000. The omissions, the newspaper announced, included 'much that is fundamental to the true understanding of Hitlerism.' Prime among these fundamental exclusions lay foreign policy, including purged sentences such as 'The aim of German foreign policy for today must be the preparation for wresting back freedom tomorrow'. For the *Manchester Guardian* the pitiful translation gave no idea of the true nature of 'Nazi expansionism' revealed in the German original.

Hitler's actions, and those of his Italian kindred spirt Benito Mussolini, soon revealed what the abridged edition of *Mein Kampf* hid. In October 1933, Hitler withdrew Germany from the League of Nations because, he claimed, it prevented Germany from making weapons and building up its armed forces. The UK and France neither protested nor imposed sanctions. Hitler had feared a stronger reaction and drew comfort from his success. In March 1935, Hitler introduced conscription and, in the process, breached the Treaty of Versailles once more. Members of the League of Nations, however, refrained from criticising Hitler for fear of deterring him from rejoining the League. In June 1935, the British signed an agreement with Hitler that allowed Germany to build up its navy, which again contravened the Treaty of Versailles. Mussolini watched carefully as the British offered this series of concessions to Germany and concluded he could force the British to march to his drum beat. Mussolini began to demand control of Ethiopia and in October 1935 his forces invaded the country. The emboldened Mussolini declared 'No one in Europe will raise difficulties, if the military situation is resolved speedily.' The Italians proved greedy to win swift success and unleashed planes, bombing raids and modern weapons against the poorly armed Ethiopians. Mussolini's son Bruno left this description of a bombing raid:

> After the bomb racks were emptied I began throwing bombs by hand ... It was most amusing ... I had to aim carefully at the straw roof and only succeeded at the third shot. The wretches who were inside, seeing their roof burning, jumped out and ran off like mad. Surrounded by a circle of fire about five thousand Abyssinians came to a sticky end. It was like hell.

Despite the hesitancy of governments to act, a growing number of observers lay in no doubt that fascism represented political terror, foreign aggression and a lust for violence. In the United Kingdom, Walter Gregory drew this conclusion and volunteered in the fight against fascism in Spain. He grew up in a working-class home in Lincoln where he gazed on as his father's name went on an employers' blacklist for union activists. Undeterred, as a young man he joined a union and then the Workers' Education Association where he took an ever-keener interest in foreign affairs. As he observed Hitler and Mussolini's aggression, he gave up on his pacifist beliefs and resolved that fascism 'would have to be met with force.' He began his fight at home in brawls with the British Union of Fascists and continued it in Spain on the battlefield against General Franco.

In the United States James Yates resolved like Walter Gregory to fight fascism in Spain. He had grown up in Mississippi in an African-American family where the state provided African Americans with miserable education and his family endured terrible wages as well as high prices while having to live in the climate of fear created by Ku Klux Klan violence. Yates escaped to Chicago where he joined a union and campaigned both for workers and the unemployed. In these struggles he stood shoulder to shoulder with white workers and quickly recognised fascism as a threat to trade-union rights, political freedom and world peace. His beliefs led him to join the League against War and Fascism and to follow events in Ethiopia and Spain. Ethiopia mattered especially because it stood out as one of the few African countries that had escaped European colonialists until Mussolini took control of the country in 1936. Spain mattered too. In 1931, it had become a progressive Republic and democracy and provided a great contrast with other countries in Europe falling under the grip of fascism. James Yates stood in solidarity with his comrades in Spain and declared in his memoirs that if the Spanish Second Republic had come to power in the United States it 'would have brought Black people to the top levels of government . . . Spain was the perfect example for the world I dreamed of.'

This book judiciously put together by Joshua Newmark tells the story of volunteers like Walter Gregory and James Yates who put their lives on the line to join the struggle against fascism in the war unleashed in Spain against the Second Republic in July 1936 by rebels including General Francisco Franco. The Spanish general enjoyed the support of Hitler and Mussolini who between them sent aircraft and tens of thousands of troops while the British and French governments quickly proved unwilling to take a stand. Unable to countenance another victory for fascism, volunteers like Gregory and Yates hoped they could end foreign aggression, prevent a second world war and protect the world from the violence and political terror they knew characterised Hitler's and Mussolini's regimes.

Peter Anderson is Professor of Twentieth-Century Spanish History at the University of Leeds. His books include *The Francoist Military Trials: Terror and Complicity, 1939-1945* (2010), *Friend or Foe? Occupation, Collaboration and Selective Violence in the Spanish Civil War* (2016), and *The Age of Mass Child Removal in Spain: Taking, Losing, and Fighting for Children, 1926-1945* (2021). He has also collaborated with the International Brigade Memorial Trust to produce materials for schools to teach about anti-fascism in the 1930s.

Introduction

Joshua Newmark

Between 1936 and 1939, some 2,500 men and women from Britain and Ireland served in the International Brigades, a force of anti-fascist volunteers from around the world who fought for the Spanish Second Republic during the Spanish Civil War. The democratic Republic was under threat from a *coup d'état* launched by right-wing generals — one of whom, Francisco Franco, would come to rule over Spain as an ironfisted dictator for more than 30 years — with support from Hitler's Nazi Germany and Mussolini's Fascist Italy. The International Brigades, organised and overseen by the Communist International (Comintern), formed the most visible and dramatic expression of international solidarity with the Spanish people's plight and of the determination of workers and progressive people everywhere to resist the spread of fascism.

In putting together this book, an edited collection of contributions to the International Brigade Memorial Trust (IBMT)[1] magazine from the past 20 years, I have aimed to reflect as best as possible the Trust's own mission — to understand and educate with accuracy about the Spanish Civil War, while also remembering and preserving the legacy of the British and Irish volunteers in the International Brigades. Historical essays from some of the foremost historians and researchers in the field of Spanish Civil War history are intermingled with thought-provoking reflections from International Brigade supporters and enthusiasts, along with a healthy dose of the voices of Brigade veterans themselves — especially important now that they are no longer with us. The book thus looks to commemorate, celebrate, but also — to an extent — interrogate, challenging a few myths and legends regarding the Spanish Civil War and its foreign volunteers even while foregrounding the spirit of solidarity, courage, and sacrifice in favour of freedom and democracy which is the invaluable legacy of the Brigaders.

Who were the British and Irish volunteers, and why did they go? Although attention has often focused on the intellectuals and writers who went to Spain — George Orwell, Laurie Lee, and Ernest Hemingway, among others, some of whom did not serve in the Brigades — the bulk of international volunteers came from workingclass backgrounds and occupations. As the essays in this book will make clear, their solidarity and ideals had been shaped by personal experiences, such as mobilising as or alongside unemployed workers in the Hunger Marches, or partaking in the mass

---

[1] Organisation founded by veterans and their families alongside activists and academics, and dedicated to preserving and promoting the memory and legacy of the volunteers for Spain from Britain and Ireland and all those who supported them and the Spanish Republic's cause at home. The magazine was formerly the *IBMT Newsletter*, subsequently *IBMT Magazine* and is now entitled *¡No Pasarán!* <www.international-brigades.org.uk>.

trespass of Kinder Scout in April 1932, described in Mike Wild's contribution to this volume — in both cases, making visible and protesting the cruel inequalities which afflicted a country barely one generation away from the trauma of the First World War. For those with a keen eye for blatant social injustice and the drive to confront it, the cause of Spain was a compelling one: the country's traditional elites (the generals, the Church, and the landowners) linking arms with Europe's fascist dictators in a violent crusade against a moderate programme of social reform.

While many of the volunteers first embodied their anti-fascist ideals on Spanish battlefields, a large proportion of them had already 'held the line' at home, disrupting the activities of the aspiring dictator Sir Oswald Mosley and his antisemitic British Union of Fascists and Blackshirt thugs — most famously at Cable Street in October 1936, where direct action blocked the fascists' attempt to march through the Jewish East End of London. In Ireland, many volunteers had also grappled with Eoin O'Duffy's fascist Blueshirts. Meanwhile, these Irish volunteers were often already veterans of one struggle for the independence of a republic — a struggle which many of them had attempted to shape in a more socialist direction. However, as Manus O'Riordan's contribution to this volume points out, Irish volunteers came from all the island's communities: in Spain, against Franco's insurgency, 'every republican was a loyalist and every loyalist a Republican.'[2]

Within the British Battalion, other minorities had their own particular experiences with opposing oppression. As Paul Philippou explains in his chapter, many Cypriots — such as Michael ('Mick') Economides, who also appears in Bob Cooney's recollections from the Battle of the Ebro — observed an overlap between fighting for Spain's independence from fascist invaders and their own struggle for national liberation from British colonial rule. And Jewish volunteers — who constituted between 10 and as many as 20 percent of the British Battalion's members, according to Richard Baxell's essay here — were often well-accustomed to fighting reactionary bigotry, whether in organised or unorganised form. As told in Jerry Harris's chapter in this volume, his father Syd, for example, had as a youth lost his job for knocking down a stockyard foreman who called him an antisemitic slur; in Spain, where he fought with the American Lincoln Battalion, his sacrifice would be greater — a bullet wound and a year's imprisonment at the hands of the Francoists.

It is also crucial to acknowledge the organisations that had helped to shape and politicise the volunteers. Most British volunteers were members of the Communist Party of Great Britain, and the Party was the main facilitator of volunteers heading to Spain. For example, Graham Davies's chapter here on the Welsh volunteers claims that 70 percent of them were Communist Party members. Christopher Hall's contribution to this volume also notes the valiant — albeit far smaller-scale — efforts of the radical Independent Labour Party (ILP) in providing volunteers (both for the International Brigades and for its own ILP contingent) and in fundraising and propaganda work back in the UK. Other volunteers were members of the Labour Party — despite the lethargy

---

[2] The Spanish Republicans were also known as 'loyalists' — loyal to the elected government, against the Francoist military rebellion.

of the party leadership in supporting the Spanish Republic — and the trade unions. In addition, many volunteers had been members of left-wing sporting clubs such as the socialist cyclists of the National Clarion Cycle Club, and the communist-aligned British Workers' Sports Federation — members of which were instrumental in the aforementioned Kinder Scout trespass. These were not, then, naive individual idealists. Rather, they came largely through their prior involvement with organisations which had given them some political education (continued in the Brigades through the work of the political commissars), a sense of comradeship, and a recognition that sincerely held ideals could only be achieved through practical action and struggle.

The tragic edge of the last point would be driven home by their wartime experiences in Spain. Even moments of glory — successfully holding the line at Jarama to prevent an early encirclement of Madrid, as retold in Ajmal Waqif's chapter, for example — had their corresponding, and heavy, costs. First-hand recollections, such as those of Cyril Sexton (Brunete) and Steve Fullarton (Gandesa) give a sense of the experience of chaos, panic, and tragic loss which was inevitable for the combat troops of an army locked into a war it would eventually lose against a better-equipped enemy: experiences at the core of Bob Beagrie's poem about the death of volunteer Wally Tapsell. Many of those who survived were subjected to the trauma of imprisonment at the hands of captors who would often haul away their Spanish fellow prisoners amid a constant tide of executions; many also suffered battle wounds. The efforts of volunteer nurses such as Margaret Powell and Madge Addy and doctors such as the New Zealander Doug Jolly were valiant and even innovative; but this testifies to the relentlessness of the deluge of wounded combatants at the same time as it signifies the heroism of the medical personnel.

Even before the formation of the British Battalion, volunteers were involved in early fighting in Aragón and on Mallorca, in the defence of Madrid which prevented an early end to the war, and at Lopera in the south of Spain. Later, the battalion was again at the defence of Madrid in the Battle of Jarama, and formed part of Republican offensives — all of which ultimately ended in failure — at Brunete, Aragón (again), Teruel, and the Ebro. An exhaustive account of the battles in which the British and Irish volunteers fought is not provided here: rather, the choice of texts included in the book aims to reflect these different realities of the war, from courage and glimpses of triumph, to failings and tragedy. In the case of the three consecutive first-hand accounts from the Battle of the Ebro (Nathan Clark, Bob Cooney, Steve Fullarton), these themes emerge more or less in sequence, as exciting early gains from the river crossing were quickly offset by supply problems and eventually swallowed by defeat. The intermingling of themes is also seen in Sam Lesser's description of an incident during his convalescence after the Battle of Lopera: despite moving on crutches due to wounds sustained in disastrous friendly fire, he was nonetheless eager to confront a Franco-sympathising Foreign Office representative, his resolute anti-fascism undimmed. Meanwhile, the lyrics of rapper David Merino's 'La Rioja 1936', translated and republished here, offer a reminder of what the Republic and its allies were fighting against: the unrelenting and brutal violence which followed closely behind Franco's forces as they progressed in their twisted 'crusade' through Spain.

Solidarity extended beyond volunteering to fight or to treat the wounded. Overseas supporters went to great lengths to raise funds for, and publicise, the cause of the Spanish Republic — as highlighted in Sheena Evans's chapter on Janet Vaughan, whose daughter could vividly recall returning home as a child to find that all the furniture had been sold off to raise money for the Spanish Medical Aid Committee. Artists, writers, and actors went to work in support of the Republic through groups like the Artists' International Association, explored here by Christine Lindey, and the Unity Theatre, recounted by Simon Breden. And some individuals exposed themselves to considerable danger and discomfort to rescue refugees — particularly the 4,000 Basque children evacuated from Bilbao in May 1937, a few weeks after the barbaric fascist bombardment of Guernica — as dramatically retold by Sarah Lonsdale. Ajmal Waqif points out that children elsewhere in Spain also received the direct solidarity of the International Brigades, whose members organised activities and established residences for refugee and orphaned children in the rearguard. Meanwhile, contrary to the examples of grassroots solidarity for the Republic, the British government supported the farcical policy of 'Non-Intervention' in Spain. In reality, 'Non-Intervention' did not prevent Franco from benefitting from a constant stream of German and Italian support, but the Republic was severely restricted in its ability to buy arms, and left largely dependent on the Soviet Union for its military supplies. Jim Jump's chapter on a strike by one group of seafarers highlights the efforts of some workers — against the will of many union bosses and bureaucrats — to resist this imparity by refusing to carry a Spain-bound cargo of nitrates which they feared would be used to manufacture Francoist bombs. And Paula Bartley's essay on 'Red' Ellen Wilkinson includes the radical Labour MP's endeavours to challenge Non-Intervention.

If solidarity extended far beyond the frontline in Spain, widening the spatial scope of the war, many of those involved felt that the conflict's temporal boundaries extended beyond 1936–1939. As British Battalion commander Bill Alexander recalled in the title of a 1989 article, republished here: 'the struggle never stopped.' After the International Brigades were disbanded in October 1938, and even after Franco declared victory on 1 April 1939, veterans and their supporters continued to battle against the dictator and support the Republican exiles, political prisoners, and clandestine opposition however they could. Although, as Fraser Raeburn explores here, their Spanish Civil War past could be an obstacle, many veterans were active in the Second World War, seeking to continue the fight against fascism. Thus would Johnny Longstaff, treated by Doug Jolly in Mataró for a facial wound from the Battle of Ebro, find himself back on Dr Jolly's operating table in Italy six years later for fresh wounds sustained there: a startling example of this continuity, mentioned in Mark Derby and David Lowe's essay here about the New Zealander doctor. While a large number of ex-Brigaders served within the mainstream British Armed Forces, others had more heterodox experiences — whether Tom Wintringham, who was instrumental in establishing the Home Guard (of *Dad's Army* fame) which he was subsequently barred from joining due to his communism, or nurse Madge Addy, whose daring wartime missions behind Nazi lines are touched on here by Angela Jackson. Like the many Spanish Republicans who fought in theatres such as the liberation of France, these ex-Brigaders often hoped, ultimately in vain, that the defeat of Hitler and Mussolini would lead inexorably to the toppling of Franco's dictatorship.

At the same time, although the British government severely limited their number, some Spanish Republicans and their families found refuge in the UK. The story of the iconic militiawoman Ramona Siles — who left Spain to accompany her wounded Brigader husband, Nat Cohen — is told by Marshall Mateer, including the later efforts by Siles and Cohen to support their local *colonia* of child refugees. While Daniel Gray's contribution to this volume describes how some of these young refugees would go on to illustrious careers in the world of football, a first-hand recollection by one of the Basque children, Herminio Martínez, offers a different perspective, focused on the difficulties and disillusionments of the early years of exile and the endeavours to preserve a connection with Spanish culture. Continuing the spirit of 'Non-Intervention', the British state did not offer an especially warm welcome to many of the Spanish refugees. Moreover, Chris Birch's essay here — written following a visit to the National Archives, many decades later — reveals that Franco's opponents in the UK were rewarded for their efforts on behalf of Spanish political prisoners in the 1940s and 1950s with seemingly relentless surveillance by the British intelligence services.

Another ongoing struggle has concerned how the civil war itself is retold — both in academia and in our public memory. Adrian Pole's essay on the Ruedo Ibérico publishing house, founded by Spanish exiles in Paris, gives a sense of the efforts to which the Francoists went in order to evade the truth of the war, and highlights the role that some British and Irish writers were able to play in helping to illuminate the recent past for a curious Spanish public living under a censorious dictatorship. Meanwhile, the IBMT and its predecessors have worked to support the legacy of the Brigades and their cause — first by supporting the veterans, and subsequently by preserving their memory. Jim Jump here recounts how the Trust was able to reunite David Lomon with a sketch by fellow Brigader Clive Branson, which dated from their shared captivity as POWs, and which helped him to reflect on his time in Spain, and Marlene Sidaway's theatrical reviews highlight recent efforts by Brigade supporters to portray the heroism of the volunteers on stage.

However, for an anglophone public, perhaps the most well-known portrayals of the Spanish Civil War are George Orwell's *Homage to Catalonia* and Ken Loach's *Land and Freedom* — both of which adopt a rather more critical posture towards the Republic and those who went to fight for it. But while Orwell and Loach's works have their own merits, we should also recognise their limitations in conveying the complex realities of the war. Whereas Loach's essay here makes a compelling case for why the particular sub-plot of the war which is treated in *Land and Freedom* was worthy of a cinematic exploration given its lessons for the Left, the critical review by Brigade veteran John Dunlop underlines the enduring nature of many of the controversies which first divided the shaky coalition fighting against Franco. Meanwhile, Jim Jump draws on the analysis of leading historian Helen Graham in applying some nuance to Orwell's account, while acknowledging the value of his personal observations as a militia veteran and witness to the war. And Helen Graham's own contribution here, an insightful review of Antony Beevor's popular military history of the Spanish Civil War, poses the question of the extent to which Cold War-era anti-communism has shaped and determined the way the war has been understood — a point upheld by her fellow eminent historian Paul Preston in his interview in this volume, which touches on many themes of interest to those with an appetite for twentieth-century Spanish history. Preston's obituary for his friend Stuart Christie — Scottish anarchist, writer, and would-be assassin of Francisco Franco — is also reprinted here, as a gesture of acknowledgement towards the anarchist movement which was such an integral part of the struggle against the Francoists.

In Richard Baxell's opening chapter, he discusses the 'nationality question' in the Brigades, where some have argued that national differences, rivalries and even prejudices undermined the internationalist credibility of the volunteers. But, as Baxell points out, none of this should or could obscure the sheer achievement of the existence of the International Brigades, filled with men and women who had gone to Spain because of a sense of international solidarity. For those who aspire to a politics of internationalism, those men and women are an invaluable example of what is possible. Shining through the historiographical controversies are the courage and sacrifice demonstrated by the Brigaders themselves, and the values they stood for. Dan Carrier, in his chapter here, explains how following in Laurie Lee's footsteps across the difficult terrain of the Pyrenees, he felt a redoubled respect for Lee and the other volunteers for the sacrifices they made in pursuit of what they believed in. As Mike Arnott describes in his essay on the Scottish volunteers, they felt that the Spanish Republic represented their progressive ideals, and they saw fascism as the ultimate threat to them. The contributions by President Michael D. Higgins, Owen Jones, John Pilger, and Ronan Burtenshaw all highlight that alongside the courageous example they set for posterity, the volunteers' values — solidarity, internationalism, socialism, anti-fascism, democracy, and freedom — are their main legacy.

The book, then, is organised into the following semi-thematic, semi-chronological sections: 'The Volunteers', 'The War', 'Solidarity', 'Aftermath', and 'Reflections'. In a process of attempting to classify and categorise pre-existing texts, many of the essays inevitably straddle more than one of these themes. Poems by Brigaders and their supporters are also dispersed throughout to add further colour to the different themes explored, along with a selection of images and illustrations. Some authors have used formal footnotes and references, whereas others write in a more informal style, but all have something to tell us about the International Brigades and British and Irish solidarity with the Spanish Republic.

Acknowledgements

This book would not have been possible without the support, supervision, and guidance of the IBMT chair, Jim Jump, for which I am very grateful. Thanks also to the IBMT executive officer and *¡No Pasarán!* editor Ajmal Waqif, and to the IBMT for allowing me to undertake this project. I am deeply grateful to all who gave permission for text and images to be included in the collection, and hope that the final work has done justice to their contributions. Thanks also to Professor Peter Anderson, my PhD supervisor in the School of History at the University of Leeds, for putting the project into motion and providing the book's preface, and to Professor Richard Cleminson, my supervisor in the School of Languages, for his guidance over the course of my PhD thesis. This work has been created as part of the Researcher Employability Project funded by the White Rose College of the Arts & Humanities Doctoral Training Partnership, funded by the AHRC, grant reference number AH/R012733/1.

> Joshua Newmark is a PhD researcher in the School of History, University of Leeds. His doctoral research is funded by the White Rose College of the Arts & Humanities (Arts & Humanities Research Council) and focuses on internationalism and international solidarity in the Spanish anarchist movement before and during the Spanish Civil War.

The Volunteers

Taken in Spain in 1938, in the front row, Brigader Sam Lesser sits between two volunteer nurses: his future wife, Margaret Powell (reading the Daily Worker) and an unknown American. In the back row, from left to right, are: British Battalion volunteers Alan Lawson and Lon Elliott, the nurses Ann Murray (reading Frente Rojo) and Ave Bruzzichesi, and the last British Battalion commander in Spain, Sam Wild. Courtesy of Ruth Muller.

Were the 'Britons' British?

Richard Baxell

Most historians now agree that around 35,000 people from some 53 nations volunteered to join the Spanish Republican forces. Of those, as many as 2,500 travelled to Spain from the British Isles. A reasonable estimate would suggest that up to 550 of them were from Scotland, between 150-200 from Wales and 70 from Northern Ireland. There were also up to 250 from what was then the Irish Free State, 60 from Cyprus, a similar number from Australia and a handful from Canada, South Africa, New Zealand and several other Commonwealth countries. There were even three volunteers from India and one claiming to come from Iraq, who volunteered under the unlikely name of John Smith (it was, of course, a *nom de guerre* — his real name was actually Gopal Mohan Huddar and he was Indian, rather than Iraqi). What is not always revealed is that somewhere between 10 and 20 percent of the volunteers were Jewish. It's hard to be more accurate than that because individuals disguised their Jewish origins by changing or anglicising their names, for understandable reasons.

When it comes to the volunteers' place of origin, as we have seen, nearly 90 percent gave addresses within England, Scotland or Wales. Therefore, at first sight it does not seem wholly unreasonable for their unit to have been called the British Battalion. However, a large number of those who gave UK addresses when they joined the International Brigades were actually not from Britain. This is particularly so with the approximately 500 who gave London addresses. As with Paris, Britain's capital city hosted — as it does today — a large transient population and a number of volunteers used temporary or 'care of' addresses, such as the Cypriot Centre in Soho, the Communist Party's headquarters in Covent Garden, or the Sailors' Home in Whitechapel. Others gave their address simply as 'London'.

The large migrant population supports the conclusions drawn by Helen Graham in her study *The War and its Shadow*, where she argued that many of the volunteers were themselves, or the offspring of, transient 'border-crossers'.[3] This may; on first sight, not seem to fit with the rest of the British volunteers, many of whom had never travelled beyond their hometown, let alone across international borders. However, it's clearly true of, for example, the Cypriots living in Soho and also true of the large number of first-generation Jews in the East End. And it is also true of many Irish volunteers, some of whom were living and working in Britain, others who had emigrated to the US or Canada. While many of these fought with the American Lincolns or the Canadian Mac-Paps, some certainly fought with the British Battalion. So it is clear that a number of volunteers in the British Battalion — particularly many of the Irish — would not have identified themselves as British. But does this matter?

---

[3] Helen Graham, *The War and its Shadow: Spain's Civil War in Europe's Long Twentieth Century* (Eastbourne: Sussex Academic Press, 2014), pp. 76-7.

After all, most international units included volunteers from several nations. In itself, perhaps not. However, as we shall see, lazily portraying all the volunteers in the battalion as 'British' was something that happened at the time and was to have dramatic consequences.

When the first English-speaking volunteers began to trickle into Spain in the late summer of 1936, they were placed within larger national units, such as the French 11th International Brigade, or the German 12th. As increasing numbers of volunteers arrived, there were soon enough to form an English-speaking company, which was placed within the La Marseillaise Battalion of the French 14th International Brigade. This unit formed the core of the British 16th Battalion, when it was formed at Christmas 1936. Alongside the British Battalion in the 15th International Brigade would be one from the US, another from Canada, and a battalion of Franco-Belge, then Yugoslavian volunteers, placed there in an attempt to bring up the numbers to something resembling brigade strength — though they were still very low in number compared with a conventional army.

Following the practice established in other international units fighting in Spain, each of the battalions took their name from a significant figure or event in the respective nation's history. A French battalion was named after the Paris Commune, the Germans had a Thälmann Battalion and the Yugoslavs were known as the Dimitrovs. The British unit was named after the Indian Communist MP for Battersea, Shapurji Saklatvala, who had died from a heart attack in January 1936. Whilst undoubtedly an influential figure in the radical politics of south London, Saklatvala's name hardly possessed the cachet of the heads of the Communist International or the German Communist Party, persecuted and imprisoned by the Nazis. So, not surprisingly, the battalion's name never caught on and the unit became universally known as the British Battalion by English-speakers, or as *el batallón inglés* by Spaniards.

At the beginning of January 1937, there were roughly 450 at the British Battalio's new base in Madrigueras, a small village just to the north of Albacete.[4] Here they began to come to terms with military training and discipline and the shortages and mixed quality of equipment. They also had to face a surprisingly cold and wet climate, unfamiliar food, no beer and deceptively strong wine.

It was during the period of training that evidence first arose of friction between different national groups within the battalion. A number of the Irish volunteers were already uneasy with having been placed in a so-called British unit, not surprising given the recent history between the two countries. Their misgivings turned to alarm and anger when it was discovered that two senior British figures in Spain — the commander of No.1 Company currently serving at Lopera, George Nathan, and the first battalion commander, Wilf Macartney—were rumoured to have played a role in British covert activities in Ireland. Worse still, Nathan was suspected as having been involved in a

---

[4] Marx Memorial Library, SC/IBA/5/2/1936/12.

hit-squad that murdered two prominent members of Sinn Féin in May 1921. Suspicions developed that he might be a Franco spy.

According to one Irish volunteer, Jim Prendergast, Nathan was, in effect, put on trial for his life. He vehemently denied that he was a spy, but admitted that he had indeed been operating as a British intelligence officer in Ireland.[5] However, he claimed that he was acting under orders and argued that, as a Jew, he was now a staunch anti-fascist and that all the volunteers in Spain were on the same side now. According to a number of accounts by Irish volunteers, the meeting responded to the spirit of his speech and actually applauded him. Undoubtedly this was due to the widespread admiration held for the military skills and courage that Nathan had demonstrated during the disastrous Lopera action in December 1936.[6] Eight of the 50 Irish volunteers had been killed and only the actions of Nathan, who coolly organised a retreat under fire, had prevented further losses.

However, resentment was to be reignited by a tactless report in the British communist paper, the *Daily Worker*, in early January, which recounted the actions of No.1 Company at Lopera, but made no mention of the Irish, instead describing them all as British volunteers. A number of the Irish at Madrigueras were furious, and it became clear that an attempt needed to be made to resolve the simmering discontent.

A meeting was called on 12 January, attended by approximately 45 Irish members of the battalion. During a stormy session, a number demanded that the group leave the British-dominated unit, while others argued vigorously 'that distinctions must be made between anti-fascist working-class comrades from Britain and British imperialism.'[7] Despite their efforts, at the end of the meeting the Irish group voted by a ratio of two to one to leave and join the Americans. While this was the most serious outbreak of discord between nationalities, it was by no means the last. As we shall see, arguments extended beyond the British unit, embroiling other national groups within the International Brigades.

Following the Irish departure, the British Battalion, and the 15th International Brigade itself, were thrown firstly into the Battle of Jarama in February 1937 and, five months later, the Republican Brunete offensive.[8] In both, the volunteers suffered appalling casualties. Over 150 were killed at Jarama and of 331 British volunteers in the ranks at the start of Brunete only 42 remained at the end. Of these, many were understandably low in morale, and pointed questions were being asked regarding the

---

[5] Walter Levine, *From Cheetham to Cordova: Maurice Levine — A Manchester Man of the Thirties* (Manchester: privately published, 1984), p. 39.

[6] Editor's note: See Sam Lesser's first-hand account of Lopera in this volume, 'Death and confusion among the olive groves'.

[7] Bill Alexander, *British Volunteers for Liberty* (London: Lawrence and Wishart, 1982), p. 69.

[8] Editor's note: See Ajmal Waqif's chapter on Jarama and Cyril Sexton's first-hand account of Brunete, both in the 'The War' section.

discipline and commitment of their Spanish comrades. The British political commissar, Walter Tapsell,[9] was incandescent: 'In plain fact, and it is hard to state this, on every occasion we were with Spanish troops in this engagement they let us down. Their behaviour on every occasion either resulted in serious casualties, or the immediate loss of positions won by us at heavy cost. This is a fact.'[10]

According to another commissar, disillusion with their Spanish comrades extended even to Bob Merriman, the commander of the American Lincolns, who remarked bitterly to him that 'the only people who do not run away are the English and the Germans.'[11] The belief that the International Brigades were used as shock-troops and were more dedicated than some of the Spanish forces seems to have been widely held.[12] At first sight it might appear strange that the Internationals were critical of the very people that they had come to help. However, to many of the Brigaders, the war was not a civil war between Spaniards, but an anti-fascist war. Thus this was just as much their fight, and the fact that it was being fought in Spain was almost immaterial. Spain was just the latest front on the European battlefield.

Unfortunately, what the leader of the Brigades — Luigi Longo — tactfully characterised as 'differences in language, military experience and customs,' also produced frictions between the international volunteers themselves.[13] A report by General Walter (General Karol Świerczewski), the Polish commander of the 35th Division, of which the 15th International Brigade was part, admitted:

> The nationality question is the weakest spot in the international units and is the main hindrance impeding the growth of our potential. Very little is said about relations between the nationalities within the international units, or more truthfully, it is completely hushed up, but it is just this which gives rise to almost all our weaknesses ... at the very same time as the volunteers were unifying, this petty, disgusting, foul squabble about the superiority of one nationality over another was going on. Everyone was superior to the French, but even they were superior to the Spanish.[14]

---

[9] Editor's note: Walter 'Wally' Tapsell's death in a tragic surprise encounter with enemy troops in March 1938 is immortalised in Bob Beagrie's poem, 'There's Wally', described and reproduced in this volume.

[10] Marx Memorial Library, SC/IBA/5/2/1937/53.

[11] John Angus, *With the International Brigade in Spain* (Loughborough: Loughborough University Press, 1983), p. 9.

[12] See Moscow 35082/1/90, reproduced in Ronald Radosh, Mary M. Habeck and Grigory Sevostianov (eds.), *Spain Betrayed: The Soviet Union in the Spanish Civil War* (New Haven and London: Yale University Press, 2001), pp. 241-2.

[13] Lisa Kirschenbaum, *International Communism and the Spanish Civil War* (Cambridge: Cambridge University Press, 2015), p. 85.

[14] Report by General Walter, 14 January 1938, Moscow 35082/1/95, cited in Radosh op cit, pp. 448-9.

Some of the German volunteers viewed the French with particular contempt. portraying them as 'drinkers, quarrelsome, and sometimes sloppy.' Meanwhile, a number of Scandinavians, Austrians and German-speaking Czechs, who had been placed in German units, complained that they were being 'oppressed' and unable to gain promotions.

There are also a number of accounts of arguments and rivalry between the national groups within the 15th International Brigade. Some Americans harboured resentments against particular British individuals, such as Captain George Wattis, who was blamed for the heavy American casualties at Jarama. Meanwhile, many British felt that the American influence in the 15th Brigade was too powerful.[15] Some Canadians felt the same way and made disparaging remarks about the Americans, whom they felt to be rather less hard than themselves. As one Canadian acidly observed: 'I think most of them would starve to death in a grocery store.'[16] When Bill Alexander, a commander of the British Battalion in Spain, later claimed that 'English, Scots, Welsh and all other nationalities mixed, with some chaffing and jokes' he was therefore giving a typically upbeat analysis. The claim by an anonymous volunteer that 'I found that national pride was one of the chief features in the life of the International Brigade' may have been an exaggeration, but it clearly played a role.[17]

It is clear that there were occasions when, despite the positive internationalist rhetoric, there was friction between the different national groups. However, it would be wrong to see this as the overarching story of foreign volunteers in the Spanish Civil War. That the International Brigades managed to operate at all, with all that was set against them, was an astonishing feat. Questions over exactly how many volunteers there were and from where they came are likely to remain. While it might seem that this is an obvious and, perhaps, over-laboured point, the issue does have contemporary relevance — and not just to academic historians. Over recent years a spate of local memorials to the international volunteers have been erected across Britain and Ireland. Part of the process usually involves drawing up lists of volunteers from the respective area, whether it be a village, town or city. Understandably perhaps, there is a tendency to include everyone connected to the area. For example, any memorial to volunteers from Oxford or Cambridge is, not unreasonably, going to include those who had studied at the universities. However, included on the plaque to volunteers from Southwark, Bermondsey and Camberwell are the Liverpudlian trade union leader, Jack Jones, the former soldier from Coatbridge in Scotland, Jock Cunningham, and

---

[15] As James Hopkins states, 'there was always considerable tension between the Americans and the British', in James K. Hopkins, *Into the Heart of the Fire: The British in the Spanish Civil War* (Stanford, CA: Stanford University Press, 1998), pp. 273-274n26, pp. 412-413 and n69, pp. 419-20.

[16] Michael Petrou, *Renegades: Canadians in the Spanish Civil War* (Vancouver: UBC Press, 2008), p. 17.

[17] John Angus op cit, p. 6.

the Jewish Latvian Dr Len Crome. Not one of these had any connection with south London before they went to Spain.

Does this matter? As a historian it matters to me. And it also matters to many family members of the volunteers and their supporters, a point amply demonstrated by continuing arguments over which national group sent the largest number of volunteers as a proportion of their total population. At the unveiling of the International Brigade memorial in Ottawa in 2001, Adrienne Clarkson, the Governor General of Canada, asserted that 'except for France, no other country gave a greater proportion of its population as volunteers in Spain than Canada.' A similar claim was made by Paul Philippou in his study of the Greek and Cypriot volunteers, *Spanish Thermopylae*,[18] which was picked up by the son of a Cypriot Brigader in a letter to the *IBMT Newsletter*: 'Some 40 to 60 Cypriots joined the International Brigades and 16 of them were killed. In the mid-1930s the population of Cyprus was 350,000 and this makes Cyprus the Country with the highest percentage of volunteers in the Spanish Civil War.[19]

This earned a swift response from Martin Sugarman of the Jewish ex-servicemen's association, who argued that the Cypriot population at the time was actually 371,000, not 350,000. He believed that the British Mandate of Palestine — including the current State of Israel, which did not exist at the time — sent a higher proportion: between 200-300 from a population of 1.38 million. He further argued that if the Arab population were excluded and only the 386,000 Jews counted, the proportion would be even higher, as only one Palestinian Arab is believed to have gone to Spain.[20] For those who wish to fly the International Brigade banner at demonstrations — both literally and metaphorically — the involvement of the volunteers in the defence of the democratic Spanish Republic was the 'last great cause' and many are understandably sensitive to what they perceive as any attempt to lessen the contribution of the International Brigades.

So, if numbers are important, what can be done to try and ensure that they are accurate? Well, there are now lists available of the men and women from a number of countries who volunteered to serve in Spain. However, as we have seen, many volunteers were migrants and their nationality was sometimes ambiguous. Some will inevitably appear on more than one list. What is needed is a comprehensive universal list of all the volunteers for Spain, where nationality is just one facet, like occupation or political affiliation. This would go a long way towards eliminating double-counting and disputes. In fact, this process has already begun. Sidbrint — Sistema d'Informació

---

[18] Paul Philippou Strongos, *Spanish Thermopylae: Cypriot Volunteers in the Spanish Civil War, 1936-39* (Barcelona: Warren and Pell, 2009), p. 3.

[19] *IBMT Newsletter*, 17, January 2007, p. 8.

[20] *IBMT Newsletter*, 20, Spring 2008, p. 2.

Digital sobre les Brigades Internacionals— is a trans-national research project based at the University of Barcelona with the aim of 'digitising the historical memory of the Spanish Civil War, the Brigaders and the International Brigades.'[21] Hopefully, Sidbrint will manage to source some more funding and can build upon what has been a valuable start. It is, I think, a fitting memorial to the sacrifices of all the volunteers for Spain, no matter how many there were and what country they came from.

Richard Baxell is a historian and the IBMT's Historical Consultant, whose books on the International Brigades include *British Volunteers in the Spanish Civil War: The British Battalion in the International Brigades, 1936-1939* (2004) and *Unlikely Warriors: The British in the Spanish Civil War and the Struggle Against Fascism* (2012). This essay appeared in issue 45 (May 2017) of the *IBMT Magazine* as 'Were the "Britons" British? Internationalism and national identity in the International Brigades', based on a lecture from the Len Crome Memorial Conference of that year.

---

[21] <www.sidbrint.ub.edu> (accessed 8 March 2017)

Rambling to Spain

Mike Wild

Sunday 24 April 2022 marked the 90th anniversary of the 1932 mass trespass on Kinder Scout, the gritstone plateau of peat bogs and heather moorland in the Peak District. It lies between the industrial cities of Manchester and Sheffield and other towns of the Pennine coalfields that powered the industrial revolution. Working people were fighting for the right to roam the moorland, for fresh air and space for recreation.

In the hungry 1930s things were grim up north. The 1926 general strike, mass unemployment, hunger marches and the rise of fascism motivated political demands for change and there was a right-wing backlash against the revolutionary movement. For young people, rambling offered a welcome relief from the dole and pollution and a chance to explore both new landscapes and discuss revolutionary ideas. They were 'free men and women on Sunday' and wanted more freedom to roam the old commons which had been enclosed under private ownership. Kinder Scout was forbidden territory dedicated to grouse-shooting interests, with gamekeepers who managed the high moors and kept trespassers off the land.

Clem Beckett, the popular dirt track motorbike rider and ex-blacksmith from Oldham, and Bernard (Benny) Rothman, an engineer and trade unionist from a Cheetham, north Manchester family of Romanian Jews were communists and vice presidents of the British Workers' Sports Federation (BWSF). From 1928 the latter was essentially a wing of the Communist Party, as part of its 'class against class' line. Clem was a vocal opponent of 'capitalist sport' and the stadium owners, fighting for fair pay and safety policies for riders. Benny, as a cyclist and rambler, saw the landowners as the enemy who represented the complete private ownership of the countryside. The trespass was to be reported in the BWSF publication, *The Worker Sportsman*. It was intended to start a wave of access events and public campaigns. Clem fired a broadside against the bosses and wrote 'Speed and Spondulicks.' Benny took on the leadership of the trespass. Young people from the regular Rowarth camp had been turfed off Yellowslacks, on the slopes of Bleaklow, by keepers. They were determined to organise a larger demo and trespass.

The ramble was advertised in the press and by leaflets and word of mouth. Word got around and about 400 assembled at Hayfield, while other parties came over from the Sheffield side to meet up with the main party. After an initial meeting in Bowden Bridge quarry, where Benny told of the history of enclosures and the struggle for access and the need for political discipline, the party moved off up Kinder Road. On a signal from a whistle they left the public footpath and headed up to Sandy Heys in the direction of Kinder Downfall. A confrontation with a group of keepers, 20 to 30 in all, and a scuffle involving trespassers Wilfred 'Woolfie' Winnick and Maurice Levine left one man injured but able to walk back to Hayfield.

After a celebratory meeting it was decided to return by the ways they had come.

Back in the village of Hayfield the ramblers halted and the police who had been alerted arrested five men and took them to the lock-up. The young men were bailed and the trial was fixed for Derby Assizes in July. They were charged with riotous assembly. Harry Mendel was acquitted but five were sentenced to various terms, up to six months maximum, initially at Leicester jail. Judge Acton made a point of mentioning the 'foreign names' of Rothman, Nussbaum and Clyne.

The jailing of the ramblers and what some established groups called the 'communist stunt' had a large impact and spread like a moorland fire, with large numbers turning up to further meetings. The ultimate goal was the establishment of national parks and legislation to allow rights of way. As the campaigns grew over the years these ambitions were eventually achieved. The Countryside and Rights of Way Act 2000 was a major landmark and the original trespassers who were prosecuted and jailed are now celebrated. The 90th anniversary celebrations were very well attended and the centenary will be eagerly anticipated.

Back in their home towns the young trespassers still had much to fight against. Oswald Mosley — heir of a prominent family of Staffordshire and Lancashire landowners — formed the British Union of Fascists in October 1932. Marches on the streets and fights on the crofts of working-class areas were common. Crowds of young people in wards like Cheetham and Hulme, including Jews and communists, fought back against the fascist Blackshirts.

From 1933 onwards demonstrations against the Blackshirts mirrored those in other communities. At rallies they chanted 'Bye Bye Blackshirt!' as a song of triumph. Meanwhile, they observed the rise of fascism in Europe and the support of the ruling class for the policy of appeasement and non-intervention at government level. Mussolini and Hitler grew ever more powerful and anti-war sentiment changed as the threat grew at home. There were more calls to meet force with force. Those same young trespassers became potential fighters and when Franco's rebel generals led the *coup* against the democratic Republican government of Spain, there was a call to 'Aid Spain' and take up arms. The Cheetham Challenge Club and other political groups organised food and medical aid ships and ambulances. Amongst the early volunteers who had been on the mass trespass to volunteer for the International Brigades were Clem Beckett, 'Woolfie' Winnick, Maurice Levine and Arthur Newsome of Sheffield. Benny Rothman volunteered to join as an ambulance driver but was turned down due to inexperience and his value on the home front.

We have delved in the archives and personal memoirs and so far have established that as many as 16 Kinder trespassers went out to Spain, of whom 10 fell in battle, a very significant number. The survivors, many wounded, came home from the Spanish Civil War and either joined the forces in the coming Second World War, which many of them had predicted, or were turned down by the authorities as 'prematurely antifascist.' They carried on their activities and supported their defeated Republican comrades.

Mike Wild is a researcher and the son of Sam Wild, the last commander of the British Battalion. This essay appeared in issue 60 (May 2022) of *¡No Pasarán!*[22]

Kinder Scout trespasser Walter Levine (left) pictured in Spain. The identity of the second individual is unknown. A poster for the popular militia can be seen behind Levine. Courtesy of the Marx Memorial Library.

---

[22] Editor's note: After the publication of this article in *¡No Pasarán!*, Kate Armstrong contacted Mike Wild, having discovered during research for her family tree that her uncle, Alexander Armstrong, had died in Spain. Mike was able to provide her with further details, including of his participation in the Kinder Scout mass trespass.

Volunteers from the valleys

Graham Davies

My engagement with the theme of the Welsh in the Spanish Civil War began a few years ago following a mesmerising assault on the senses from the masterpiece by Pablo Picasso — his *Guernica* — after a visit to the Museo Nacional Centro de Arte Reina Sofía in Madrid, Spain's national museum of 20th century art.[23] Not long after, I discovered in the corridor of the Burry Port Institute in Carmarthenshire a plaque commemorating those men from South Wales who were killed in Spain fighting against fascism. This engagement has now produced my book targeted at the general reader on the Welsh volunteers — *You are Legend*, published by Welsh Academic Press.

The classic descriptions of the Welsh in Spain were written by Hywel Francis in 1984 and Rob Stradling in 2004. Both are rigorously researched by competent historians: the former reflects the first hand knowledge of the volunteers extrapolated from extensive personal interviews; the latter has the advantage of further reflection and access to the Russian archives on the International Brigades.

The Welsh involvement in the Spanish Civil War began a little earlier than some realise. As the last dramatic acts of the death of the Spanish Republic unfolded with the murders of Castillo and Sotelo and the cryptic telegram from General Mola which signalled the uprising in Morocco, another piece of the jigsaw was emerging.[24] At 07.15 on the morning of 1 July 1936, Captain Cecil Bebb, a commercial pilot, took off from Croydon Airport, London, in a Dragon Rapide aircraft, bound for the Canary Islands. His mission was to make contact with General Franco and fly him to Tetuán

---

[23] Editor's note: Guernica (in Basque 'Gernika') is a town to the east of Bilbao, considered to be the spiritual capital of the Basque people. Ahead of the Francoist advance in northern Spain, on 26 April 1937, German and Italian planes repeatedly bombed the town, killing hundreds of civilians in attacks which drew global attention to the horror of aerial bombing. Pablo Picasso painted *Guernica* after being commissioned by the Spanish Republican authorities to create a mural for the Spanish pavilion at the 1937 World's Fair in Paris, applying his inimicable cubist and surrealist style in a powerful and evocative depiction of the bombing.

[24] Editor's note: Historians treat these two assassinations as emblematic of the rising political violence and the breakdown in the rule of law which preceded the generals' illegal military *coup* against the Spanish Republic. José del Castillo Sáez de Tejada was a police Assault Guard who was involved with socialist and anti-fascist organisations; hours after his murder by Spanish Falangists on 12 July 1936, fellow Republican Assault Guards and socialist militia members detained the right-wing monarchist parliamentary deputy José Calvo Sotelo under false pretences and murdered him as a reprisal. Less than a week later, the generals began their *coup*.

in Spanish Morocco, where he would meet up with Spain's Army of Africa.[25] Bebb was from Church Village, near Pontypridd, in Wales, and so it seems the first action of a Welshman in the Spanish conflict was to facilitate Franco's role. To what extent MI6 was complicit in this secret journey is a continuing matter of conjecture. It has been alleged that Franco was accompanied by one of their agents, Major Hugh Pollard, with two other women and that the plot was planned over lunch at Simpson's in the Strand.

Ironically, there is another story to tell about the first Welsh volunteer to engage in battle in the Spanish Civil War. Frank Thomas was born in Pontypridd and brought up in Cardiff. Bored with life as a travelling salesman he admits he was attracted to Spain in a thirst for adventure and glory. Politically right-wing and strongly anti-communist, he writes that he was touched by the sacredness of General Franco's cause and joined El Tercio, the Spanish Foreign Legion, linking up with them in October 1936 before the attack on Madrid. There would not have been many of Thomas's countrymen who would have appreciated his presence in Madrid's Casa de Campo, the Parque del Oeste or the University City, throwing bombs at the members of the International Brigades who were bravely defending the city. They would not have been impressed to hear that his company at the Battle of Jarama had taken the village of San Martín de la Vega, a stone's throw from the British at Morata de Tajuña. Nor would the Welsh in the Battle of Brunete have enjoyed knowing that at Villanueva de Cañada, Frank Thomas had been strengthening the barbed wire defences before their attack. Thomas was a Welsh volunteer for the Francoist cause who, by his own admission, deserted and returned home with O'Duffy's Irish Brigade. His ideology had little to commend it then and has even less currency today.

Before the International Brigades had been set up there were already hundreds of volunteers from outside Spain who had attached themselves to various militias. James Albrighton was a young student from Salisbury who enrolled in the Republican Army on 2 October 1936. He wrote a diary (of which I obtained a personal copy) of those early experiences and mentions a Welshman named Sydney Lloyd Jones, who joined a couple of days later. They became part of the Spanish MM (*Muerte es Maestro*; Death is Master) Centuria who were involved in 'special duties,' which included searching out and executing the fascist spies of Madrid. They fought in the attempt to stem the Nationalist advance from Toledo to Madrid at San Martín de Valdeiglesias and Navalcanero.

According to Albrighton, Sydney Lloyd Jones died on 14 October in actions against the Moors and the Spanish Foreign legion at Chapinería, about 30 miles west of Madrid. He describes how three of the men, Sidney Lloyd Jones among them, were killed while repulsing a fascist attack on their flanks. He writes: 'Their bravery and courage in continuing their fighting, despite all being wounded was not in vain — it gave the new Centuria time to reach us.' Sydney Lloyd Jones, about whom nothing else

---

[25] Editor's note: The Army of Africa was Spain's colonial army in its Moroccan protectorate. It included the elite Spanish Legion and a large force of Moroccan indigenous infantry under the command of Spanish officers.

seems to be known, was the first Welshman to die in combat against fascism in Spain. He was buried with his comrades in a ditch that ran through the grove where they were fighting.

Of the other early arrivals we know that at least Will Lloyd and Bob Condon of Aberaman and Pat Murphy of Cardiff had linked up with a battalion of French volunteers and were in a unit that was sent on Christmas Day by train to the Córdoba front and in January to Las Rozas. However, it was not until December of 1936 that the group began to expand. Indeed, when the newly formed British Battalion went into action at the Battle of Jarama it was likely that there were about 30 Welsh volunteers among the 600 British. Other Welsh volunteers failed to get into service in Spain for a number of reasons, including being captured or failing a medical. Also among these early arrivals were David Joseph Jones of Llwynypia, W.J. Davies, John Williams and Sam Morris of Ammanford, Bill Coles and Jack Taylor of Cardiff, Tom Davies of Bedlinog, Michael O'Donoghue of Merthyr Vale and William Foulkes of Treorchy.

I have listed almost 200 'Welsh' volunteers who served in Spain in the appendix of my book. They are men and women who served on the Republican side in Spain, for whom I found a recognisable footprint and who were either born in Wales or had strong Welsh connections. About 70 percent of these were members of the Communist Party and over half of the total were miners. My estimate is that 35 of these died, two more than the number usually cited. Despite the view expressed by some that it was allegiance to the Communist Party as opposed to Republican Spain that motivated most of the volunteers, the strong anti-fascist motives of the Welsh volunteers were echoed by the comments of socialist leaders and politicians, and replicated in the debates and discussions of political groupings in the UK. For example, in a local council meeting in Llanelli on 10 September 1936, Councillor Brinley Jones argued that the victory of Italy and Germany in Spain would mean the downfall of the British Empire and the end of a democratic chamber in Llanelli.

The views of the Welsh volunteers followed a common pattern. Typically, Jim Brewer was convinced of the need to fight fascism as part of an international movement. Outraged by Hitler's military intervention in Spain, for him silence meant acquiescence. Morien Morgan had interrupted the last year of his honours degree at university to volunteer for Spain. A radical and intelligent thinker, he was appalled that Mussolini's actions went unchallenged, amazed at military might when he was visiting the Rhine and felt helpless at growing German military expansion. Another volunteer, Will Paynter, went to Spain initially as the Communist Party organiser for Wales in order to look after the British Battalion's interests at the International Brigade headquarters. He regarded himself as part of a battle, not merely to defend a people from a savage aggressor, but to destroy something that could eventually crush the people of all democratic countries.

What, then, was the legacy of the Welsh volunteers? Certainly the Comintern regarded the Brigades as a highly disciplined force that played a huge part in resisting fascist aggression, and their contribution was possibly decisive in some battles for the survival of the Republic. They were seen as the embodiment of international and proletarian solidarity and future revolutionary warriors, as well as potential Soviet spies. For many their sacrifice 'stands as an eternal rebuke to those in power in Western bourgeois democracies whose preference for collaborating with fascism in the 1930s rather than confronting it made inevitable the horrors of the Second World War …'

British Battalion commander Bill Alexander argued that the volunteers understood that fascism led to war, and the three-year resistance gave time for people everywhere to learn lessons and prepare for their own struggle against fascism. He believed that the lessons to be learned were that fascism must be exposed and that it could only be defeated by struggle and that ordinary people had the potential to be realised in a truly free and democratic society.

It is true that compared with the Irish contingent of volunteers, the Welsh did not develop a strong corporate identity, although they tended to find their place together in No.1 Company. Yet Will Paynter was also keen that there should be no separation by nationalities — only close cohesion and better relationships with Spanish comrades. The Welsh did not get much of a mention in the XVth Brigade's newspaper *The Volunteer for Liberty*, nor did they feature much in *The Book of the XV Brigade*, which was written by many different volunteers and edited by Irishman Frank Ryan. Yet there were Welshmen who were company commanders, political commissars and who had attended officers' training schools, and certainly their largely militant coalfield background, digging experience and singing ability left their mark.

Fred Copeman specifically mentions the lift given to the multinational group on the way to Brunete by the singing of the Welsh miners, and Miles Tomalin composed a limerick about the confusion caused by similar Welsh names:

> There was a young fellow named Price.
> And another fellow named Price.
> And a fellow named Roberts.
> And another fellow named Roberts.
> And another young fellow named Price.

Hywel Francis points out that the special regard, even reverence, in which Welsh International Brigaders were held is illustrated by both the numerous memorial meetings and the kind of welcomes organised in their communities for those who returned. He states: 'They were in the same tradition as the Chartists at Newport and were to be celebrated in spite of their respective defeats, because they were all men before their time.' However, it is ironic that while the Welsh Dean of Chichester declared that the Brigaders had given their lives for something of eternal value and that God would not forget such sacrifices, Pope Pius XII had sent a telegram to Franco at the end of the war giving thanks to God for the long-desired Catholic victory in Spain.

For Alun Menai Williams, he had been part of a truly international force of volunteers spurred on to action by the heartfelt tries of '*ino pasarán!*' of a beleaguered nation and its people. They fought for an ideal but lost out to superior force. In 2009

Carles Casajuana, Spanish ambassador in London, told the group of veterans receiving Spanish citizenship: 'Your efforts were not in vain. Your ideals are part of the foundations of our democracy in Spain today.' There is no more fitting tribute to the Welshmen and all other volunteers of the International Brigades than the memorable words from the speech of La Pasionaria, from which the title of my book derives: 'You are history. You are legend. You are the heroic example of democracy's solidarity and universality . . . we shall not forget you; and, when the olive tree of peace is in flower, entwined with the victory laurels of the Republic of Spain — come back.'[26]

>Graham Davies is a freelance writer and researcher whose books include *You are Legend: The Welsh Volunteers in the Spanish Civil War* (2018) and *Outwitting Franco: The Welsh Maritime Heroes of the Spanish Civil War* (2020). This essay was published in issue 46 (September 2017) of the *IBMT Magazine* as 'Welsh at War.'

---

[26] Editor's note: 'La Pasionaria', 'passionflower', was the name given to Dolores Ibárruri, a leading Spanish communist politician and one of the Republic's figureheads. She was a legendary speechmaker and is often credited as the first to deploy the phrase '*ino pasarán!*' (they shall not pass) during the civil war.

The Connolly Column
Manus O'Riordan

The sheer viciousness of the propaganda and hatred faced by those Irish who took such a courageous stand against fascism in Spain was summed up in a series of articles that ran all week in the *Irish Independent* in the new year of 1937, and concluded with the following fascist curse pronounced on those Irish International Brigaders who met their deaths.[27] These began with Achill islander Tommy Patten in December 1936 and ended with Jack Nalty and Liam McGregor in September 1938:

> In concluding these articles, I wish to state that the present Government of Madrid is 100% Red and violently opposed to the Catholic Church. Any Irishman preparing to fight for or defend vicariously this regime is defending the enemy of his faith.

The International Brigade Memorial Trust honours the memory of all those who had the moral courage to confront unpopularity on the home front in Ireland through their defence of the Spanish Republic. They were led in the south by that brave republican priest who had read the invocation on the occasion when the freely-elected First Dáil met to ratify the Irish Republic in 1919 — the former vice president of Sinn Féin, Father Michael O'Flanagan. And they were led defiantly in the north by the then chairman of the Northern Ireland Labour Party and future Unionist Party Minister for Education in the postwar government of Northern Ireland, Harry Midgley.

As for those who volunteered to go to Spain to fight, the wording of a plaque unveiled in Belfast in September 2006 was broad enough to encompass both strong and weak, because we knew what it cost each and every one of them to take the stand they did. It was dedicated to those volunteers 'who stood against Fascism.' It was pleasing to note that this wording was unequivocally solid enough to exclude any honours for the man who claimed to have been the first Irish volunteer, Charlie McGuinness of Derry. He initially did go out to Spain but, when offered the opportunity to actually fight for the Republic, he promptly returned home in December 1936 and during that same month, while the first Irish International Brigaders were being killed in action, he commenced producing such scurrilous — but all too influential — fascist propaganda for the *Irish Independent*.

It was none other than that same McGuinness who had been the author of that fascist curse quoted above. Despite his betrayal of Irish International Brigaders, we will

---

[27] Editor's note: As Manus O'Riordan mentioned in a note accompanying the original version of this article, there was no organisation called the 'Connolly Column' in Spain; rather, he and Peter O'Connor first deployed the term as a blanket name — like the 'Abraham Lincoln Brigade' for American and Canadian volunteers — to honour all Irish volunteers in the International Brigades.

always honour those heroes. To mention just two of them, named in Christy Moore's song 'Viva la Quince Brigada':

> Bob Hilliard was a Church of Ireland pastor
> From Killarney across the Pyrenees he came
> From Derry came a brave young Christian Brother
> Side by side they fought and died in Spain.
> Éamon McGrotty was that Derryman's name.

I accompanied McGrotty's late brother John in 1994 and 1996 to the mass grave of 5,000 fighters where Éamon is buried near Jarama. John brought soil from their parents' grave to mix into that mass grave and brought some of Jarama's soil back to their grave. He carried his brother Éamon's own missal with him on both occasions, and retold the double hurt experienced by his family when they sought to have a mass said after Éamon's death in February 1937 and the Bishop of Derry refused them, saying that a mass would be no benefit whatsoever to Éamon, as he was 'now in Hell'. McGuinness's dirty work had borne fruit.

Thanks to research undertaken by Ciarán Crossey and Jim Carmody, we have an ever-expanding roll of honour for the Irish volunteers. Of the northern volunteers on the roll published by the International Brigade Commemoration Committee in Belfast, six of them had served alongside my father, Michael O'Riordan, in the British Battalion in the 1938 Battle of the Ebro. One Ulsterman who survived that battle was the first of my father's immediate comrades-in-arms that I remember from early childhood, Hughie Hunter from Ballyclare, Co Antrim, who always brought his mouth organ down with him from Belfast to play tunes for us in our Dublin home and whom my father brought to life in an interview with Ciarán Crossey. He recalled Hughie carefully saving his few *pesetas* at the front in order to send home a regular donation to the Communist Party of Ireland's unity fund in Belfast.

Anybody fortunate enough to have heard the 2006 BBC Radio Ulster programme by Diarmaid Fleming could not fail to have been moved by the accounts of volunteers from the north: Peggy Mount talking about her brother Dick O'Neill from the Falls Road; Liz Shaw talking about her father Joe Boyd from Co Tyrone; Harry McGrath being recalled by his Shankill Road nephews. Such volunteers came both from Catholic and Protestant religious backgrounds; from republican, communist, labour and loyalist political traditions. People from all those traditions have come together at a succession of events to honour the memory of the volunteers. Such coming together does not abolish real political differences but it does enhance the human relationships that make dialogue possible. And while such events provide no solution for the Irish question, in our coming together to honour all who defended the Spanish Republic we might note that in that one particular struggle there was in fact an interchange and identity of language used in Spain itself, where every republican was a loyalist and every loyalist a Republican.

The volunteers who hailed from the south were all Irish republicans in the

Wolfe Tone tradition — Catholic, Protestant, Jewish and atheist. There is space only to name a few. Bill Scott came from a Dublin Protestant working-class tradition that had seen his father take up arms as a member of the Irish Citizen Army alongside James Connolly in the 1916 Rising. Frank Edwards was a Waterford teacher who had already been victimised by the Christian Brothers and who, on his return from Spain, found himself blacklisted by Catholic schools for his Spanish Republicanism and by Protestant schools for his Irish republicanism, but who also found that one school prepared to employ him was Dublin's Jewish National School. Frank had been born in Belfast in 1907 to a Catholic family that was subsequently forced out of its home by sectarian conflict and then settled in Waterford. Another Irish volunteer was Maurice Levitas — known to family and friends as Morry — from a Dublin Jewish working class tradition, his parents being refugees who had fled Tsarist antisemitism in Latvia and Lithuania. During the course of the Second World War, Morry's maternal aunt Rachel and her family would become Holocaust victims in Riga. His paternal aunt Sara, her family and neighbours would be locked into their own Lithuanian village synagogue and burned to death. A paternal uncle in Paris, whom Morry had visited on his way to Spain in 1938 and again on his way back in 1939 following his release with Bob Doyle from the San Pedro de Cardeña concentration camp, and who thought he had emigrated far enough west to be safe, would also be murdered on his own doorstep by the Gestapo at the very end of the war.[28] Christy Moore's song speaks of 'the rising fascist tide', and it was that tide which those International Brigade volunteers — so derisively referred to by the British and American establishments as 'premature anti-fascists' — had fought so hard to halt.

Another volunteer, originally from Kerry but for a number of years intimately linked with the city of Belfast as a Church of Ireland clergyman, was the Reverend Robert M. Hilliard, who was to fall at Jarama in February 1937. Hilliard was a Protestant republican, not only in respect of the Spanish Civil War, but also in respect of his native Ireland. Hilliard had in fact been an IRA volunteer in Kerry during the Irish Civil War. In 1931 he was to serve as a Church of Ireland curate in Christ Church, Derriaghy, and in 1972 that church was presented with a communion chalice, paten and cruet in his memory by a fellow International Brigader who was himself an agnostic, the Co Tyrone Independent Labour Party volunteer, Joe Boyd. After he had been appointed to the Belfast Cathedral Mission in 1933, Hilliard became greatly radicalised by the social

---

[28] Editor's note: Bob Doyle, who lost an eye as a youth in a fight with fascist Blueshirts, was an Irish Republican Army (IRA) veteran and member of the left-wing Irish Republican Congress who went on to volunteer for the International Brigades in 1937. In Spain, he trained recruits and saw action at Belchite before being captured at Gandesa and suffering 11 months of imprisonment and torture at the hands of the Francoists. However, he survived and saw Second World War service in the British merchant navy. As a communist and a trade union shop steward with the Sogat (printing) union living in Britain in the post-war period, he also helped to organise underground trade unions in Spain. Bob Doyle's extraordinary biography was summarised in an obituary by Richard Baxell following his death in 2009: <https://www.theguardian.com/uk/2009/feb/16/obituary-bob-doyle>.

upheavals in Belfast at that time. Personal problems saw him subsequently leave for London where he became even more radicalised in later years, joining the Communist Party of Great Britain and volunteering for Spain in December 1936.

Hilliard's last message to his family was dated 24 January 1937 — a fortnight before his death. He wrote:

> My dear, Five minutes ago I got your letter. There is a Daily Worker delegation here who will take this back. They leave in ten minutes so I have time for no more than a card which will have an English postmark. Teach the kids to stand for democracy. Thanks for the parcels, I expect they have been forwarded to me, but posts are held up very long & especially parcels. Do not worry too much about me, I expect I shall be quite safe. I think I am going to make quite a good soldier. I still hate fighting but this time it has to be done, unless fascism is beaten in Spain & in the world it means war and hell for our kids. All the time when I am thinking of you & the children I am glad I have come. Give my love to Tim, Deirdre, Davnet & Kit. Write when you can, it will help. Love to you, Robert.

The very last Irish volunteer to reach Spain was an Ulsterman, James Patrick Haughey from Lurgan, Co Armagh, who had fought shoulder-to-shoulder with my father, Michael O'Riordan, in the Battle of the Ebro during July and August 1938; and who was captured and imprisoned that September in the concentration camp of San Pedro de Cardeña. As with the letters of the Reverend Bob Hilliard, the following extract from a letter written from Canada after Haughey's release from that fascist hell brings us still closer to the great humanity of all such volunteers. The letter from Jim to his sister Veronica is dated 25 May 1939:

> It would be impossible to describe the humiliations we suffered after that [capture] until we arrived in the concentration camp. Here we met some more international prisoners of war. There were 36 different nationalities including Irish, British and Americans (some time I will describe this camp, it was very interesting). Here I had my head dressed and settled down patiently to await the day when we should be liberated. There were 400 of us in a room which would hold 50 comfortably, no smokes, no books, 1 toilet and one water tap for 400 men, abundance of lice, very little food, beans twice a day. For the last 3 months before we were released we were fed on bread and water, nothing else.

Jim Haughey went on to prove his continuing anti-fascist valour. He volunteered for the Royal Canadian Air Force in June 1941. He was killed in a plane crash on 12 September 1943, and his name is engraved on Canada's World War Two *Book of Remembrance*. Like Charlie Donnelly, he had expressed in verse the anticipation of his own death, which also occurred at the age of 23. On 31 October 1943 the *Times of London* posthumously published Jim's poem — simply entitled 'Fighter Pilot' — over the name of Séamus Haughey. These verses have echoes of the W.B. Yeats poem 'An Irish Airman Foresees his Death', but possess the greater authenticity of being the actual premonitions of a real airman, rather than Yeats's attribution of his own imagined thoughts to Robert Gregory.

What I hadn't realised until 2005 was that Jim had already lost his father a year before. Able seaman James Aloysius Haughey had been killed at sea — torpedoed by a Nazi German submarine — on 1 February 1942.

Reflections on his father's death at sea are also present in the first verse, where James Patrick speculates about his own forthcoming death.

> I think that it will come, somewhen, somewhere
> In shattering crash, or roaring sheet of flame;
> In the green-blanket sea, choking for air,
> Amid the bubbles transient as my name.

The final verse is a tribute to him and to all of his internationalist comrades who stood against fascism in defence of the Spanish Republic.

> When peace descends once more like gentle rain,
> Mention my name in passing, if you must,
> As one who knew the terms — slay or be slain,
> And thought the bargain was both good and just.

> Manus O'Riordan, the son of Irish International Brigader Michael O'Riordan, was a trade unionist, activist, and researcher of the International Brigades. This text first appeared in issue 52 (September 2019) of *¡No Pasarán!*

The legacy of the Scottish volunteers

Mike Arnott

The principles of social justice, health, education, women's and workers' rights, on which the fledgling 1931 Spanish Republic was based, chimed loudly with progressives around Europe and beyond. But it was these principles which were to come under brutal assault by Spain's forces of reaction, including the army and the Catholic Church. It was also these principles, as well as the recognition that Spain was perhaps a prelude to another world war, which drew many from the politicised working-class to the ranks of the International Brigades, formed by the Comintern in the autumn of 1936.

Scotland's working-class was no different. The vast majority of the 549 Scots who volunteered were working-class and mostly communists, some already blooded in fighting fascism at home, such as in Edinburgh's Usher Hall or on Aberdeen's Castlegait. Glasgow-born Jock Cunningham, Aberdonian Bob Cooney and nurse Annie Murray were amongst the Scots who became rightly renowned for their leading roles in Spain. But it is within the lived experiences of the unheralded fighters, nurses and the Aid Spain volunteers on the home front where revealing, untold stories can be found.

Accounts of the Scots in Spain, from Ian MacDougall's *Scottish Voices from the Spanish Civil War* to Dan Gray's *Homage to Caledonia* and STV's documentary *The Scots who Fought Franco*, all combine to present a group portrait of those involved. Forged in austerity, on hunger marches and in street battles with the Blackshirts, the honesty and sincerity of their witness resonates across the years. These are not the dupes of Moscow or the Stalinist dogmatists portrayed by lazy historians or those with an axe to grind. These are humane, often funny, free willed but disciplined individuals, full of life and optimism, all driven by a desire to defeat fascism. Many more joined the largest community-based international solidarity movement the country had ever seen. From beetle drives in elegant Edinburgh terraces to collection prams pushed around the cobbled pit rows of Fife and Lanarkshire, money, food, bandages and clothes poured in.

The first organised group to leave for Spain was actually the Scottish Ambulance Unit, organised by a former Glasgow Lord Provost, Sir Daniel Stevenson. On 17 September 1936, six ambulances, a supply lorry and male and female medical and support staff left George Square in the city. One of the drivers, Thomas Watters, would become the last surviving Scot who served in Spain, dying aged 99 in February 2012. The diary of one of his fellow SAU volunteers, Donald Gallie, has just been published by Sussex Academic Press, edited by his daughter.[29] The military volunteers

---

[29] Donald Gallie, *The Spanish Civil War: the Road to Madrid*. Transcribed and edited by Nina Stevens (Eastbourne: Sussex Academic Press, 2019).

followed, building in number as Christmas 1936 approached. In all more than 200 from Glasgow and over 60 from Dundee made up half of those who were to go from Scotland, the last not leaving Scotland until April 1938 when the bad tidings from the front line must have been known to them. One of these, a teenage Steve Fullarton, was the last Scottish combatant to die, in February 2008.[30] Four volunteered from his street alone in Shettleston in Glasgow.

A few were involved in the late 1936 fighting around Madrid, but all of Britain and Ireland's volunteers in Spain were brought together at Albacete following Christmas that year to join the new arrivals who would form the new British Battalion. They left for the front line, 600 strong, in early February 1937, to Jarama. Since 2011, a memorial to the 39 Scots Brigaders who fell at Jarama has stood in the cemetery of the town of Tarancón in Spain, where some of those remembered died in the hospitals of the Republican medical services. It is a touching coincidence that Len Crome served as a doctor in Tarancón. Every year, as part of the Asociación de Amigos de las Brigadas Internacionales (AABI) annual Jarama commemoration, hundreds who gather at the memorial also learn about those medical services and about a local campaign to preserve one of the original hospital buildings. This has attracted wide support from locals and visitors alike.

As many fell in the successive battles: Brunete, Teruel, Gandesa, Caspe and the Ebro, more arrived, but in fewer numbers. Eventually, in September 1938, the Brigaders were withdrawn and arrived back in the UK in December that year. They left over 120 Scots behind, to rest forever in Spanish soil. The words of Dundonian Mary Brooksbank's poem 'Graves of Spain' recall how their sacrifice was remembered at the time; 'Tread softly, señoritas, o'er their lonely graves, / Spaniards mute your voices for our dead; / Stars shine steadfast, eternal vigil keep, / Light soft the soil around each valiant head.'

In the years since the end of the civil war, physical memorials to that same sacrifice have arisen across Scotland: from those almost epic in their scale, at Glasgow and Motherwell, to iconic symbols in small communities, such as Renton's famous Spanish bull, they act to this day as focal points for the growing numbers of annual commemorations that continue to populate the calendar. Dundee in February, Edinburgh in April, Renton in May, Motherwell in July, Glasgow, Irvine and Kirkcaldy in September. Popular culture has also celebrated the legacy, with last year's play *549 Scots of the Spanish Civil War* by Wonder Fools joining the Maley brothers' *From the Calton to Catalonia* from the previous generation to create a proud theatre tradition inspired by the Scots Brigaders. In music, the Lanarkshire Songwriters continue a fine tradition stretching back through Ewan McColl to Glasgow Brigader Alex McDade, who penned the original lyrics of 'Jarama Valley'.

Mike Arnott is a trade unionist and political activist. This essay was first published in issue 53 (January 2020) of *¡No Pasarán!*

---

[30] Editor's note: See Steve Fullarton's first-hand account from the battle for Hill 481 (part of the Ebro campaign) in this volume: 'You fool, you fool, why did you have to shoot me?'

A Glasgow memorial to the International Brigades, topped by a fibreglass statue of Dolores Ibárruri. Known as 'La Pasionaria' ('passionflower'), Ibárruri was a key Communist Party politician, one of the leading figures of the Republic during the Spanish Civil War, and a legendary speech-maker. The statue was designed by Arthur Dooley and unveiled in 1980; it looks out across the River Clyde. Courtesy of the IBMT.

From an English Guest

Christopher Caudwell

O wad some pow'r the giftie gie us
To read your Burns, at least in parts.
But we are simple Sassenachs,
We do not understand your cracks –
For instance, what the hell are 'airts'?

And then we'd understand your lingo –
Give 'stane' for 'stane' and 'hame' for 'hame'.
Instead we smile or shake the head
And trust it fits with what you said.
Of course we know you do the same.

But never mind – we're anti-Fascists:
We tread the same grey Spanish dust.
We know you're fighters, like your ways –
And though we don't know what he says
We'll take your Rabbie Burns on trust –

As soldiers' poet – full of failings,
And of your famous Scottish pride,
Poet clear as Highland spring
Through whom ten million Scotsmen sing –
A people's poet till he died.

>Christopher Caudwell was the pseudonym of Christopher St John Sprigg, a poet, novelist, intellectual, and influential Marxist theoretician. He was killed in action with the British Battalion in February 1937, during the Battle of Jarama. This poem was originally written as a tribute to the Scottish comrades during the Battalion's Burns Night celebration at Madrigueras in January 1937 and was published in issue 21 (September 2008) of the *IBMT Newsletter*.

Inspired by the struggle for national independence

Paul Philippou

Cypriot volunteers in the International Brigades served predominantly in the British Battalion and the American Abraham Lincoln Battalion. Based on materials found in the main archives, around 57 Cypriots served in the International Brigades. Two Hellenic volunteers, brothers Costas and Hercules Avgherinos, the children of refugees from Constantinople, both of whom served in the British Battalion, have generally been placed within the Cypriot contingent, thus taking the total to 59. Cypriot volunteer recruitment was centred around two geographic locations, London and New York, both important Cypriot diaspora migration points. Significant Cypriot emigration to Britain occurred in the 1920s and early 1930s — a response to global economic depression and contingent economic and political circumstances in Cyprus. circumstances in Cyprus.

    In Britain, Cypriot migrants settled in and around St Pancras, Camden, and the West End of London where jobs were to be found in the hotel, catering and tailoring industries. Greek emigration to the US began tentatively in the 1880s and 1890s. A community of 18,000 at the turn of the 19th century reached half a million by 1940. It is more than understandable that in the US, Cypriot immigrants found a place within the well established Greek community. Twenty-seven volunteers have been identified as residing in Britain prior to their passage to Spain, 22 in the US and four in Canada, of whom three — Toula Ioannou, Maria Nicolaou, and Eleni Nikiphorou — served as nurses in Spain. The political situation in Cyprus, especially in regard to the difficulties faced by the Communist Party of Cyprus at that time, meant that direct volunteering and/or travel from Cyprus was very difficult. Had it not been so, it is worth suggesting that the size of the Cypriot volunteer contingent in Spain might have been much higher.

    All members of the Cypriot contingent were Greek-Cypriots. No evidence of Turkish-Cypriot involvement has as yet come to light. This is perhaps a reflection of the then size of the Turkish-Cypriot community in Cyprus, Britain, and the US. This is not to say that there may not have been Turkish-Cypriot volunteers within the small Turkish volunteer contingent. The UK-based Cypriot volunteers were in the main active members of the Communist Party of Great Britain, operating within a 'Cypriot section' and producing their own Greek-language propaganda. Several, including Yiacoumis Georgiou, had been members of the Communist Party of Cyprus.

    Key to the political and social development of the UK-based Cypriot volunteers was the Cypriot Political & Cultural Club in London's Soho district. At least 8 Cypriot volunteers gave the club as their contact address in their International Brigades records. This *kafenia* operated as a cultural and political workers' centre, from which communist literature, activity and ideas disseminated among the Cypriot community. The US-based Cypriot volunteers were politically active in the CPUSA and in

Pankypriaki, the main Cypriot cultural organisation in the US during the 1930s. A number of the Cypriot volunteers, including Georgios Pantazis, Antonis Thomas, Jacovos Koumoullos, Jimis Joannou, Panayiotis Katsaronas, Vasilis Pattikis and Christos Christodoulou, were part of the Pankypriaki leadership.

Cypriots in the US also came within the orbit and influence of the political and cultural organisations of the substantial Greek-American community, including Spartacus, which, as Dan Georgakas and Paul Buhle have argued, was 'the organizing hub of what emerged as the largest and most important radical current in Greek America'. Spartacus operated a club close to the 'Greek tavern scene of Eighth Avenue' and the fur and garment districts of New York, which maintained heavily unionised Greek employment. *Empros*, its communist newspaper, ran from 1923 to 1938.

Volunteers in the English-speaking units of the International Brigades were in almost all cases politically active or politicised individuals — the adventurer or dilettante, whilst not unknown, was a rare beast. There is clear evidence of the involvement of many of the Cypriot volunteers in the National Unemployed Workers' Movement of the 1930s in Britain. Nicholas Vasiliou, for example, interviewed by the Imperial War Museum, testified to his radicalisation by the Hunger Marches of 1932 and 1934. Similar evidence exists to confirm Cypriot activity within the US labour movement and the great unemployed marches of the 1930s, especially those of 1933 and 1934 when US unemployment ran at over 20 percent. The London-based volunteers Antonis Theodoulou, Michael Economides and Ezekias Papaioannou have all testified to their involvement in pro-Republican rallies and in demonstrations against the British Union of Fascists prior to volunteering.

Cypriot volunteer motivation also included resistance to an imperialism experienced first-hand; specifically, it included a linkage between the struggle against fascism and the achievement of 'national independence' for Cyprus. Britain in the 1930s was still very much an imperial power, one that had held Cyprus as a protectorate/colony since 1878 and one whose governance in the 1930s became increasingly despotic. International Brigader Michael Economides, writing in the *Volunteer for Liberty* in 1938, drew heavily on the Cypriot colonial experience under British rule: 'The fight of the Spanish people for the defence of their democratic liberties and their national independence is at the same time the struggle of all the oppressed colonial peoples and oppressed national minorities.'

Thirty-eight Cypriot volunteers were either wounded or killed in Spain, a casualty rate of 68 percent. About a third of the total were killed. Both these figures were significantly higher than the equivalent rates for the British Battalion, for which casualty rates were around 50 and 25 percent respectively. On 21 September 1938, Juan Negrín, the Spanish Prime Minister, announced the withdrawal of the International Brigades. British Empire citizens, amongst them many Cypriots, were camped at Ripoll in the Pyrenees before repatriation to Britain. Other volunteers crossed over to France, where they were initially interned. Not all Cypriot volunteer repatriation went smoothly. For example, the British consul in Spain was determined that Nicholas Vasiliou be sent to Cyprus. Intervention by the International Brigades

Commission in Paris secured his return to Britain. Evanthis Nicolaides, on the other hand, was prevented by the British consulate in France from travelling to Cyprus. Most surviving US-based Cypriots found little difficulty returning to New York. However, in common with the other American volunteers their difficulties began in the decades after the Spanish Civil War as a result of increasing anti-communist attitudes within the American state apparatus.

In 480 BC, 1,400 Spartans, Thebans, and Thespians defended the pass at Thermopylae against an invading Persian army. The Cypriots who travelled to Spain held the passes of that country against reaction and fascism. The Persian army was victorious at Thermopylae — and Franco captured Madrid on 28 March 1939. Ultimately, Xerxes's second invasion of Greece was defeated. Fascism too was defeated in Europe.

> Paul Philippou is a historian and the author of *Spanish Thermopylae: Cypriot volunteers in the Spanish Civil War, 1936-39* (2009). This article first appeared in issue 55 (September 2020) of *¡No Pasarán*

Cloudless Day in Spain

Jimmy Moon

It does not seem thirty long bleeding years this weekend
That the bloody rising started in Spain,
And of my comrades and companions of those days
Very few now remain!
There was a band, the Samurai of the West,
Some odd two thousand from these British Isles
Who sprang to arms, made the Pyrenean passes
And like knights of a new order
Would win their spurs in the cause of freedom.

You today, who would remember us, the common men,
Have heard much from intellectuals,
Who would call us tilters of windmills,
And cynically laugh at Don Quixote,
But it is better to have fought and lost in a good cause,
If you can say, in our losing, we have lost at all!

I well remember that weekend thirty years ago
For my brother and I, young lads in our teens,
Set off on our bikes, our steel steeds,
Heading for the other side of Leicester,
Father called us early,
Mother gave us good food for saddle bags,
In our strong youth we sped
Through the sultry countryside of July.

Wheels hissed on tarmac, the sun shone down,
With high gears and on well-oiled wheels we sped
Out into the country, passing the haymakers
And sweating over our bars,
Eventually reaching our destination,
And slept as only young men can.
Next day, the Sunday, we must return,
And in fickle July the sun shone brassy and burning,
Yet the night before the golden yellow moon hung over the forest.

I remember we stopped for tea at a roadside café
And I chided my brother for his lack of speed
Who much later was to singe his wings like Icarus
And falling to his death blazing in his bomber
Missing somewhere over Germany.
And all through that hot Sunday we pedalled
Hard the hundred and twenty miles home again.

Meanwhile we wondered how two of our comrades fared
Who at this very time were cycling through southern France
Down to Barcelona to that romantic warmer clime,
For down there, in Catalonia, they hoped
To test their young manhood in the Workers' Olympiad!

What did we know of Spain in our youth?
Oranges, pomegranates, the castanets,
The wild gypsy dancing, of dark eyed beauties,
The rousing call of flamenco heard on the radio.
We knew of the Spanish Main
Of tales of lofty galleons,
Laid low by our pirate ancestors.
Of recent times there was a legend
Of miners with their dynamite in Asturias
Who had made a desperate stand to defend their liberties.
This is all we knew,
We who were to know so much for so long.

And all the time our wheels sang
And echoed our youthful song.
That evening late we arrived home
Stripped to the waist
My Mother said:
'Good God you did not come through London like that!'
'All the way from Leicester' we laughingly replied,
And after supper we prepared the bed.
'There is a rumour' father said
'That there's a rising in Spanish Morocco,
'Gainst the Spanish Republic, the fascist generals rise.'

So Nat and Sam in Barcelona,
What tales they'll tell on their return!
They were not to come back,
But stayed to fight in the first centuria.

Red, yellow and violet was to be their banner
And with three pointed stars on berets
All our friends one by one would go to Madrid
Where stood the International Brigade
To give their blood to Spain,
And now only some two hundred of us remain.

Last week I heard that Martin
Had died of cancer of the lung,
And Alan of leukemia had lost his only son.
Of those who laid not down their lives
Amongst the olive groves or were maimed, some
Returned to suffer once more in the bloody world war.
And others died foolishly and without cause:
Archie drank himself to death, Jock is a tramp, Guy went mad.
They say Geordie's wife has left him,
Or is it the other way?
Paddy's on the road, is still working very hard,
Oh my dear comrades, life is sometimes sad.

Where is black Sam?
Who drove the ration truck and had frostbite?
Or almond-eyed Chang,
Whose father kept a laundry
And once taught English in Peking?
The brown-skinned Turk from Istanbul,
Whose pseudonym was Smith?
So brave, I well remember him and
The golden-voiced Cuban who sang to us at night
They were just a few of us who went to Spain, to fight.

Of the other brave battalions and brigades
Formed of all the tribes of men
Bards in other lands shall often sing of them,
The high-stepping girls and brave boys of our youth
You'd hardly recognise them in their children,
This is the truth!

The youth today ride motorbikes,
The girls no skirts at all.
Their hair is long and flowing
To be with it or on the ball.
But underneath this rebel show

Against all cant and power
They may still find in Spain's freedom
Their best and finest hour.
Oh yes, I well remember that evening long ago
And perhaps of Tom, Dick and Harry you'll say
I just remember them —
They fought in Spain
That we might hold our heads higher today.
Will tomorrow bring another cloudless day in Spain?

> Jimmy Moon was a stretcher-bearer and later a machine-gunner in the British Battalion before his capture at Calaceite, Aragón on 31 March 1938. After ten months' imprisonment at San Pedro de Cardeña, near Burgos, he was repatriated in February 1939. This poem was published in issue 37 (July 2014) of the *IBMT Newsletter*, believed to be previously unpublished. It was discovered in the papers of International Brigade supporter Martin Cantor, with a dedication 'To Martin Cantor from Jimmy Moon, 10th February 1990. Salud.' It was written on the 30th anniversary of the Francoist uprising.

Jimmy Moon (left) and Dr Reginald Saxton, who served as a doctor in Spain after volunteering through the Spanish Medical Aid Committee. They are photographed raising the British Battalion banner at the unveiling of an International Brigade memorial in Reading in 1990. Courtesy of the IBMT.

The War

Painting of the XV Brigade's Anti-Tank Battery by Thomas Chilvers, one of the battery's veterans. The battery's accurate, high velocity guns were a key asset of the Brigades until they were destroyed during the retreat from Belchite in March 1938. Courtesy of the Marx Memorial Library.

Not such a quiet front

Marshall Mateer

In the early hours of Sunday 19 July 1936, the last peacetime train to Barcelona made its way along Spain's coast. From his carriage window, the *Daily Worker* reporter Frank Pitcairn heard Spanish youths shouting: 'Shooting! Barcelona!' By the time the train neared the city cries of 'Long live democracy! Long live the Republic!' thundered up and down its corridors. Barcelona, still echoing to the sound of gunfire, was crowded with people silently listening to radio bulletins from the loudspeakers of the pavement cafés and bars.

    Against the large numbers of people soon scrambling to get out of Spain, a few pushed determinedly the other way: 'Germans, Italians, Swiss, Austrians, Dutch, a few Americans,' reported Pitcairn (real name Claud Cockburn), and a handful of British. 'All languages are spoken . . . an indescribable atmosphere of political enthusiasm . . . absolute confidence in speedy success.' Some were already in Spain for the People's Olympiad that had been planned as a counterfoil to the Berlin Olympics hosted by Nazi Germany. Others made their own way to Barcelona and sometimes straight to the front. By mid-August three tailors from Stepney, Nat Cohen, Sam Masters and Alec Sheller, and artist Felicia Browne had passed through the Karl Marx Barracks in Barcelona. Masters was now at the front and the poet John Cornford had enlisted in the militia of the revolutionary POUM (Partido Obrero de Unificación Marxista / Workers Party of Marxist Unification) in Lecina.[31] The British consulate was reporting to the Secret Intelligence Service the presence of 'known British Communists,' including Tom Wintringham established the Tom Mann Centuria; Kisch was wounded and invalided home.

It was common for individuals to move between militia units of their own volition — mostly for practical reasons. On 18 August the Thälmann-Gruppe were approached by two Germans and Sam Masters, who asked to join them, as they had lost contact with their own unit in the fighting. A major deployment of troops from the Karl Marx Barracks was delayed. Felicia Browne transferred to another that was ready to move. In Tardienta, 100 miles from Barcelona, in Aragón, she volunteered for a 'shock unit' and died behind enemy lines alongside the Italian comrade she had tried to help. Nat Cohen went on an ill-fated expedition to Mallorca, as did the young Richard Kisch and

---

[31] Editor's note: The POUM was a revolutionary Marxist party primarily concentrated in Catalonia. During the Spanish Civil War it was part of the broad alliance against Franco and the fascists, but clashed with the Moscow-aligned Communist Party of Spain (PCE) over questions of strategy and how to balance war and revolution, as well as the PCE's accusations that the POUM was part of a 'Trotskyist' fifth column to sabotage the Republic. The POUM leader, Andreu Nin, was murdered in June 1937, ostensibly on orders from Moscow.

The iconic photo of the Tom Mann Centuria at the Karl Marx Barracks in Barcelona, September 1936. From left to right, the individuals are: Sid Avner, Nat Cohen, Ramona Siles García, Tom Wintringham, Giorgio Tioli, Jack Barry and David Marshall. Courtesy of the IBMT.

his friends. Back in Barcelona Cohen and Tom Wintringham established the Tom Mann Centuria; Kisch was wounded and invalided home.

In Barcelona an agency reporter scanning the crowds waiting to sign for the POUM militia saw Bill Peel. Standing 6ft 6ins and weighing 16 stone, he must have stood out even more than George Orwell would do three months later. Secretary of his Labour Party branch and Spanish relief committee, Peel had been sent to Spain to write a report on the situation there. At home his mother fretted for his well-being, while his father, a cotton magnate, was opposed to his son's politics, though he 'admired his courage.' He joined a workers' militia, but Peel himself, a direct descendant of Prime Minister Sir Robert Peel, was 'depressed about his ancestry.'

William Martin delivered an ambulance, funded by the Independent Labour Party, to Barcelona. Amongst those on board when the vehicle went to Tierz in Aragón was a German volunteer Eva Laufer, who later settled in Britain. Before an attack on Huesca she recalled: 'We were given rum in our coffee and marijuana cigarettes' but 'neither affected me . . . I was terrified!' Martin, who had army experience, joined an anarchist column and was immediately put in charge of an artillery unit.

Meanwhile, on 20 September in Hyde Park thousands gathered for the 'The March of English People's History.' They greeted Richard Kisch with a great cheer. They stood in silence while a portrait of Felicia Browne passed, her story already part of the wider narrative. 'Miss Felicia Browne, the artist, was in the ranks of the government army and she was killed,' Willie Gallagher informed the House of Commons during the first full parliamentary debate on Spain (29 October). 'Let us face up to this question, which is of significance to the whole of Europe, and make sure that victory goes to the people's government.' The *Evening Telegraph* had informed its readers that the British government was making every effort at 'ensuring non-intervention in Spain.' Steps to prevent volunteers from leaving Britain were under 'active consideration.'

The high plateau of Aragón has its own climate: glaring sun and radiating heat; biting cold and permeating damp. At the British hospital at Grañén, Kenneth Sinclair-Loutit noted that 'treatment [for] wet, cold and exposure in the Sierra Alcubierre was our main task for several days.' 'It was very cold,' Laufer recalled, 'and we were given long underpants.' Winter was setting in — a last chance to attack.

Greville Texidor, originally from Wolverhampton, joined the POUM militia. She and her partner Werner Droescher took part in the Battle of Almudévar (November 1936) in the Italian Rosselli Brigade. They reached the barbed wire entanglements on the town's edge but were beaten back. The attack, a carefully planned operation, was launched at daybreak across a wide arc of the front. But the promised planes did not arrive till the afternoon after the ground troops had already attacked. The artillery made some mark, but for a period fired on its own troops. The backup promised by the communist forces for the Italian brigade did not materialise; and a flanking unit became lost in the hills during the night. Perhaps worst of all, communication between the different sections and the command during the two days was intermittent, confused and often non-existent.

As Texidor and Droescher were under fire, a few miles further along the ridge Nat Cohen and Sam Masters, in the communist militia, were storming 'The Hermitage', a fortified machine-gun placement on a promontory which commanded the region. It had been fought over many times. The attack failed, the casualties were high and Wintringham's angry cry: 'That bloody Hermitage!' carried all the way back to Britain. Cohen and Masters were amongst the wounded taken to Grañén. Aragón is often described as 'a quiet front.' John Cornford used the phrase as a refrain in a poem: 'This is a quiet sector of a quiet front.' Ralph Bates, with years in Spain, saw beneath the surface and sensed the 'grim tranquility' of the region.

In the Spanish Civil War visitors' centre at Robres, a memorial records 8,500 names spelled out in pure white on a stark red ground — those from the Los Monegros region who died in this quiet front between 1936 and 1946 (the end of guerrilla activities in the region). On his return home William Martin implored his comrades at Ruislip-Norwood Labour Party: 'Unless [it] was stopped in Spain it would happen to this country,' and Bill Peel called on the labour movement 'to oppose utterly the present policy of the National Government.'

Peel joined the Durham Light Infantry and died fighting in France in 1940, one of those who fought fascism three times: on the streets in Britain, in Spain, and on a Second World War battleground. Emmanuel 'Manny' Julius was part of the first British Medical Unit: young, Jewish, a member of the Communist Party and enthusiastic to get to Spain, though 'disgruntled' with his role as quartermaster. To one colleague he 'seemed second rate and rather schizoid.' He drove an ambulance but was sometimes 'reckless.' Julius 'deserted' from the medical unit, joined a military column and was killed in action in the Sierra de Robres.

Irish volunteer Bill Scott later remembered: 'A friend of mine named Julius, a Londoner, was killed on the 8th of October. He was leader of a Column although only twenty-four. He was leading an attack on a machine gun nest and was killed in the fight that followed. I was talking to him three days before he died. He was on leave in Barcelona and went back to the front of his own accord. He said he wanted to be with the boys when they captured Huesca.'

Marshall Mateer is an artist, film-maker, writer, and educator, who has researched the earliest British volunteers in the Spanish Civil War. This essay was featured in issue 43 (September 2016) of the *IBMT Newsletter* as 'Aragón: not such a quiet front'.

Death and confusion among the olive groves

Sam Lesser

The battle at Lopera was perhaps the smallest of the bitter battles against fascism in Spain, and the shortest in duration, but it was crucial nevertheless. And in the record of the British volunteers in Spain, it was a baptism of fire.

Earlier in the fighting in Madrid's University City, the Casa de Campo and Boadilla del Monte, the first two groups of British volunteers had helped defeat Franco's first attempt to take Madrid. The survivors of those groups, and they were few, were then withdrawn to the International Brigade base at Albacete. But by Christmas 1936 a critical situation had arisen in Andalusia, where the fascist general Queipo de Llano was directing a general offensive from Córdoba and Granada.

To deal with this emergency it was decided that the formation of a complete English-speaking battalion would have to be delayed and the No.1 Company of 145 men, including the [Madrid] survivors John Cornford, Jock Cunningham, Joe Hinks, Joe Clarke, Edward Burke and myself, were detailed to form part of the French 12th Battalion, later called the Marseillaise, and part of the 14th International Brigade commanded by the Polish General Walter — Karol Świerczewski. That No.1 Company, which included English, Irish, Scots and Welsh volunteers, most of whom of course would not accept being called 'the English company,' but they were inevitably called '*los ingleses*' because they all spoke English. The company, as part of the British Battalion, was later given the title of the Major Attlee Company in honour of the Labour Party leader when he visited the battalion. The company was commanded by the legendary George Nathan, later killed at the Battle of Brunete [in July 1937].

One night [in December 1936] the word went round that the fascists had broken through on the Córdoba front and everybody, cooks, the lot, was taken to the local railway station at Albacete, put on a train and sent across Spain to a place called Andújar, where we detrained. As we were getting out of the trains we came under attack from the air — machine-gunned from the aircraft — and I remember our first casualty at that time was a man from the East End who had been at Cable Street — Harry Segal. He was killed as he was getting out. I saw him as he was hit and his body fell to the ground.

We underwent more training at Andújar, then went on trucks to the front. There was a very bitter battle at a town called Lopera and, personally, I was not in very good shape, although I had survived Madrid. But we advanced there, as ordered. As we advanced we came under very heavy fire and had to keep our heads down. I did my best but, not far from me, John Cornford and Ralph Fox were killed. There were heavy casualties, and I was wounded. I didn't know at the time where I'd been wounded — in which part of my body — except that when I tried to get up I couldn't. I just fell down — there was something wrong with my legs. Our losses during the battle were heavy.

It was not only arms that we lacked in that Battle at Lopera — and much of the armaments we did have seemed to have come from a museum. We also lacked a proper medical service and our wounded from that battle, myself included, had to be taken away in farm carts at first and then in open trucks. Nor shall I ever forget as I lay there hearing the calls during the night of '¡camillero!' and '¡brancardier!', the Spanish and French words for stretcher-bearer. Fortunately for me, my comrade Jock Cunningham managed to drag me clear from the crest of the hill where I was caught and he helped me along until we found a cart.

It was a long time later that I was told that people started looking for me, and Jock Cunningham, who'd been with the Argyle and Sutherland Highlanders, had become a great friend of mine during the Battle of Madrid, said he was going out to look for me. Apparently they said: 'It's no use, Jock, he's a dead'un, a goner, and if you go out you'll be a goner too.' Jock, to his credit, said he was going anyway. He looked around and found me — then literally dragged me in, because he couldn't find a stretcher.

I'd got a bullet in my left leg, and also in my back — because I had an early encounter with what in World War II came to be called 'friendly fire.' Our French comrades, who were on our right flank to support our advance, were sending over crossfire. We had apparently advanced too quickly and when they saw us they opened fire.

The biggest surprise came when, at the end of a journey through the night, we [the injured] finished up at what turned out to be a hospital in the town of Linares de Jaén, at that time a lead and silver mining town controlled by the British company Rio Tinto. As we were taken from the trucks we saw a huge crowd packing a courtyard of the hospital and they cheered as we were lifted off and taken into the hospital where we were to be nursed by Spanish 'sisters of mercy,' nuns who were devoted to their duty. But the following day we were in for a bigger surprise when, as it seemed to us, the wards were packed by ordinary men and women bringing gifts of all sorts from elementary things like toothbrushes and toothpaste, soap, combs, underwear, pyjamas and trays and trays of succulent Spanish pastries and bottles of sweet Málaga wine.

Later when some of us had recovered sufficiently to go into town we discovered that it was impossible to buy a drink or a meal, for the people insisted on treating us as guests. At that time I could not get out but some of the Irish comrades did, and Joe Monks told me that there was a so-called British consul in Linares who was chatting up some of our people and encouraging them to desert. As soon as I was equipped with crutches I went to the office of what is called an 'honorary vice-consul,' a local inhabitant recruited by the Foreign Office to look after British interests in the area. In his office this man was blatantly displaying on his wall pictures of Hitler and Mussolini. I gave him a piece of my mind — but by then he had managed to organise the desertion of a couple of our people. After Lopera, the No.1 Company and the 14th Brigade, as well as the Marseillaise Battalion, took part in other engagements at Las Rozas and Majadahonda. When the company returned to Albacete the 67 survivors of the 145 men who had left the base were given a heroes' welcome. We had left our finest under the olive trees on what used to be called Calvary Hill around Lopera, as we were to leave so many more at Jarama and Brunete, Teruel and Belchite.

> Sam Lesser was wounded in action in the International Brigades but lived to become one of the last surviving Brigaders upon his death in 2010. After the war he married the volunteer nurse Margaret Powell and later served as IBMT chair, receiving honorary Spanish citizenship alongside other IB veterans in 2009. This extract from Sam Lesser's memoir was reproduced in issue 43 (September 2016) of the *IBMT Newsletter*, as 'Lopera: Death and confusion among the olive groves'. Reproduced here with kind permission of Sam Lesser's daughter, Ruth Muller.

The original memorial to English-speaking members of the XV Brigade at Jarama. Erected in 1937 adjacent to the graves of numerous volunteers, it was destroyed following the Francoist victory. Although new memorials have been installed since the transition to democracy in Spain, the tireless efforts of Spanish researcher José María Olivera Marco have led to the original location being identified, which has in turn led to the approval by Spanish authorities of a project to survey the site and potentially exhume the remains of the fallen Brigaders. Courtesy of the IBMT.

Madrid lived!

Ajmal Waqif

This February marks the 85th anniversary of the Battle of Jarama, when the International Brigades, as part of the Spanish Republican Army, repelled Franco's forces south-east of Madrid. After days of bloody and chaotic battle, they checked the enemy advance along the Jarama River. After failing to take Madrid in late 1936, Franco made a renewed attempt to surround the city by cutting the road to Valencia, which was the seat of the Republican government at the time. The Republican forces stationed south of Madrid, including the 14th and 11th International Brigades, met the rebel assault on 5 February. They gave ground over the next few days and by 11 February the Rebels had taken the west bank of the Jarama River and begun their crossing. Very early in the morning of 12 February, the XV Brigade, consisting of the British Battalion, the Balkan Dimitrov Battalion and Franco-Belgian units, were mobilised and moved to the Pingarrón Heights, which was part of the ridge of hills overlooking the Jarama River valley. Behind them were the groves of olive trees that have become an enduring symbol of the battle. Facing off against the elite troops of the Army of Africa, the Battalion's lack of training and equipment took its toll, with the number of casualties growing at an alarming rate.

By early afternoon, the battalion was in a desperate position, its flank unprotected, the machine-gun company without ammunition and numbers decreasing by the minute. The hill where they made their stand came to be known as Suicide Hill. The remaining volunteers were faced with little choice but to pull back to the battalion's headquarters on the plateau behind them. The enemy rushed to occupy their position on Suicide Hill but were quickly forced to duck for cover by the machine-gun company, which at last had managed to reload and arm their weapons. As the first day of the battle came to an end, the battalion found itself with less than half the number that had set out from Madrigueras. Scottish volunteer Frank McCusker later said: 'It wasnae a battle at all, it was a bloody slaughter as far as we were concerned. They had everything and we had nothing.'

The next day, 13 February, was no less terrifying. The battalion waged a desperate struggle to hold back the rebel forces. As their flank once again came under attack, the commander of No.4 Company pulled his soldiers back and the machine-gun company, situated on a knoll to the battalion's right, became isolated and were surrounded. Over 30 volunteers, including company commander Harold Fry and adjutant Ted Dickenson, were captured and several of the battalion lost their lives in an ill-judged attempt to rescue them. Somehow, the remaining volunteers in the battalion held on until nightfall.

On day three, under a sustained attack from a hugely superior force supported by artillery and tanks, the line finally broke. In small disorganised groups the exhausted volunteers drifted back to the farm cookhouse which they had established as a base. There they were addressed by Lieutenant Colonel Gal, the commander of the XV Brigade. He explained to them that they were now the only troops between the Rebels and the Valencia road. Despite their physical and mental exhaustion, 140 volunteers marched back, led by Jock Cunningham and Frank Ryan, to try to recapture their lost positions. They sang 'The Internationale' as they rallied, picking up stragglers along the way. The enemy forces, fooled into believing them to be fresh reinforcements while also suffering vigorous attacks from the Dimitrov Battalion to the right, retreated back to their earlier positions. 'A battalion that does not know how to be defeated deserves an occasional stroke of luck,' reflected Tom Wintringham, battalion commander at Jarama, a few years later.

Then, during the night of 14 and 15 February, the Republicans brought up actual reinforcements and the gap in the line was finally plugged. The Rebel advance ground to a halt. Both sides dug defensive fortifications and a stalemate ensued, which neither side was able to overcome. The Republicans' repeated counter-attacks over the course of the month failed to push Franco's forces back over the river. The last of these attempts saw the newly-formed American Abraham Lincoln Battalion cut down by machine-gun fire while attempting a frontal assault on the enemy positions. Charlie Donnelly, one of the Irish volunteers attached to the battalion, while crouching for cover, reportedly said: 'Even the olives are bleeding.' Shortly afterwards he was shot and killed among those olive groves.

After February 1937 the positions at the Jarama front remained virtually static for the rest of the war. The bloody sacrifices at Jarama meant that Franco was never able to conquer Madrid militarily. As Wintringham later wrote: 'The biggest and best organised drive that Franco had so far made had been stopped — within a few miles of its starting place . . . Madrid lived.' The Battle of Jarama epitomises both the horror and the heroism of the volunteers' experience of Spain's civil war. It served as a baptism by fire for the XV Brigade who, barely trained, under-equipped and following chaotic orders, somehow managed to hold back the full ferocity of a professional army. Their sacrifice continues to resonate down the years, remembered in memorials, song, poetry and art.

Ajmal Waqif is the executive officer of the IBMT. This essay appeared in issue 59 (January 2022) of *¡No Pasarán!*

Panic at Brunete

Cyril Sexton

One day towards the end of July the Spaniards yelled that the Fascists were coming.[32] Harry Gross sprang upon the parapet firing at the enemy. John Ireland and I were firing as fast as we could with our rifles. On the right there was an enemy officer or NCO directing the troops forward. I set my sight for 200 yards and took a bead on him. To my satisfaction I saw him go down.

We seemed to have held them to our front, but we could see our right flank was crumbling. Then we no longer heard the sound of our light machine gun and found that Harry was dead. We tried to fire the gun but the pan was empty. After fitting a new one we tried again, but it still would not fire. It looked like it had been dropped in the sand and grit and needed a good clean. We were too pressed for things like that. Our Spaniards were now all either dead or wounded, and the wounded were trying to make their way to the rear.

The enemy had by now outflanked us and were beginning to climb the ridge behind us. With our machine gun out of action, they began to advance towards us. They were throwing hand grenades. Others followed with rifle and bayonet. John Ireland and I were now being fired on from the front, the right flank and the rear. My rifle became so hot that I had to knock the bolt up with a stone to insert more cartridges. Our two rifles did not seem to be making much difference to the advancing troops.

We could only retreat down to the Guadarrama and up the ridge further down the valley. We agreed that since we were on our own and being shot at from three sides it was no use staying. We went down into the valley with bullets cracking around our ears and puffing up the dirt around our feet. We climbed the hill to the right, went down the other side and up another slope. When we reached the top we found some of the British Battalion there, taking pot-shots across the valley.

Further up the ridge we were on to our right there appeared some figures and I started firing at them. I knew this must be the enemy that had outflanked our previous post. Someone said: 'Don't fire. They're on our side.' In fact they were an enemy fighting patrol with a spotter for their artillery as well. Soon shells began to fall amongst us. Those that remained moved back down the reverse slope, though still followed by the shelling.

---

[32] Editor's note: At Brunete, on the western outskirts of Madrid, the Republicans had attempted a July 1937 offensive which intended to disrupt the Francoists' progress in northern Spain and take some of the pressure off besieged Madrid. However, within a few short weeks the Republicans had stalled in their advance and were then forced into retreat by a massive counter-attack. The International Brigades sustained significant losses over the course of the Battle of Brunete.

John and I moved down and found a deep dug-out, which we occupied, taking turns to rest or to be on lookout. Around this time John was wounded in the upper arm. I went with him to what we thought was the rear and found an ambulance, which took him, leaving me on my own. Stuck with no one to talk to, no knowledge of where anyone was and not a soul in sight, I felt really lonely. It was the enemy airforce that made me pull myself together. They came over and started dropping bombs around me, and that concentrated my mind in a moment.

I began making my way back to where I thought our reserve position would be. Going along the woody valley of the Aulencia river towards Villanueva de la Cañada on the left, I was overtaken by lots of panic-stricken troops dragging their mules with them. I stood aside to let them pass and went on myself. When I came to the head of the valley there were mounted military police trying to get some order into the troops. It didn't seem as if they were having any success, when another lot of planes came over and dropped their bombs, causing more panic.

Leaving this turmoil I continued along the road to Villanueva and found a couple of others from the battalion and joined up with them. In the meantime, the enemy airforce was having a field day, dropping their bombs on vehicular traffic and with their fighters straffing anything that moved. We crossed the road and the other two said they knew where the cookhouse was and this was always the rallying point. When we arrived there we were soon joined by the rest of the battalion. How few of us remained. When we were counted there were only 42 of us.

Cyril Sexton was a gardener who became a machine-gunner with the British Battalion. He was wounded twice, at Jarama and at the Ebro, but survived and was also a veteran of the Second World War. This edited extract from Cyril Sexton's unpublished memoir features in issue 61 (September 2022) of *¡No Pasarán!*. Published with the kind permission of his son, Clive Sexton.

There's Wally

Bob Beagrie

My poem 'There's Wally' was inspired by reading the developing manuscript of *I Sing of My Comrades* by Tony Fox (now published), a booklet to accompany the unveiling of the Stockton memorial to the eight members of the International Brigade born in Stockton-on-Tees.[33] I was particularly struck by one particular incident which occurred during the Aragón Offensive. On 31 March 1938, during the second Battle of Belchite, the British Battalion was being escorted to their forward positions and came across a group of six tanks which the men mistook for Republican tanks. As Bob Cooney recalls in *Proud Journey*: 'We were soon disillusioned. With terrifying suddenness the tanks opened fire on us. Another group of tanks emerged from the wood on the right, and simultaneously hoards of Italian infantry appeared yelling their heads off. It was a shambles!'

The account goes on to describe how the British Battalion commissar Wally Tapsell was shot immediately by a fascist officer in the first tank. Tony Fox writes in his upcoming history:

> The British managed to return fire, some men tried throwing empty cans, in an attempt to fool the tank crew that they had grenades, this gave enough respite for the Battalion to scatter. The men made their way back to Republican lines in small groups: Walter Gregory led one group, Malcolm Dunbar another, Lewis Clive led a handful of men who took several days to make their way back, Bob Cooney had been captured initially but managed to escape with another handful of men.

This incident and the flight back to Republican lines would make a strong and dramatic screenplay. In an attempt to begin a rudimentary exploration of the ambush I focussed it into a poem, trying to use each line as a cinematic style close-up of accumulating details, which paint a bigger picture and capture the shock, drama and tragedy of the event. The pictorial nature of the poem led to the conceit of using the refrain 'There is the . . .' which renders the event in a kind of fixed eternal moment, one which we might view from afar, study intensely but never fully understand. I realised the approach bore similarities to illustration and remembered the children's *Where's Wally?* picture puzzle books by English illustrator Martin Handford. These books ask the reader to locate 'Wally' among the extraneous details and other figures within a certain location. The connection between Wally Tapsell and Handford's 'Wally' is meant to be one of ironic tragedy given the poem begins with Tapsell's sudden death, described using the simile of the bull at the *hora de la verdad*, a sacrificial bull at 'the moment of truth' in a bullfight, when the matador makes the killing thrust of his sword between the horns.

---

[33] Editor's note: Self-published in 2022 as Tony Fox, *I Sing of My Comrades: Remembering Stockton's International Brigaders*.

The poem tries to capture the 'shambles' and panic of the situation and towards the end returns to focus upon the prostrate, still body of Wally Tapsell and the necessity to leave him if they are to survive the ambush and avoid capture.

There's Wally

There is Wally toppling like *toro* in the *hora de la verdad*
There's the dead glare in his eyes even before he hits the ground
There is the small cloud of gun smoke from the barrel of the pistol
There is the rosette bullet hole flowering in the soil of his flesh

There's the stricken, disbelieving stare of his comrades in ideals
There is the turret of the tank from which the shot was fired
There is the flush of panic in the faces of the ambushed Brigaders
There is the frantic, headless chicken-run as realisation kicks in
There are the boys ducking and diving as if caught oggy-raiding

There is the sporadic yell and splutter of hastily returned fire
There are the Italian infantrymen emerging from the tree line
There are the British throwing tins of food as if they were grenades
There is Lewis Clive barking orders like a starting gun, 'Regroup! Retreat!'
There is the scatter and scramble for escape into the woodlands

There is Bob Cooney shouting, 'I thought they were ours!'
There is Malcolm Dunbar dragging Bob behind a tree trunk
There is Bob insisting they can't leave their Commissar like that
There is Malcolm pointing at Wally Tapsell lying still in the dirt

There's his voice saying, 'He's gone! Now run! Run, or we're done!'

> Bob Beagrie is a poet and playwright. He is senior lecturer in Creative Writing at Teesside University. This poem and accompanying explanation appeared in issue 56 (January 2021) of *¡No Pasarán!*

Members of the British Workers' Sports Federation, a Communist Party-aligned sporting organisation, in Moscow in July 1928 to attend the first Spartakiad — an international sports event held in the Soviet Union. The photo, taken at a Moscow station, is from a cutting from an unknown Soviet publication. The original owner, one of the individuals in the photograph, identified future British Battalion commissar Walter 'Wally' Tapsell in the foreground on the left, with both hands visible. Courtesy of the IBMT.

4am: the great advance begins

Nathan Clark

Four o'clock is zero hour[34], and the boats push off. The fascist guards hear us and turn on a machine-gun sweeping the river. The bullets splash in the water, and land in the sand of our bank with a 'plop'. The light comes up rapidly and they see what is happening. Other machine-gun teams are roused and eight or ten begin blazing away furiously, but, in their panic, their aim is bad; so far our casualties are nil. Now our anti-tanks come into action. They fire high velocity 3-inch shells directly at their objective and, if one of them lands near you, that's just too bad.

With the growing light they can see the machine-gun emplacements and the shells are landing all round them. That cascade of brick, concrete and sand was a machine gun nest — it's twisted iron and dead fascists now. 'The home wires must be red hot over there; the avions won't be long now,' someone remarks. The first lot are over; several fall and lie still as they run for cover, but move steadily up the hill, from rock to rock, giving as good as they get. The boats are back again and a fresh load goes across; the fascists must feel a bit like King Canute, except that he knew what he was in for, and they are totally unprepared for such an invasion. The engineers begin their operations, and work with speed and skill, only possible with the fiercest discipline and organisation under such trying conditions.

There is a distant drone; everyone strains eyes to see where they are coming from. Those Germans certainly don't waste time — five Junkers in formation, then three and another three. The men in the boats blaze away hopefully with their automatic rifles. Suddenly bright flashes and white puffs appear all round them, the anti-aircraft have come into action. They twist, turn, bank, and fly off into fascist country — and reappear much higher. They begin to drop stuff; one lands half a mile upstream and the waves set the boats rolling. Another drops inland somewhere; another on the far bank, but the anti-aircraft are keeping them too high for accuracy, so we don't pay much attention. By this time the anti-tanks have accounted for a third of the machine gun nests, hand grenades of our advance column for a few more, and

---

[34] Editor's note: In late July 1938, the Republicans launched a surprise mass offensive, crossing the Ebro river at two locations in Catalonia and Aragón in an attempt to stave off the Francoist advance on the Republic's wartime capital in Valencia and to demonstrate to the international community that the Republic remained in the fight. Lasting until November of that year, it was the biggest battle of the civil war in terms of scope, length, and manpower, and ended in a costly loss for the Republicans. Nonetheless, as Clark's recollection implies, the offensive had a promising start. It also inflicted huge and disruptive losses on the Francoists. Some controversy over the wisdom of the decision to launch the offensive endures: see Helen Graham's review of Antony Beevor's *Battle for Spain* in her contribution to this volume.

the rest have retreated in haste to positions further back; panic seems to reign on the other side!

In what seems an incredibly short time, a temporary pontoon bridge spans the river. Tonight it will be replaced by a steel and timber one, but it will serve to take the first tanks and trucks. The tanks lurch on first, and the great cork floats sink deep into the water; the trucks and artillery follow. The great advance has begun; everything has gone off better than we dared hope.

>Nathan Clark was the great-grandson of the founder of Clarks Shoes. A Quaker, he volunteered as a driver — first of an aid lorry, then an ambulance — in Spain. This excerpt of an August 1938 despatch was published in issue 35 (July 2013) of the *IBMT Newsletter*

Across the river and into the fire

Bob Cooney

We crossed the river on the morning of 25 July. On the eve of our great adventure we held a battalion meeting at which every man present pledged himself to give his life if necessary for the honour and glory of the battalion and the victory of the Republic. Revolutionary songs and old-time choruses were sung, and in each song could be sensed the feeling that the singers were on the eve of a great adventure and were bound together by a great hope and a great comradeship. Our men were lifted out of themselves. Stirring speeches were spontaneously made by Spaniards and Britishers from the ranks. The evening concluded with *'vivas'* and cheers that gave a clue to the manner of fight we would wage on the other side of the river. Then we were on the march.

We crossed at Mora where once a long narrow bridge had carried the main Gandesa road across the river. The only opposition came from the air, from which wave after wave of Italian bombers dived on the boats and on the troops waiting to cross. The first troops to cross had met with heavy machine-gun fire from fascist strong points but, going in with great determination, they mopped up the machine-gun posts before the enemy aircraft had time to operate. Half of our battalion crossed in small boats. The remainder crossed by the first pontoon to bridge the river. In front of us went the battalion colours borne proudly aloft by Frank Bush, alongside the Spanish and Catalan flags.

Striking across country, we made for the Corbera highway. As we moved up a sunken dirt road an old peasant ran to meet us. He knelt down and with tears in his eyes kissed the Catalan flag. We were deeply moved by the incident, which brought home to us what the crossing must mean to the men, women and children who had lived for three months under the yoke of fascist tyranny. How proud and happy we felt as we pushed on in our mission of liberation. As we neared the road the bombing intensified, and in the vicinity of the Ascó-Flix crossroad it became really terrific. Marching in artillery formation, one column on either side of the road, we escaped with a few minor casualties, though most of us were showered with stones and earth.

Our sudden attack had obviously created a panic in the fascist ranks. Hundreds of prisoners came smilingly to us, obviously glad to be out of the war. A large number were Moors who amused us by holding their clenched fists high above their heads in what they fondly imagined as the 'Red' salute. *'Viva Rusia,'* they chanted. They had been quite convinced that Franco was defending Spain against a Russian invasion. All foreigners were 'Russians' — unless they were on Franco's side, in which case they were German or Italian 'volunteers.'

Late in the afternoon we were two kilometres from Corbera — the town from which we had set out on the fateful 30 March. This time the tables were turned. The

13th Brigade were preparing to storm the town, but their rear was threatened by a strong body of Moors who occupied the hills to the north-east. So our battalion deployed for action against the Moors. The fight for the hills raged all night. There was no stabilised front. The Moors, experts in hill-warfare, established themselves in caves, behind rocks or any other cover the hills afforded. Their snipers cost us some good lads, amongst them Mick Economides, a brave Cypriot, who had been one of the early volunteers. He had a severe wound in the back from which we did not expect him to recover, but his tough constitution and unquenchable spirit combined to effect a complete recovery.

We drove the Moors from the hills, thus clearing the road to Corbera which the 13th Brigade occupied without further opposition. Bloody battles lay ahead of us. The rough mountainous country had been well fortified by the enemy, and offered several advantages to the defenders. 'He who has the heights commands the valleys.' Besides these natural advantages the fascists had enormous superiority in equipment, and had no problems of communication in their rear as we had. In the first days of the offensive nearly 600 Italian planes and huge quantities of artillery, machine-guns etc were transferred to the Ebro front. The ferocity of the counter-attacks were said by veterans of the First World War to beat anything they had yet experienced. Del Vayo, the Republican minister for foreign affairs, stated:

> Reliable witnesses who took part in the European war assure us that in certain aspects these attacks have exceeded in violence the historic German assaults against Verdun. Day by day our soldiers have endured incessant bombardments by 500-kilo (1,200-pound) bombs and by artillery, which, firing day and night, gave its discharges the tone of an incessant drum-roll. Our soldiers have hung on to the soil like parts of the soil itself, and hardly did the invading infantry come out to engage in hand-to-hand fighting than all their efforts were turned into invariable defeat.

Our army stood firm against these assaults and even advanced to the gates of Gandesa. Enraged at his humiliating defeat at the hands of the ill-equipped People's Army, Franco threatened the civilian population 'without whose complicity,' he said, 'the crossing could never have taken place.' A tactless admission of the place he held in the minds of the Spanish people. He contradicted himself later when his airmen dropped leaflets amongst us, telling us that our offensive had actually been planned by Franco agents in our ranks. We had been lured across the river in order that *El Caudillo* could entrap and crush us once for all. But there was one way out, one way by which we could win *El Caudillo*'s forgiveness. We were given categorical instructions as to the date on which we should rise and shoot our officers and commissars. Only thus could we save ourselves from the wrath to come. Our officers and commissars were not noticeably alarmed.

Our supply problems intensified as the days went by. Not only did we lack equipment. The food situation was serious. When men are being tested to the limit day after day, toiling up rocky hillsides which blister inadequately shod feet; when water is so scarce it has to be doled out in minute quantities brought to the lines under enemy fire; when throats are parched and choked with dust; when under these conditions men are asked to make superhuman efforts against a strongly entrenched and well-equipped enemy, food becomes all important, for food means strength. Yet such was the strain imposed upon our slender supply lines that a week passed before our brigade *intendencia* and battalion kitchens managed to cross the river. We relied entirely on captured food dumps. Under these conditions we entered the battle for Hill 481 — the bloodiest battle in the Ebro campaign and an epic ranking with the battalion's first great struggle at Jarama.

>Bob Cooney was an Aberdonian communist and anti-fascist who served as a political commissar in the British Battalion of the International Brigades. This extract from Bob Cooney's memoir was featured in issue 49 (September 2018) of *¡No Pasarán!*. The memoir was published as *Proud Journey: a Spanish Civil War memoir* in 2015 by the Marx Memorial Library and Manifesto Press. The manuscript is held in the Marx Memorial Library, Spanish Collection, Papers of Robert Hunt Cooney, 'Proud Journey' manuscript, SC/VOL/RCO/1, reproduced here with kind permission of the Marx Memorial Library.

You fool, you fool, why did you have to shoot me?

Steve Fullarton

The place: Hill 481, near Gandesa; 1 August 1938. The battle was over and our attempt to take the summit of Hill 481 by frontal attack had failed. Small arms fire from both sides had stopped and only the artillery from afar kept firing, though at a much lesser frequency. I looked around and everyone without fail was on the ground either wounded or killed. I seemed to be the only one left unscathed. I started to give the help I could to those behind me and worked my way along and upwards, until I came to Paddy (O'Sullivan). A broken left arm and a broken right leg was his own diagnosis. For something to say I simply said: 'I was trying to help the comrades down there.' He said: 'I know, I was watching you.' Probably he was not the only one watching me. It's possible that the enemy was watching me too.

I thought back to that day when we recruits caught up with the British Battalion at Reus. I heard Paddy's voice giving orders to his men and I thought: 'He's too strict for me. I hope I don't get posted to his section.' But I was, and I asked around about Paddy and with almost one voice they told me: 'He's a good man to be up the line with.' Dusty, Peter, Den, all of them were of the same opinion, so that was good enough for me. I soon settled down and accepted my lot and had no trouble at all. Michael (O'Riordan) used to come from his side of 'Chabola Valley' to our side to chat with Paddy, and they both stood so erect. Paddy always looked the soldier and was always dressed as though ready for parade. He and Michael stood more or less face to face when they chatted, but not exactly. It was more left shoulder facing left shoulder or right shoulder facing right shoulder. I never could understand this stance and many years later I asked Michael about it. He laughed and said it was the IRA training: you can look forward and watch your back at the same time. I never did find out if he was joking.

Paddy told me to put a tourniquet on his left arm and another on his right leg, which I did, and checked that with his right hand he could release both if and when he thought it necessary. 'Find a safe place until it's dark, then come and get me,' he said. Find a safe place! He told me to have a good look around so I could identify the area properly. It was quite easy because a nearby tree had been cut in two and the upper part had fallen, pointing to Paddy. I started to make my way down to a depression I had seen from my higher level and was just getting into it when I heard a short burst of machine gun fire — and I felt the thud. I had been hit and I fell into the hole. 'You fool, you fool, why did you have to shoot me?' I thought. The battle was over and only the artillery was active.

I lay there for several hours waiting for dark, and when it did get dark, I heard Jimmy calling from our line and coming out towards me. He was calling for Paddy and I called him over to me and told him exactly where to find Paddy. I watched his back as he disappeared in the dark. I now had to consider my own position. How would I get back? Well, I made it, dragging my machine gun with me which was taken from me when I got back, and I was taken to the first aid post. It was not until some weeks later when I was convalescing that I learned that Paddy had not been rescued and was now listed as killed at Hill 481. You fool, you fool, you bloody fool, why did you have to shoot me?

>Steve Fullarton was wounded at the Battle of the Ebro but survived and later served in the RAF. When he died in 2008 he was the last surviving Scottish veteran of the Spanish Civil War. This recollection — transcribed by Marlene Sidaway from a tape recording by Steve Fullarton — appeared in issue 19 (February 2008) of the *IBMT Newsletter*.

'Michael O'Riordan, Irish International Brigader, crossing the Ebro at Vinebre with a senyera [Catalan flag] on the 25 July 1938', painted oil on canvas by the Barcelona-based fine artist Pere Piquer. Michael O'Riordan's late son, Manus, is one of the authors in this volume. In July 2018, the painting was donated by the Comissió de la Dignitat (Dignity Commission), an organisation promoting remembrance and justice for the victims of Francoism, to the Centre d'Estudis de la Batalla de l'Ebre (Centre for Battle of Ebro Studies), and now hangs in the Memorial Museum of the Battle of the Ebro in Gandesa, Catalonia. Courtesy of Pere Piquer.

The experience of imprisonment

Jerry Harris

My father, Sydney Harris, was born in Leeds in 1916 to working-class Jewish parents. His father had been a medic with the British Army in the First World War and suffered lung damage from mustard gas, and his mother died in the influenza plague in 1919. Travelling to America, Syd's father put him in a Jewish orphanage in Chicago at the age of five, where he stayed until he graduated from high school. Leaving the orphanage in the middle of the Great Depression wasn't easy. Syd began to box at the Golden Gloves level, and when his stockyard foreman called him a 'kike' Syd knocked him to the floor and got fired.

Syd had begun to hear about fascism — its antisemitism and its threat to democracy. So, in 1937, he joined the Young Communist League and decided to volunteer for the Lincoln Battalion. When Syd got on the bus for the trip to New York, Eddie Balchowsky came walking up, his arms around two girls and a bottle of champagne in hand. Eddie was from a well-off Jewish family and had been studying to be a concert pianist at the University of Illinois. But Eddie was on his way to Spain too, and so the working-class, orphan kid and the radical, privileged student were to become life-long friends. On their way to Communist Party headquarters in New York, Eddie heard someone playing Mozart from a second story window. Eyes bright with passion he turned to Syd, pointed to the window and said: 'That's why I'm going to Spain!'

The two young men got to Spain in late November 1937. Eddie was assigned to scout for the Canadian Mac-Paps and Syd stayed with the Lincolns. Syd grew up reading Rudyard Kipling and said, at the training camp in Figueres, that it broke his heart to learn that Kipling was a big imperialist. But years later he still liked to quote the ending of 'Gunga Din'. 'You're a better man than I,' said the British officer to the water boy Gunga Din. That's the lesson he took from the book.

Syd became a sergeant and fought at Teruel in the winter of 1937/38. But in April 1938, during the retreat, he was shot and captured. For a month the Lincolns had battled and conceded ground, first from Belchite, to Albalate, Caspe, and Maella. Finally, they tried to break through fascist lines to reach the Republican-held city of Gandesa. Failing the charge, the Lincolns retreated to a hill overlooking a small valley.

Syd was ordered to take three men across the central valley road, up the facing hill to look over the heights and report back on enemy activity. But while separated from the battalion, a company of fascist cavalry came riding through the valley. The Lincolns opened fire, forcing the fascists up the opposite hill, riding straight towards Syd and his comrades. Firing from behind a tree, he heard a rustling from behind. Quickly turning he saw a soldier on horseback aiming his rifle straight at his head. Syd's quick movement spooked the horse into rearing, causing the shot to hit his ankle.

Knocked off his feet, he went tumbling down the hill and smashed into a boulder, with the cavalryman in quick pursuit. But to get a shot the fascist would have to expose himself to fire from the Lincolns, and so instead he retreated up the hill.

The battle was soon over and both fascists and Lincolns abandoned the area. Syd found himself alone, with two grenades, a gaping wound and unable to move. As the sun was going down, he spied two women clothed in Spanish black walking down the road. One was an older woman and the other, Susana, was just 17 years old. They were Republican supporters. They promised to come back and, as night set, Susana reappeared with an orange and an egg. By this time Syd was going into shock and shaking from the cold. Susana held him throughout the night, keeping him warm in her comforting arms. It was the first time Syd had spent the night in the arms of a woman.

In the morning she went to seek help, but before she returned, Italian fascists appeared picking up the dead. Spying Syd, they rushed up shouting: 'You red bastard we'll kill you right here, you fucking Russian Bolshevik!' Syd cried out: 'No, no I'm American from Chicago!' Suddenly the shouting stopped. The Italian lieutenant cocked his head: 'Chicago?' Syd replied: 'Yes, for Christ's sake Chicago!' Suddenly a broad smile broke out on the lieutenant's face. He fired off his machine gun into the air, looked at Syd, and said: 'Chicago, home of Al Capone! Take him alive!' Dragged into town, Syd was thrown into a barn and fell into an exhausted sleep. A little while later he woke to shouts and kicks with German soldiers standing over him yelling: 'You red bastard we're going to kill you right here, fucking Russian Bolshevik!' The Italians rushed in and an argument raged over who owned the prisoner. Luckily for Syd, in Italy's first victory over Germany since the Roman Empire, they managed to expel the German troops.

He was sent to a prison hospital in Bilbao where he spent four months. While there, the Spanish authorities were letting a German doctor experiment on the patients. In a letter Syd wrote that the 'fascist hospital reminded me of the slaughter and butcher houses back home ... Injections were given only to the Internationals to "make your blood better".' After two died and a third went out of his mind the prisoners rioted and tore up the ward, and the hospital administration finally removed the German doctor.

Syd was sent to the prisoner of war camp at San Pedro de Cardeña. As the 700 inmates lined up for review, a colonel led them through salutes to fascist Spain. The last was a straight-arm salute to Franco. But instead of shouting Franco the men let out the cry 'Fuck you!' The colonel looked sternly at the men, and then smiled. '¡Otra vez!' 'Fuck you!' '¡Uno más!' 'Fuck you!' Syd turned to the guy next to him: 'What the hell is going on?' 'The colonel doesn't speak English, and to him "fuck you" sounds like Franco with an English accent.' But life at the prisoner of war camp was anything but easy. Syd recounted his experience, writing:

> Cold cement floor full of holes, broken stairs, thousands of mice, rats and vermin of all kinds ... As we drove in we received our first view of what was later to be a daily

occurrence: a sergeant with a long leather, reinforced, twisted cane-whip, lashing out among a group of men. We all had our share of beatings from shell-shocked sergeants who didn't even try to give any reasons in explanation of their actions. Too many of us bear scars from sticks, rifle butts, fists or boots, they used them all. They got a genuine pleasure and joy in making and seeing us as miserable as possible.

Always hungry, unable to concentrate, to exercise, lying on louse and flea-ridden mattresses all day waiting for a ladle full of beans and two rotten sardines. Clothed only in pants, shirts and slippers in a cell with damp and windy climate; no wonder 10 of our comrades died and most of the others were sick all the time. Three water taps for 700 men to wash themselves, their clothes, and plates in ... planning for the day when once again we could be MEN. Freedom. Liberty, how we appreciate those words now. But in the midst of that feeling comes the thought of our comrades, especially those from the countries dominated by fascists, who are still in national Spain. Always picked upon to receive the worst treatment by the guards, they have the courage, self-discipline, and intestinal fortitude that belongs to men convinced of the righteousness of their actions and a deep and everlasting love of liberty and democracy. May the day be soon that they also can once again breath the fresh air of liberty and freedom for which they sacrificed so much to defend; until then salud comrades.

When he went to Spain Syd was still not an American citizen, and so was released with the Canadian volunteers. He returned to the US by way of Toronto, married Rose Fine, and became a well-known labour photographer and journalist. He served as head of the Lincolns' Veterans' Lodge and often organised security for Paul Robeson when he sang in Chicago, acting as his personal bodyguard. During the McCarthy period the FBI threatened to deport him back to the UK, but Syd held strong, remained politically committed and active, and became a US citizen in 1957. He named his first son Paul after Robeson, his middle name Aaron, after Aaron Lopoff. Lopoff was Syd's commander in Spain who he described as the 'bravest man he ever knew.' After five sons his last child was a girl. He named her Suzanne after Susana.

> Jerry Harris is a researcher and writer in global political economy, and the son of IB veteran Sydney Harris. His publications include *Global Capitalism and the Crisis of Democracy* (2016). This chapter originally appeared as 'UK-born Lincoln volunteer who survived shooting and prison' in issue 57 (May 2021) of *¡No Pasarán!*

A revolution in battlefield surgery

Mark Derby and David Lowe

Many years after working as a nurse with Spain's Republican Army medical services, Aurora Fernández clearly recalled the outstanding qualities of a young surgeon from New Zealand. Doug Jolly, she said:

> does honour to his name — a man more 'jolly' it would be difficult to find. I remember once, waiting [for] an order to leave for the front, all of us nervous and tense, fearful that planes would arrive ... Dr Jolly began to tell jokes and seeing that the Spaniards did not understand him, began to dance and sing in the style of the Maoris and he inspired the group of spectators and all were smiling and tension went down.

At the time of writing, with much of the world locked down to control the spread of a deadly virus, it is timely to recall the work of this dedicated physician, who developed innovative techniques for treating trauma injuries during the civil war, and never wavered from the principles of Christian socialism which first sent him to Spain. Jolly was aged 32 and studying in London for qualifications in surgery when the civil war broke out. He belonged to the Christian left, a circle that included Rev Donald Grant and his wife Irene (whom he had first met as a medical student in New Zealand), the moral philosopher John Macmurray, and the Austrian-born economist Karl Polanyi. To join the second team of volunteers organised by the Spanish Medical Aid Committee meant abandoning his surgical studies just before the final exam, yet he seems to have done so without hesitation.

In December 1936, Jolly arrived at the International Brigades headquarters at Albacete bearing a personal letter of introduction from British Communist Party head Harry Pollitt: 'This comrade is not a member of the Communist Party, but is a very warm sympathiser with the cause of the Spanish Government, and has been highly recommended to us.' Soon afterwards Jolly was spotted at a café by Tom Wintringham, later the commander of the International Brigades' British Battalion. The New Zealander appeared to be 'thoroughly lost, having come out on his own from London with a minimum of papers and less knowledge of foreign languages than even an Englishman of his sort can usually muster.' The two men soon became friends, and Wintringham later came to appreciate Jolly's surgical skills. 'I have to thank him (and a clean bullet) for much the neatest among my scars.'

That winter the Madrid front was under heavy attack from Nationalist forces trying to cut its only road link to Valencia. With the rank of lieutenant, and heading a surgical unit comprising seven nationalities, Jolly established a mobile field hospital just behind the front line. For the next two years his team was sent wherever the fighting was most intense, 'to Andalusia in the South with its semi-tropical heat, away to Upper Aragón with its snow-covered mountains and finally taking part in the government offensive which involved the crossing of the Ebro from Catalonia into Aragón in July 1938.'

Jolly deeply admired the local people he met, such as 'the peasants with their strange carts drawn by long strings of mules and donkeys,' who brought food and firewood that was often as vital to his work as anaesthetic. 'It was amazing also to see the people in the towns and cities with their over-riding contempt for falling bombs. In the early days they scorned to take shelter. One has to go to Spain's national sport in the bull-ring to find the analogy of this seeming indifference to death.'

One of his nurses, Hungarian-born Anna-Marie Basch, found that Jolly 'did not belong to any political party, he was simply a doctor who was anti-fascist through extraordinarily high ethics. That is what brought him to Spain.' Those ethics compelled him to treat his patients without regard for their military affiliation. He operated on Franco's Moorish troops in Madrid, and Italian fascists in Guadalajara. This indiscriminate approach in the face of overwhelming demands for medical care provoked outrage from other doctors, such as the Czech Frantisek Kriegel. He saw that Jolly had developed a novel method of triage, numbering each patient in order of urgency, and that the No.1 label had been given to a Nationalist prisoner. Kriegel ordered Jolly to treat one of the many wounded Republicans first. Jolly replied: 'I refuse, and if you insist I'm going home tomorrow . . . the reasons that brought me here are the same reasons which will make me operate on that prisoner first, because he is in the most need of salvation.' Kriegel conceded, and apologised the next day.

Over two frenetic years Jolly performed thousands of operations, winning deep respect for his professional skills, his good humour and his courage under fire. Nurse administrator Gusti Jirku remembers driving with him towards a newly captured village in the Guadarrama, when four Junker fighter bombers appeared. A bomb landed 30 yards behind their car. '"What lousy shots," Mr Jolly said, without turning his head.' Arriving at their new field hospital, he performed a stomach operation with bombs falling 50 yards away. 'Mr Jolly worked on in complete silence and with perfectly steady hands, while the Czech doctor assisted and Anne-Marie [Basch] passed instruments with the precision of a machine. But she was no machine; she treated every patient like her own son.'

Jolly and his ever-changing team set up field hospitals in abandoned farm houses, tents, railway carriages, tunnels, and eventually a large natural cave — wherever they could conceal their patients from Franco's bombers. On the banks of the Ebro river in 1938, the British nursing administrator Nan Green classified the day's casualties according to the type of wound, and the weapon that caused it. She then made handcoloured graphs to show which medical supplies were needed, and priorities for treatment. This system proved so effective that Jolly revived it in the hospitals he ran during the Second World War.

The Republican Army's hard-pressed but resourceful medical services pioneered profound and long-lasting clinical innovations, including the first widespread use of blood banks for transfusions. 'The blood was delivered daily to the field hospitals,' Jolly later recalled, 'in special vans equipped with refrigerators run by small petrol motors (rather like a milk delivery service.) ... This is the first time that conserved blood had been used on a large scale.' He noted that this development would eventually transform peace-time trauma medicine.

Following the disbanding of the International Brigades in late 1938, Doug Jolly returned to Britain but continued to work on behalf of Republican Spain. During 1939 he addressed more than 60 public meetings in Britain and in France, urging support for former colleagues such as Kriegel whose home countries were now under Nazi control and who therefore faced imprisonment or worse if they were repatriated. He also drew on his frontline experience to warn British leaders of the vital need to prepare for an entirely new form of warfare. The *British Medical Journal* reports him saying that 'The character of war had changed by reason of mass attack by aeroplane. The medical officer could no longer sit behind the lines and await his cases.'

Jolly realised that the available texts on war surgery dated from 1918, and were written from 'the viewpoint of the base hospital.' He decided to produce a surgical manual aimed at 'younger, inexperienced surgeons, who will be operating in this [coming] war in the casualty clearing stations.' The resulting volume, *Field Surgery in Total War*, became an essential item of kit for military surgeons for the next several decades.

With the rank of lieutenant-colonel, Jolly served in the Second World War in the Middle East and Italy, occasionally encountering patients familiar to him from Spain. As a Stockton teenager, Johnny Longstaff had fought in the Battle of the Ebro and received a facial wound. He was treated by Jolly at the International Brigade hospital at Mataró, north of Barcelona. Six years later Longstaff was wounded in Italy, and again found himself on Jolly's operating table, at the New Zealand hospital near Naples. As issue 48 of *¡No Pasarán!* reported, in 2018 a plaque to Jolly was unveiled in his hometown of Cromwell, Central Otago, on the wall of a store founded in 1870 by his grandfather.[35]

David Lowe is a doctor and intensive care specialist in Sydney, Australia. Mark Derby is a New Zealand historian whose books include *Kiwi Compañeros: New Zealand and the Spanish Civil War* (2009) and a forthcoming biography of Dr Doug Jolly. This essay appeared in issue 54 (May 2020) of *¡No Pasarán!* as 'Doug Jolly: New Zealand doctor who revolutionised battlefield surgery.'

---

[35] Editor's note: The authors have also published this research in an academic article: Mark Derby and David Lowe, 'Douglas Waddell Jolly (1904-1983) – New Zealand pioneer of modern battlefield surgery', *Journal of Medical Biography* 28. 4 (2020), 224-32.

Dr Doug Jolly (seated, wearing a singlet), likely on an excursion somewhere in rural Catalonia during preparations for the Battle of the Ebro in mid-1938. The woman with glasses sat by his side is Anna-Marie Basch, Hungarian operating theatre nurse and Jolly's lover. The other individuals are unknown International Brigaders, likely also from Hungary. Courtesy of Eva Cserháti.

A nurse's notes from the Aragón front

Margaret Powell

After spending several months in a small village on the Aragón front serving at an urgent surgical centre, the division to which we were attached became a 'shock division' moving from place to place; we, as the mobile surgical team, moved with it. We reached the end of our journey, which was high up in the Pyrenees at midnight and for the rest of the night we heard mules and trucks go by towards the front line — in some places less than four miles away.

Early next day we commenced making our preparations, selecting for the theatre a shed which had been used as a slaughterhouse (there was no other choice). At least it had the virtue of a roof, even if some of the walls were missing. Blankets were hung where the walls should have been, whilst the remaining walls were white-washed and the mud scraped off the floor . . .

All the afternoon and evening we heard the sound of battle, and we knew that soon our period of 'idleness' would cease. The wounded began to arrive at about six o'clock in the morning, a grim contrast to the loveliness of the Pyrenees, and we started our work without doing more than struggle into our clothes and washing our hands.

In addition to being surgically responsible for our own division of over 10,000 soldiers, we were also detailed to attend another 3,000 men because their division had no surgeon.

All the wounded, many of whom had to be brought down from the mountains on mules, were first treated at the first aid stations and then came on to us. Ambulance after ambulance — 'six abdominals and a couple of heads — all for operation.' Next one: more abdominals, more heads, compound fractures, 'all for operation.' And for all this, only one surgeon — Spanish — who just goes on and on, speaking only to enquire what is next; making anxious enquiries about the state of the last case; asking about the stock of sterile material, and above all passing never-failing words of encouragement to the wounded, even after 24 hours of constant work!

We had no electricity, but worked with primus lamps and candles and when all the mantles broke, just candles. Imagine if you can, a surgeon performing a laparotomy, finding and suturing a liver wound, or maybe 24 or more intestinal perforations, performing a nephrectomy, removing a spleen, all by candlelight. Meanwhile we grope around the table for instruments, thread needles, break catgut capsules all in the flickering light . . .

Blood transfusions were given whenever possible, but we could not employ the tubes of blood because we had no refrigerator in which to store them, so the direct method was always used. There were times when it was impossible to find a donor, for everyone within reach had given as much as they could.

We were, I suppose, always in some sort of danger, but somehow when one is surrounded by danger one does not think of it, and in any case we did not have the time to worry. The only fear which haunted us was the fear that we should not have enough material with which to work. There are things which the Spanish people are able to supply us with, but there are many necessities they cannot provide. We depend on our [Spanish Medical Aid] Committee for these, and so far they have not failed us. The thought that some day they might have to stop supplies through lack of funds is too terrible to contemplate . . .

If you could know the Spanish people as I have come to know them, you would find the ordinary people brave and kind, fighting not because they love bloodshed as many people would have you believe, but because they know that they MUST fight to save their homes and for the right to live peacefully and decently. They feel and indeed they know that the victory of the Fascist force would mean tyranny and oppression for them and for Spain.

Margaret Powell volunteered as a frontline nurse during the Spanish Civil War and was the last British nurse to leave Spain. She later married Brigade veteran and former IBMT chair Sam Lesser, whom she had met in Barcelona. This recollection appeared as 'Notes from the Aragón Front' in issue 27 (September 2010) of the *IBMT Newsletter*, having originally been published in the April 1938 issue of *British Nursing Journal*. A longer version of these notes from the front is available at <cohse-union.blogspot.com/2008/06/margaret-powell-welsh-international.html>. Reproduced here with kind permission of Margaret Powell's daughter, Ruth Muller.

La Rioja 1936

David Merino

Cries of 'Long live Christ the King!' and 'Up with Spain'. Engine noise from a convoy of cars and lorries. Shouts open up a black abyss along the road . . . an open abyss, a deep wound, deliberately meant never to heal, so that our people would be forever torn in two.

These were summer days, not so long ago, when nobody believed what they'd heard on the radio about that far-away military *coup*. Then came men from nearby towns with guns, blood in their eyes, menacing gestures, and in their hands a blank and revengeful piece of paper, ready for a list of names.

This was a war without front-lines, without battles. Life stood still. Taking the villages was more than just shoring up the rearguard. With gusto they set about their task. A line of fire was drawn to separate the 'bad' people from the 'good'. Street by street, house by house, everyone would be judged. Trust was smothered under a blanket of hysteria, of divine providence . . .

From the pulpits came the injunctions, the proclamations handed down from on-high: 'Choose between the Devil or Spain.' Cowardice was branded as courage, allowing denunciations to be made, triggers to be pulled in this holy crusade to save Spain, vomiting names, filling the death lists of men, women, neighbours who didn't go to church, who didn't humour their betters, who spoke out of turn, who read books . . .

Terror exploded out of nothing, the earth darkened and the light dimmed. The executions began, a liturgy of rifle-shots at dawn. Lives were shattered and decades of rights trampled on by those who couldn't care less about the sight of corpses scattered in ditches. It was that easy to die, that easy to kill.

Such was the dark system of terror set loose in those days turned into night by black dawns. Here there was no war — only groups of men killing unarmed people, their friends from the classroom, the dance hall and the *pelota* court — all the while averting their eyes and holding their tongues before an abstract foe.

Death-squads collected their nocturnal cargo, those named by the local well-heeled thugs. It was a chillingly effective scheme: 'I didn't pull the trigger, I just named him,' 'I didn't know his name, I just pulled the trigger' — a simple division of labour, a perfect way to commit genocide.

The lists ran out, but had to be replenished. The spiral of massacres spun faster still.

Soon blood-lust took over, so did jostling for position, entertainment and showing-off. Individuals count for nothing, only the group now master of the night — a master with absolute power. Fired up with alcohol, testosterone and gun-powder, the exterminating beast roared and the killing continued.

There were months of mass slaughter, unexpected but unspontaneous — a massacre plotted by the military high command and blessed by the Church hierarchy.

They didn't kill randomly, only those who questioned the established order of work and property. And they made sure the tortured corpses would be seen by others, warning them not to follow the same path — dumping bodies at daybreak on the land controlled by the old guard, protecting feudal privileges, making it clear that some thoughts were unthinkable.

And the families and widows were called scum, and sentenced to live in eternal terror. Torture, castor oil, shaven heads, stripped of their belongings and land. They were robbed even of their pain, not even able to mourn in black, nor whisper to the bones, condemned to suffocate in the poisonous fear of each memory.

Over the mass graves and the silence of the bereaved emerged Franco's new Spanish state, like a colossal stigma. And the bitter rain of blood of those years remains in our earth. The bodies are still in our earth. The fascist beast prevailed, but the wounds of death will not heal.

History is blowing in the wind and written in the books, and to hell with anyone who says we have to forget. We will not forget, we'll never forget, never forget.[36]

> David Merino is a member of the Spanish rap group Perro Lobo. These lyrics from 'La Rioja 1936' were translated by Jim Jump and published in issue 43 (September 2016) of the *IBMT Newsletter*, after Perro Lobo performed the original at the IBMT's annual commemoration event in July 2016, followed by a reading of the translation by the actress Maxine Peake.

---

[36] Editor's note: The original song (in Spanish) is accessible online at <perrolobo.bandcamp.com/track/la-rioja-1936>.

Frank Farr (left) with an ambulance belonging to the first British medical mission to Spain. Courtesy of the Marx Memorial Library.

The lessons of Spain

Frank Farr

To those of us who came back from Spain at the end of that war to be involved only months later in World War II, the whistle of bullets and the crash of bombs were easily forgotten. Spain was a low-key war of meagre armament compared with what came later and our memories of it are more of people and politics than battlefields. I went out early, in 1936 with the first British ambulance unit, and came back finally more than two years later with the British Battalion of the 15th International Brigade. When I went we were confident of victory against Franco's army rebellion; when I returned we all knew that the war was lost. But the experiences in between led not so much to disillusionment as to a realistic awareness of what was militarily and politically possible.

Never before has there been such international unity in a single cause. Men of 50 nations made their way to Spain just to take a hand in someone else's war. Although mainly of the political left, there were men of all parties and none among the volunteers on the Republican side. Only a handful of committed fascists supported Franco in the field, except from the interventionist German and Italian forces.

When I arrived at the Aragón front with the first ambulance unit the line was held by volunteer militia units. They were organised into *'centurias'* of 100 men each and commanded by centurions elected from their ranks. Everything was idealistically democratic and tactical decisions were taken by rank and file vote after endless discussions.

On one occasion when rain turned our crude trenches into muddy ditches, the Spanish *centuria* on the right flank of the sector voted themselves out of the mud and back to the comparative comfort of the village behind us. The German *centuria* on their left woke up in the morning to find their flank completely exposed. If the fascists facing us had known, they could have walked right through the lines without hindrance.

From this sort of anarchy to the organisation of a trained and disciplined army was a long step and it was not fully completed when the war ended. It looked strange to us to see huge posters around, well into the second year of the war, saying: 'The People's Army is necessary.' It seemed obvious to us. But to the Spanish anarchist and syndicalist elements the idea was not easy to swallow. Military organisation and discipline were alien to their ultra-democratic ideals.

When the International Brigades were formed, divided mainly into language groups, they set comparatively high standards of discipline. But cooperation with the new People's Army was bedevilled by political divisions and jealousies. The Internationals always felt that they got less than their fair share of help from the over-stretched supporting arms, aircraft, tanks and artillery, to say nothing of simple small arms ammunition.

After I had left the ambulances to join the Brigade in the last year of the war I found the [British] Battalion about 80 percent composed of raw young recruits straight out of home. For two or three weeks we camped around the countryside armed with quite good new Czech rifles but no ammunition at all. Then we handed them in and received a consignment of 'Mexicanskis' plus ammunition. Training consisted of firing five rounds per man. Then we went into our first action at Gandesa and the new rifles got hot and jammed in the first few minutes of firing.

This was my first and last action as an infantryman. I was wounded, spent three months in hospital, nearly died of typhoid and associated illnesses, and finished up in the central barracks outside Barcelona as *comisario de guerra* for all the XVths, a post carrying duties a cross between adjutant and chaplain to all members of the Brigade passing through, from new recruits to wounded coming out of hospitals and back into the line.

By this time the depleted ranks of the Internationals were being filled up with Spanish conscripts. They were not too keen to go to war and, despite the strident propaganda designed to keep up morale, few of them believed any longer that the Republic could win.

Our own men, too, were war-weary and thinking only of getting home alive. Pep talks by political activists met a cynical reception and a distribution of cigarettes seemed more important than a battle. It was not until we came home, excited and happy, that we realised what a great historical event we had taken part in. Those huge cheering crowds at Victoria Station when we came off the train, the bands and banners, hysterical relatives and spontaneous public reactions woke us up to the fact that we represented far more in the political arena than our puny numbers had meant in the battlefield.

Only much later on, after serving in London through the Blitz and then in North Africa and Italy, did I realise fully what we had lacked in Spain in the way of organisation, equipment and sheer military experience. Looking back on it I would not have missed the Spanish experience for anything. The friends I made and lost alone made it worthwhile. But if such a situation arose again I could not honestly encourage my son and his contemporaries to go. Soldiering is for soldiers, not for enthusiastic amateurs.

Frank Farr served in Spain with the first ambulance unit and later with the International Brigades. This article was written in 1975, seemingly intended to be included in Philip Toynbee's *The Distant Drum* (1976) — a collection of memoirs about the Spanish Civil War — but remaining unpublished until it appeared in issue 45 (May 2017) of the *IBMT Magazine*. Held in the Marx Memorial Library, Spanish Collection, Papers of Frank Farr, SC/VOL/FFA. Reproduced with kind permission of the Marx Memorial Library.

Solidarity

Undated photo of activists from a 'Milk for Spain' campaign which worked to alleviate the hunger afflicting the population of Republican Spain during the war. The man in the middle is Arthur West, of Nottingham; the other individuals' names are unknown. The photo was colourised to highlight the use of the colours of the Spanish Republic to decorate the van. Courtesy of the IBMT.

The women who helped rescue Basque children

Sarah Lonsdale

Just before the lockdown shutters came clanging down in spring 2020, I went on holiday to northern Spain, visiting the coastal towns of Santander and Bilbao, and also Guernica, historic ancient capital of the Basques. In Bilbao I strolled into a quiet square, fringed with tall plane trees, their leaves just starting to emerge into the Spanish sunshine. The name of the square intrigued me: Plaza de Mrs Leah Manning, and I wondered why the people of Bilbao had named this leafy square, surrounded by schools, after an Englishwoman of whom I had never heard.

It turned out there was a pretty big reason: in the spring of 1937, while the Spanish Civil War was raging, and as General Franco's troops were bombing towns up and down the Basque coast, Mrs Leah Manning helped 4,000 Spanish children escape on a ship, the *Habana*, to England. The night of their departure, 21 May, Franco's bombers attacked Portugalete, Bilbao's harbour where the children were being loaded. They almost didn't make it at all. When I started to investigate Leah, I discovered that she was not the only British woman who tried to help the Basques in the spring of 1937. Many women joined the Aid Spain movement, raising money to help send clothes and food, and also to try and help rescue Spaniards, whose worlds were being bombed to smithereens by the fascist *coup* that was taking place in the country. This is the story of just three of those women.

In March 1937, Florence Roberts, aged just 20, was helping her widowed father, merchant seaman William Roberts, take his Cardiff-registered *Seven Seas Spray* to Barcelona to pick up a cargo of olive oil, almonds and barrels of cognac. Once the valuable cargo of sun-drenched goods was loaded, the ship's orders changed and Florence and her father changed direction for Bilbao. The residents of Bilbao were starving — General Franco had blockaded the harbour and the roads into the town so no food could get in. People were eating their dogs and cats. French and British merchant vessels were trying to run the blockade to deliver food to the Basques but none had so far managed to get past the Italian cruisers guarding the port — Mussolini had sent his navy to help Franco.

On the night of 19 April, the *Seven Seas Spray* left the French port of St Jean de Luz. With her navigation lights off, she passed, unseen, close by an Italian cruiser shortly after leaving France, but after that, had an uneventful voyage. After 10 hours' sailing the *Seven Seas Spray*'s arrival in Bilbao was feted by the Basque authorities. English newspapers celebrated the 'pretty, 20-years-old' captain's daughter sporting a jaunty sailor's cap. Florence briefly became a journalist and she reported, in her first despatch for the *News Chronicle*:

I have seen children and even women run after lorries leaving one ship with loads of salt and snatch a handful of it. Hordes of children gather round the food shops from early morning till dusk pleading for food. What they prize most are pieces of white bread . . . despite their hardships they would rather starve than surrender.

Florence and her father ran the blockade all through the spring and summer of 1937, taking in food, and taking out refugees. Then in August, while in Santoña, the *Seven Seas Spray* was boarded by Italian soldiers and Florence, William and the crew spent the next two months as prisoners. While Florence and her father were secretly making food deliveries in small ports along the coast, it soon became clear that a larger operation was needed.

Guernica had been bombed — causing international scandal — killing hundreds of people. It was clear that Bilbao would be next, and the citizens had only days. But while a French ship had succeeded in evacuating some children, Britain's Prime Minister, Stanley Baldwin, had been unwilling to offer help for fear of looking like Britain was taking sides. Leah Manning had arrived in Bilbao on 24 April. She drove straight to the British consulate to ask for help in persuading the government to approve the evacuation. She was seen, she later wrote, as 'an officious busy-body.' But Manning wasn't to be dissuaded. Briefly a Labour MP in 1931, she had been a teacher since she left school and her whole life was dedicated to helping children.

On 17 May, while the British consul was away from Bilbao, Manning sent a telegram to London from the consulate, more or less claiming that the evacuation of the children was so well underway that it would be impossible to stop. While the British government thought her a busy-body, Manning had public opinion on her side. The large amounts of money now raised by the Aid Spain Committee for the children's upkeep meant that Whitehall objections over the cost of caring for the children were neutralised. On 21 May the yacht *Habana*, with a capacity of 800, began loading the young passengers, with the help of British doctors Audrey Russell and Richard Ellis, and nurse Aileen Moore.

Aileen Moore volunteered to help the evacuation because she could speak Spanish. When she flew from Biarritz into the Spanish war zone, it was the first time she had ever flown in her life. She wrote in the *Nursing Mirror and Midwives Journal*:

> The little monoplane was perched, glittering, in a field of clover and daisies against a background of blue, snow-covered Pyrenean peaks. Her weight was 25 kilos . . . Up, up, up, so high that the rolling Atlantic seemed only a corrugated gleaming blue surface, broken by deep patches of shadow . . . far down, miniature destroyers rode on the white specked blue sheet of sea.

Waiting for final embarkation orders, she ate rice, beans, cat and donkey steak, dodging German air raids as she escorted distraught children away from their weeping mothers. Before the *Habana* was fully loaded, the Nationalist air raids on the port had become so intense that the ship left without all of the children on board.

Apart from severe bouts of seasickness ('for two dreadful days and nights Richard, Audrey and I slipped and slithered from one pool of vomit and diarrhoea to another') they arrived safely in Southampton on 23 May. Two weeks later, Bilbao fell and many of the children's parents were killed. Manning had literally snatched the nearly 4,000 boys and girls out from underneath Franco's nose. Once they arrived and had been put in temporary tents outside Southampton, Manning did not give up fighting to find them homes and schools. The children, when adults who either returned to Spain or settled in Britain, remembered her fondly. One woman, Esta Nickson, who had been on the *Habana* wrote in 1991: 'I remember her very well, we all loved her. She always had a smile and a cuddle for all of us.' Leah, Florence and Aileen's stories tell us how compassion for children in danger can turn even 'ordinary' people — a nurse, a teacher and a merchant sailor's daughter — into heroes.[37]

Dr Sarah Lonsdale is senior lecturer in Journalism at City University of London. Her research includes the history of journalism and the depiction of journalism in fiction. This essay was originally published as 'Leah Manning and the women who helped rescue Basque children', in issue 58 (September 2021) of *¡No Pasarán!*

Basque refugee children at a camp in Eastleigh, Hampshire, in spring 1937 shortly after arrival in England and prior to being dispersed to the colonias around the country. Courtesy of the Martínez family.

---

[37] Readers can learn more in Sarah Lonsdale, *Rebel women between the wars: Fearless writers and adventurers* (Manchester: Manchester University Press, 2020).

The seafarers who went on strike against Franco

Jim Jump

Much has been written and said in the past few years about those seafarers who supported and in some cases gave their lives for the Spanish Republican cause. A memorial to the British crews who ran the fascist blockade of Spanish Republican ports was unveiled in Glasgow in 2019. In 2018 a plaque was erected in Alicante to Archibald Dickson, master of the *Stanbrook*, the last ship to rescue Republican refugees in the dying days of the country's civil war. Scores of British and Irish merchant seamen also volunteered to join the International Brigades, often jumping ship in Spain to do so.

When remembering this proud record we should not overlook the story of the merchant ship *Linaria*, whose crew risked prosecution and their livelihoods for refusing to take ingredients for explosives to Franco-held Spain. They went on strike in Boston, Massachusetts, on 23 February 1937, announcing that 'we will not take out the ship if it means helping to kill people in Spain.' This was not a simple case of industrial action. It was against the law for seafarers to go on strike in a foreign port. By deciding on their 'stay-in strike', the *Linaria* crew were breaching the draconian provisions of the Merchant Shipping Act. What they were doing was tantamount to mutiny. Seventeen of the crew, most of them from Tyneside and the North-East, were arrested and charged under the 1888 Act on arrival in Liverpool a month later.

Abandoned by their own union, the National Union of Seamen (NUS — now part of RMT), which was then under right-wing, pro-employer leadership, they relied on local Aid Spain activists, as well as a defence committee set up in Tyneside to help them raise money for their legal costs and for travel and accommodation. On Merseyside their defence was organised by Jack Jones, a local docker and union activist who would go on to join the International Brigades — and to become one of Britain's outstanding trade union leaders of the last century. He worked with local Labour MP and lawyer Sydney Silverman to launch a financial appeal, put together a legal team and looked after the welfare of the men.

The crew decided to take a stand shortly after they were berthed in Portland, Maine, on 20 February, with a cargo of anthracite from the Soviet port of Mariupol). They learned then that their next port of call would be Boston, where the 3,385 ton Stag Line ship would load nitrates to take to Seville. They immediately made a united protest to the master, Capt James Robinson. According to a report in the *Daily Herald* on 22 February, under the headline 'British steamer crew's cargo protest,' the nitrates were 'for use in the manufacture of explosives.' The report went on to say that the crew had agreed to proceed to Boston, where there would be talks 'to thrash out the matter' with the owners and officers. They meanwhile elected a negotiating committee, headed by Alex 'Spike' Robson, a ship's fireman. He said: 'We do not want to help deliver nitrates because we do not want to be a party to the killing of women and children by bombs and shells.' Robson later explained to *The Shieldsman* on 22 April that, despite assurances that the nitrates were to be used as fertilisers, 'we decided that the only course was to go on strike, which we did.' The US dockers' union, the ILA, was reported as saying it would see to it that the cargo of nitrates would not be loaded.

On 26 February the Board of Trade in London ruled that the cargo for Seville did not contravene Britain's policy of non-intervention in the war in Spain. The seafarers disagreed and their sit-in strike in Boston lasted 10 days. During this time the NUS representative in New York strongly advised the men to proceed with the voyage, subject to the inclusion of a special clause in their terms that would provide additional wages and indemnity in the case of injury. When this was rejected by the crew as 'blood money,' the NUS complained that the men were being led by 'a well known communist' — a reference to Spike Robson. Fearful no doubt that the example of the *Linaria* crew might inspire other seafarers to take industrial action against trade with Francoist Spain, the British consul-general in Boston warned the strikers that they would find it very difficult to get another job. He told them that 'every British captain and every British shipping company in the world will know that you are of the *Linaria* crowd.'

The *Linaria* strike took place against the background of efforts initiated by Scandinavian maritime trade unions to agree an international trade boycott of Franco's Spain. By the end of 1936 plans for the boycott had been drawn up by the International Transport Workers' Federation (ITF). However, backed by the Trades Union Congress (TUC), the NUS and the Transport & General Workers' Union, representing dockers, immediately objected. ITF general secretary Edo Fimmen said after hearing their objections at a meeting in Paris in 1936: 'It was just as if they were representing their own government.' Meanwhile, the Norwegian seamen's union began telling its members to prevent the departure of ships to Franco-held ports. Several were stopped in Cardiff and Newcastle when Norwegian crews walked off their ships. Rank-and-file union activists on Newcastle Trades Council supported the action. But as Fimmen noted in January 1937: 'The British unions not only do not join the action, but indirectly try to hinder it by allowing their own people to load [the ships] for the rebels and man them.'

Though facing hostility from their own union, the *Linaria* crew did receive backing for their stand from Labour leader Clement Attlee. Raising the dispute in the House of Commons on 26 February, Attlee asked whether the government had sent instructions to the consul-general in Boston to support the crew. The future prime minister went on to ask what the position was of seafarers 'who are asked to load supplies which are obviously war supplies.' In response, the government reiterated its view that the nitrate cargo was not prohibited.

In a hopeless position, however, the *Linaria* crew eventually agreed to be paid off and repatriated, with money deducted from their wages for their time on strike. On arrival in Liverpool they were charged with 'neglect of duty and wilful disobedience of a lawful order.' Their case came to court in Liverpool early in May 1937. They presented evidence from an analytical chemist, who pointed out that nitrates are essential for the manufacture of munitions. The magistrate declared their action justified, but fined them each 40 shillings (about three days' pay) for impeding the progress of their ship.

Though let off relatively lightly, the men and their supporters launched a successful appeal, which saw their fines quashed. As Jack Jones later recalled: 'A good case was presented before the Recorder, E.G. Hemmerde, KC. The defendants were lucky because Hemmerde had strong socialist sympathies.' The *Daily Herald* reported on 6 June: 'Holding that they were justified in refusing to sail to Spain, the Recorder of Liverpool, Mr E.G. Hemmerde, KC, allowed an appeal by members of the crew of the North Shields steamer, *Linaria*. Fifteen had each been fined £2, and the other two, apprentices, discharged under the Probation Act, for refusing to sail the *Linaria* from Boston, USA.' In an interesting aside, the report noted: 'The captain, James Robinson, agreed that the men constituted the best crew he had had in 30 years.'

The *Daily Worker* gleefully declared on 15 June that 'the Recorder showed himself more progressive than the leadership of the NUS.' Not surprisingly the shipowners were unhappy with the verdict and the case ended up in the High Court in April 1938. Renowned socialist barrister D.N. Pritt defended the crew and Spike Robson defended himself. The appeal was thrown out and all costs awarded against the owners. Robson, however, paid a price for his role in the strike and was blacklisted from the shipping industry. But with the outbreak of war in 1939, he found work on auxiliary Royal Navy ships crewed by merchant seamen. As a footnote, Robson was elected in 1947 to the NUS's executive council, the first communist to serve in that capacity. He later became a mentor for Jim Slater, a future NUS general secretary, who was one of the key figures on the North East coast in the militant National Seamen's Reform Movement of the 1950s and 60s.

Though an important legal victory was achieved, the story of the *Linaria*, when seafarers challenged what one historian has dubbed 'an unholy alliance' of government, shipowners and the men's union, also answers a question which has been posed by labour historians: why was direct solidarity action by British maritime workers so limited during the Spanish Civil War? Robson and his shipmates took a unique stand — and in doing so fully exposed the implacable opposition such action faced.

Jim Jump is the son of IB veteran James 'Jimmy' Jump and is the current IBMT chair. He is the former editor of the *The Seaman*, journal of the National Union of Seamen and the RMT, and has written and edited various publications about the Spanish Civil War and the International Brigades. This story was published in issue 58 (September 2021) of *¡No Pasarán!* as 'When British seafarers went on strike against Franco shipment.'

For more information see: Jack Jones, *Union Man* (London: Collins, 1986); *Spike: Alec 'Spike' Robson 1895-1979: Class Fighter* (North Tyneside TUC, 1987); Dieter Nelles, 'The ITF and the Spanish Civil War' in Bob Reinalda (ed.) *The International Transportworkers' Federation 1914-1945* (Amsterdam: Stichting beheer IISG, 1997), pp. 174-99.

Red Ellen in Spain

Paula Bartley

In November 1934 'Red' Ellen Wilkinson visited Spain with Lord Listowel as a representative of the Relief Committee for the Victims of Fascism, a communist front organisation.[38] The visit, Ellen's first to Spain, had been orchestrated by Otto Katz, a Czech communist secret agent who later became the controller of Soviet propaganda and spymaster in Western Europe. A month beforehand, a socialist republic had been founded at Oviedo, Asturias, but troops under General Franco were brought in from north Africa to overthrow it.[39] Ellen reported that army repression had been brutal and there had been victimisation on a terrible scale: prisoners were tortured, workers were imprisoned and the socialist press censored. Moorish troops, 'maddened with drink had been let loose in the first terrible days,' doing things that no Spanish soldier would dare do. Soon after Wilkinson and Listowel arrived they were bundled into a car by the Francoists 'for protection' and driven to the Spanish border. Ellen insisted that they had been kidnapped.

In 1936 her support for Spanish socialists was further tested during the Spanish Civil War. Ellen, now the Labour MP for Jarrow, believed, as with others on the left, that the civil war was part of an international struggle against fascism and argued that military help should be given to defend the Spanish government. British Tory prime ministers, first Stanley Baldwin and, from May 1937, Neville Chamberlain, fearing that the civil war might precipitate a European war, hid behind the principle of non-intervention. To their discredit, the TUC and initially the Labour leadership agreed.

In April 1937, in another visit organised by Otto Katz, Ellen travelled to Spain with a cross-party section of women, Eleanor Rathbone, the Duchess of Atholl and

---

[38] Editor's note: Wilkinson was a trade union organiser, left-wing suffragist, and a founding member of the Communist Party of Great Britain before becoming a Labour MP in 1924. She took part in the Jarrow March in 1936 and later served as Minister of Education in Clement Attlee's reforming post-war Labour government.

[39] Editor's note: In October 1934, a revolutionary movement was triggered by the inclusion of ministers from the conservative Spanish Confederation of the Autonomous Right (CEDA) in the government. Working-class organisations — already frustrated by the slow pace of reform under the Republic and by the victory of right-wing parties in the 1933 elections — interpreted the CEDA's ascension as a sign of the advance of fascism in Spain. The main events took place in Catalonia, where a short-lived Catalan Republic was proclaimed, and in the northern region of Asturias, where thousands of armed workers (mainly miners) took control of territories including the regional capital of Oviedo and began to organise a revolution which was soon crushed by troops brought in from Spanish Morocco.

Dame Rachel Crowdy. In Madrid she reported that 'shells from rebel six inch guns, smashing in the street outside, tearing through the roof of a theatre, blew mangled bodies of women and children' through the doorway of the hotel where she was lunching with the other members of the delegation. Their car was standing nearby. Before they could drive away, the body of one of the victims had to be wiped off it.

The four women returned with a new commitment not only to organise relief schemes but to convince the British government that Franco and his army were being assisted by German and Italian forces. One of their notable successes was persuading the government to allow nearly 4,000 children from the Basque Country to come to Britain as refugees. Ellen was also successful in getting her trade union, the NUDAW shopworkers' union, to raise a voluntary levy for a period of three months to help finance the initiative. Soon people were calling Ellen the 'pocket Pasionaria.'

Shortly after Ellen's return from Spain, the cultural capital of the Basque population — Guernica — was destroyed in one afternoon by the bombing of the German airforce. On Thursday 8 May, identifying with the fate of the Republicans and frustrated by Parliament's reluctance to do anything to help, Ellen broke down and sobbed during a debate on Spain in the House of Commons. The bombing of Guernica changed the Labour Party's attitude towards the Spanish government. It denounced the bombing as an 'outrage upon humanity, as a violation of the principles of civilisation, and a manifestation of the merciless and inhuman spirit' of the fascists.

At the next Labour Party conference Ellen's analysis of the situation in Spain was, at last; accepted. The Labour Party reversed its policy; advocated supplying arms to the Republic and organised a series of mass demonstrations in support of the Spanish government. In that same month, October 1937, Labour also set up a Spain Campaign Committee to further its aims. Ellen, along with William Gillies, was elected joint secretary. The committee immediately organised an intensive publicity campaign: public meetings and demonstrations were held; letters and telegrams were sent to MPs and to the government; the press was bombarded with propaganda; and posters were plastered around towns and cities. Franco, the committee maintained,

> is a rebel. His troops are invaders. His ships are pirates . . . The war in Spain is an international war . . . We are not neutrals in this conflict. We have never been neutrals; we will never be neutrals; we cannot be neutrals.

The committee called for the immediate withdrawal of foreign troops in Spain and insisted that the legitimate government be allowed to purchase weapons. In December 1937, Otto Katz organised another visit to Spain for Ellen, this time with Clement Attlee. In Madrid, they visited the frontline trenches under artillery fire and carried out an inspection of the British Battalion.

Starvation threatened to undermine the Spanish government's war efforts, so the main focus of Ellen's work back in Britain was arranging humanitarian relief. She helped set up the Milk for Spain fund and persuaded the Co-operative Union to get involved. Customers at the 20,000 co-operative shops were encouraged to buy a sixpenny token to help towards the purchase of cost-price condensed milk and milk powder to be sent to Spain. In Barcelona, for example, the fund served 33,000 glasses of milk and a biscuit to children each morning.

Ellen, however, was fully aware that the Spanish government needed more than milk and food to win. Everywhere she could, in the House of Commons, at conferences, public meetings, demonstrations and in newspaper articles, she spoke of the need for arms. Ellen and Eleanor Rathbone constantly asked questions in the House of Commons about the so-called non-intervention pact, the plight of refugees and the role of Germany and Italy in providing arms to the rebel forces. If the Spanish government were given the freedom to buy airplanes, anti-aircraft guns, artillery and tanks, Ellen urged, Franco's insurgents could not win. If fascism triumphed over democracy, she prophesied, it would mean the consequent destruction of Europe.

On 1 April 1939 Franco declared victory over the democratically elected government of Spain; a few weeks earlier Chamberlain had recognised Franco's regime. The fight against fascism ended ignominiously: until September.

Paula Bartley is a historian and author of *Emmeline Pankhurst* (2002), *Ellen Wilkinson: From Red Suffragist to Government Minister* (2014), and *Women's Activism in Twentieth-Century Britain: Making a Difference Across the Political Spectrum* (2022), among many other publications on women's history. This essay appeared in issue 42 (May 2016) of the *IBMT Newsletter* as 'Red Ellen and the Spanish Civil War'.

Minor role, massive effort: the Independent Labour Party

Christopher Hall

Even after 80 years the role of the Independent Labour Party in the Spanish Civil War is a controversial topic. George Orwell's *Homage to Catalonia* is still the most famous and most read book about the war; equally, Ken Loach's *Land and Freedom* is its best known cinematic portrayal. Both works cover a very small and distinct part of the civil war — which virtually ignores the war as a whole and the role of the International Brigades. The ILP, like the Communist Party, threw its energy and resources into fighting fascism in Spain, and the ILP and its members were involved in far more than the events depicted by Orwell and Loach.

In the 1930s the ILP was a revolutionary socialist party in sharp decline. It had left the Labour Party in 1932 in an argument over 'standing orders' and had seen its membership fall from around 16,000 in 1932 to about 4,000 in 1936. Its four MPs, led by the charismatic James Maxton, gave the ILP a greater profile than its influence on the ground merited. Like the Communist Party and left-wing members of the Labour Party and trade unions, the ILP was involved in the Hunger Marches and was also part of the resistance to Oswald Mosley's Blackshirts at Cable Street in 1936.

When the Spanish Civil War began in July 1936 the ILP belonged to an International known as the London Bureau, which consisted of small left-wing socialist and dissident communist parties. Her sister party in Spain was the POUM (Partido Obrero de Unificación Marxista / Workers' Party of Marxist Unification), an anti-Stalinist communist party which supported the revolution that had broken out in Catalonia in response to the military uprising. In Newport ILP members worked closely with the local Communist Party. In Aberdeen the ILP and Communist Party also worked together, up until June 1937, when the POUM was declared an illegal political party in Spain and relations between the local members broke down.

The ILP was involved in the Spanish Civil War in three main areas: humanitarian aid, military volunteers and political lobbying. From the beginning of the war the ILP began to raise money to help her sister party in Spain. There was even a 'self-denial' week in which individuals had to give up a luxury and the money saved was donated to Aid Spain. Funds were forwarded to John McNair, who had been sent to Barcelona to set up an ILP office and make contact with the POUM executive. McNair passed on the money to the POUM to buy medical supplies. Once over £1,000 had been raised the ILP bought a van, which was turned into an ambulance, filled with medical supplies, driven to Spain along with two nurses, and given to the POUM. One of the drivers, with First World War artillery experience, stayed behind to command a militia artillery unit.

In 1937 the ILP raised funds to fill a food-ship to help with feeding the people of Bilbao in the Basque Country. When the Spanish Republican government refused the offer, the money was used to send further medical supplies to Spain and to finance the care of Basque refugee children — 4,000 of whom had been evacuated to the UK. The ILP housed 40 of them at The Grange in Street, Somerset. The house was supplied by the Quaker Clark family (as in Clarks Shoes).[40]

ILP volunteers fought in a variety of military forces in Spain. These included the ILP's own unit, the 'ILP Contingent', militias, the Republican army and the International Brigades. In autumn 1936 Bob Edwards, a member of the ILP executive (National Administrative Council), won agreement to raise a military force to help the POUM. In all, around 25 men left the UK for Spain in January 1937 and were joined in Spain by more British volunteers, including Orwell, bringing its strength up to a high of around 40. Military training was virtually non-existent and, after two weeks of mainly marching up and down, the volunteers were taken by bus to the front, where they received antiquated rifles and very limited ammunition. They stayed there until late March 1937. The front was a quiet one and the ILP Contingent took part in no major battles and only a single trench raid. As Orwell famously exclaimed: '... nothing happened, nothing ever happened. The English had got into the habit of saying that this wasn't war, it was a bloody pantomime.'

In late March 1937 the ILP unit was on leave in Barcelona, where they met Walter Tapsell, commissar of the British Battalion of the International Brigades, to discuss joining them.[41] The 'May Days' made this impossible: the POUM and the Anarchists of the CNT-FAI [National Confederation of Labour - Iberian Anarchist Federation] took up arms when government forces attempted to retake buildings and services controlled by the revolutionaries.[42] The ILP volunteers were involved in a passive way in the May Days, guarding POUM-held buildings. One ILPer took to his hotel room with a large quantity of beer, hoping to sit out the troubles, but was arrested. After the May Days some volunteers went home, some joined other units and around half returned to the front with the ILP Contingent. In June 1937 the POUM was outlawed and most of the ILP volunteers returned home to avoid arrest. Several, though, joined other Republican units. The last ILP volunteer to leave Spain was Reg Hiddlestone in February 1939.

Like the British Battalion, the bulk of the ILP Contingent were party members; most were of working-class origin and active trade unionists. A few had previous military experience either in peace-time or in the First World War. One man even

---

[40] Editor's note: Nathan Clark, great-grandson of the founder of the Clarks shoe company, was a volunteer ambulance driver in Spain; one part of his despatch from the Battle of Ebro is included in this volume — see '4am: the great advance begins'.

[41] Editor's note: See the above contribution by Bob Beagrie — the poem 'There's Wally' about the ambush which saw Tapsell killed in action.

[42] Editor's note: See Jim Jump's chapter here about George Orwell's description of the May Days, in 'New perspectives on Orwell's memoir'.

deserted from the Tank Corps to join the ILP Contingent in Spain. The vast majority of the volunteers were dedicated anti-fascists, with only a handful there purely to support the revolution. Two men even applied at the same time to join both the ILP Contingent and the International Brigades, but joined the ILP unit because it replied to them first.

Two members of the ILP Contingent were killed in Spain. Bob Smillie died from untreated appendicitis in a Spanish prison, where neglect and incompetence seemed to be the cause of death rather than any deliberate action.[43] Arthur Chambers was killed fighting in an anarchist unit in July 1937. In all, 13 members of the ILP unit were wounded and two hospitalised.

At least 15 and possibly as many as 100-plus ILP members joined the International Brigades. Two leading Merthyr ILPers served in the British Battalion: Evan Peters and Lance Rogers, who joined the Communist Party while in Spain, but re-joined the ILP on returning home, after which he was a conscientious objector in the Second World War. Three Merseyside ILPers fought in the International Brigades, with one, James Stewart, being killed at Jarama in February 1937. Swinton (in Salford) Branch ILP member Walter Sproston was killed at Calaceite in March 1938.

Up to June 1937 the ILP supported the POUM politically. ILP MP John McGovern visited Spain on a propaganda tour in the autumn of 1936. After the POUM was banned the ILP continued to support the Spanish Republic, but also attempted to get POUM prisoners released and were involved in three delegations to Spain in 1937-38. In addition, David Murray, who was in Spain investigating the death of Bob Smillie for the ILP, helped Scottish International Brigaders who had been imprisoned for indiscipline and insubordination. He gave them clothes, food and cigarettes and passed messages to their relatives.

The role of the ILP in the Spanish Civil War was a very minor one and did little to affect the course of the war. In addition, its support for the POUM meant it was ostracised by other left-wing parties. But considering the size of the ILP and its very limited financial resources, party members put a tremendous effort and huge amounts of energy into fighting fascism and helping the POUM in Spain. Their contribution and sacrifice need to be remembered.

Christopher Hall is a researcher, and author of *Not just Orwell: The Independent Labour Party Volunteers and the Spanish Civil War* (2009). This essay appeared in issue 42 (May 2016) of the *IBMT Newsletter*.

---

[43] Editor's note: Smillie's death, reportedly from appendicitis, in Valencia's Modelo Prison, following his arrest close to the French border for being without possession of the correct papers and for carrying 'war materials' (two empty grenades he likely wanted to keep as souvenirs), has long been a topic of suspicion and controversy given the wider context of political tensions between the POUM and the Communist Party.

Artists for Spain

Christine Lindey

The early 20th century's momentous upheavals politicised many people and artists were no exception. The mechanised carnage of the First World War, the 1920s Hunger Marches, the increased immiseration caused by the Great Slump of the 1930s and the concurrent rise of fascism galvanised the left's calls for peace and social justice. The Bolshevik Revolution and its fledgling worker state offered hope and inspired many to discover Marxism. Clive Branson, Betty Rea and James Boswell were among several artists who joined the newly formed Communist Party of Great Britain. Rea and others travelled to Russia to see for themselves, and Pearl Binder and Cliff Rowe were among those who stayed on as working artists. Unlike in Britain where the Depression dried up sales and commissions, work for artists in the Soviet Union was plentiful. Meanwhile, working-class artists such as James Fitton and Percy Horton were already politicised by the British socialist and labour movements.

For socially committed artists the question was: how best to put their work at the service of political change? One way was to organise and in 1933 a handful of artists founded the Artists International (AI). Rowe initiated it on returning from the USSR, having been impressed by the professionalism and internationalism of Soviet artists' organisations and the country's egalitarian cultural policies and social integration of artists. The AI was also influenced by socialist and communist artists' groups in Mexico, France and the US. In 1934 as membership grew to 32, the AI defined itself as: '. . .The International Unity of Artists Against Imperialist War on the Soviet Union, Fascism and Colonial Oppression . . .'[44] It outlined its intention to spread Marxist beliefs through exhibitions, the press, lectures and meetings and by collaborating on posters, illustrations, banners and stage designs and maintaining international contacts with similar groups.

Just as the AI opposed establishment politics, so it challenged the dominant Art for Art's Sake aesthetic. Preached by Roger Fry and Clive Bell, this held that art should address purely formal problems and not be tainted by politics; whereas politically committed artists depicted the realities of working-class life and opposed individualism with collectivism. Influenced by William Morris's socialist aesthetic, they challenged the hierarchy which placed 'pure' Fine Art above the Applied Arts. Indeed some artists rejected easel paintings for being unique, exchangeable commodities, and turned to socially useful public arts such as banners and prints which democratised art. Boswell gave up painting in 1932, and he, Binder, Fitton and

---

[44] *International Literature*, 1934, p.151, cited in R Radford, *Art for a Purpose: The Artists' International Association 1933-53* (Winchester: Winchester School of Art Press, 1987), p.22.

Poster for a week of exhibitions, meetings and cultural activities in support of Spain in London in November 1937. It was designed by the artist Priscilla Thornycroft, a member of the Artists International Association, and painted in the red, yellow and deep purple of the Spanish Republican tricolour. In 2017 Anna Cordon was able to reunite her Aunt Priscilla — who was by then 100 years old and living in Germany — with her sketchbook containing the original poster design. Courtesy of Anna Cordon.

James Holland contributed biting condemnations of poverty and fascism in illustrations for *Left Review* (1934-38).

In 1935 Mussolini's invasion of Abyssinia and Hitler's increasingly threatening belligerence caused the AI to temper its Marxist stance in the inclusive spirit of the Popular Front.[45] Renamed the Artists International Association (AIA), it widened membership, including attracting established artists such as Laura Knight and Henry Moore, so gaining public gravitas and funds. But it was the outbreak of the Spanish Civil War which truly united and galvanised artists into action. Appalled by the French and British governments' unjust refusal to aid the Spanish Republic, numerous artists rallied to its defence in the belief that a second world war could only be averted by defeating Franco, Hitler and Mussolini in Spain. AIA membership surged to 700 in 1937 and had increased to 1,000 by the Second World War.

For politicised artists the question was not whether to, but how to defend the Spanish Republic. Some, including Julian Bell and the communists Clive Branson and Felicia Browne, argued that in times of such political urgency direct political action superseded artistic commitment. They joined the British volunteers of the International Brigade, in which Browne became the only British woman combatant. She was killed in action, as was Bell. Other artists argued that they could be most useful by raising public consciousness and funds. The AIA arranged numerous events including exhibitions such as Artists Help Spain. Organised in 1936 by women in just two weeks, it raised the enormous sum of £500 for the Artists' Ambulance and its medical supplies.

Artists produced numerous leaflets, posters, floats, illustrations and fundraising events such as public lectures, a cabaret and 'Portraits to Help Spanish Medical Aid.' The British Battalion's silk banner was made collectively, as Phyllis Ladyman embroidered Jim Lucas's design and Rea carved a clenched fist for its carrying pole. Some works, such as Peter Perí's emotive relief sculpture *Aid Spain*, conveyed anti-war content through traditional means. Two hundred artists marched as a contingent in the 1938 May Day parade, including the street action by four Surrealists, who dressed and masked as the Prime Minister Neville Chamberlain and danced minuets with his trademark furled umbrella. In 1939 Priscilla Thornycroft collaborated with Fran Youngman to paint 'Spain Fights On, Send Food Now', from tall ladders on a gigantic public hoarding, knowing that this action by two young women would publicise the cause by attracting the press. Even artists such as Henry

---

[45] Editor's note: 'Popular frontism' became official policy in the international communist movement in the wake of the Nazi takeover of Germany, urging communists to unite with other political groups — including middle-class liberals and moderates — in anti-fascist alliances. This could involve rolling back the discourse of revolution and class struggle in favour of the language of democratic freedoms. The military *coup* occurred in the middle of the July following the election of one such Popular Front coalition — including socialists, communists, left-wing republicans, and even some moderate anarcho-syndicalists — in Spain in February of 1936. During the civil war the *frente popular* grew to include Catalan nationalists and the bulk of anarcho-syndicalist movement organised in the CNT-FAI.

Moore and Julian Trevelyan, whose works normally avoided overt political content, contributed posters or banners.

AIA artists were not alone in producing art for Spain. But the AIA was the largest and most organised group to do so. And its clear political focus acted as a forum for the exchange of ideas, particularly during collaborative projects such as banner-making and staging exhibitions. While most artists still remained in their ivory towers, this minority took the radical view that artists could not escape the issues of their time. Rea explained: 'The future of art hangs on the future of civilisation. It is time the artists began to think what sort of future they want and what they can do to get it.'[46]

>Christine Lindey is an art historian and *Morning Star* visual arts critic, whose publications include *Art for All: British Socially Committed Art* (2018). This text was published in issue 49 (September 2018) of *¡No Pasarán!*

---

[46] B. Rea, *5 on Revolutionary Art* (London: Wishart, 1935), p. 1.

Spain in the heart

Sheena Evans

When the International Brigade memorial on London's South Bank was unveiled on 5 October 1985, *The Guardian* mentioned 'an old grey-haired woman' speaking of medical aid for Spain. This was Dame Janet Vaughan, aged 85, whose activity during the Spanish Civil War had been largely forgotten by then. But her story can still be found in papers and sound recordings, mainly in the Marx Memorial Library, the Imperial War Museum and the Hull History Centre.

Born in 1899, the daughter of a public school headmaster, Janet was expected by her parents to have a conventional middle-class life and marriage. Instead, she became a doctor and — having seen as a student the poverty of London's slums — a socialist. In 1930 she married David Gourlay, a socialist and conscientious objector. They lived in a flat above the travel agency David ran in Bloomsbury's Gordon Square. The sisters Vanessa Bell and Virginia Woolf were her cousins; and she was related to Amabel and John Strachey, both prominent socialists. By 1936 Janet was an eminent medical researcher: the second edition of her classic book *The Anaemias* was published that year, and she was promoted to senior lecturer at the British Postgraduate School of Medicine at Hammersmith. She also had two children, Mary and Priscilla, both under five.

Then came the rise of fascism. Janet wrote later that the Spanish Civil War 'became for many of us the great opportunity to take a stand against fascism.' The Spanish Medical Aid Committee (SMAC) was set up in August 1936 through the Socialist Medical Association, at the instigation of Communist Party activist Isabel Brown — soon to be one of the committee's leading fundraisers. By September, Janet was chair of one of its most effective local committees: Holborn & West Central London. Its first public meeting was held on 5 October; and the pamphlet it published in November included contributions from writers such as J.B. Priestley, Rebecca West and Stephen Spender, all arguing against the government's policy of non-intervention.

Janet drew in her friends to support the cause. Vanessa Bell wrote in October 1936: 'For the last few days we have all been trying to do posters for a meeting . . . to get money to send medical help to Spain — Janet Vaughan asked me and Duncan to do some — and Q[uentin] and A[ngelica] have done one each too . . .'; and again in November Janet was one of those who 'pestered' her 'by every post' to help with a show of Spanish art. In its first three months, the committee raised more than £684 (around £35,000 in today's money), of which it gave £600 to the national SMAC. Janet herself remembered walking in poster processions, speaking on soapboxes at street corners and in 'huge public meetings' and selling 'many treasured possessions,' Her daughter Mary (aged 4 ½ in May 1937) stood alongside such soapboxes on Saturday afternoons and has a vivid memory of returning one day to find the flat dark and empty, the car and much of the furniture sold for Spanish Medical Aid; and of her mother's 'absolute delight' at the amount of money she had raised. Although Janet had resigned as chair of the local committee by March 1938, she continued as one of the national vice-presidents of SMAC, and addressed an all-London women's meeting as part of a huge campaign around Britain over the autumn and winter of 1938-39 to fill foodships for Spain. She was also delegated, with other women, to lobby the Foreign Office (unsuccessfully) for more government help.

In January 1939, SMAC called a meeting at which doctors returned from Spain shared their experiences. Janet took the chair for questions and discussion — a long session, mainly about the then innovative practice of using stored blood for transfusions. This had been pioneered in Barcelona by the Spanish doctor Frederic Durán Jordà, and Dr Reginald Saxton spoke at the meeting about using stored blood provided by Jordà for the International Brigades. Janet had worked for SMAC in sending personnel and medical supplies — including blood transfusion equipment — to Spain. She had studied the literature and experimented herself with stored blood. She also learned personally from Dr Jordà, when she helped him and his family settle in England after their escape from Spain. With world war now looming, she saw the need to act quickly to use this knowledge. Between April and July 1939, she was the driving force behind a group of pathologists who met on her initiative in her flat, at first unofficially, and planned what was to be the wartime blood transfusion service for London. When war came in September their plan was put into effect. Similar arrangements followed in the provinces. The service was to save thousands of civilian lives.

Janet was the principal of Somerville College, Oxford, from 1945-1967. She never forgot Spain. She gave money to help dissidents under Franco and, into her old age, to the International Brigade Association. The pendant she wears in a 1985 portrait by Victoria Crowe, now at the National Portrait Gallery, is a stone she treasured, picked up in 1981 from the Jarama battlefield. At the unveiling of the International Brigade memorial in 1985, many listeners were moved to tears as she recalled some of her colleagues in Spanish Medical Aid — Isabel Brown, Leah Manning, Audrey Russell and Richard Ellis, and Vanessa's son Julian Bell who met his death as an ambulance driver — and urged all present to fight 'for our democratic rights, for our social services, for our health service, for our children's right to full education and full employment. We can say as the Brigades said in 1936: "¡No pasarán!"[47]

Sheena Evans is an independent researcher and biographer. This chapter appeared in issue 29 (June 2011) of the *IBMT Newsletter* as 'Janet Vaughan: Spain in the heart'.

---

[47] A fuller account of this research is available in Sheena Evans, 'Give till it hurts: Janet Vaughan and Spanish Medical Aid', *Women's History Magazine* 69 (2012), pp. 18-25.

Portrait of Dame Janet Maria Vaughan by the artist Victoria Crowe, dated 1986-1987. In the portrait, which is in the National Portrait Gallery's primary collection, Vaughan is wearing the pendant with the stone picked up from the Jarama battlefield. Courtesy of Victoria Crowe.

Forgotten plays about the civil war

Simon Breden

Relatively little has been written about British theatrical responses to the Spanish Civil War. Perhaps this is due to the ephemeral nature of theatre, but most examinations of literary responses to the war have focused on poetry and prose. However, at the instigation of Professor Emilio Peral Vega of the Complutense University in Madrid, as part of a government-funded project, *Métodos de propaganda activa en la Guerra Civil* (Methods of Active Propaganda in the Civil War), seeking to discover unpublished works on the subject from around the world, my research has uncovered a strong and prolific theatrical current in the UK that had largely been forgotten.[48] My recently published collection compiles a selection of eight plays staged by Unity Theatre companies around the UK between 1936 and 1946, all but one previously unpublished and located in archives in the UK and the US. All these plays focused centrally on the Spanish Civil War, seeking to inform working-class audiences about what was going on, or on the International Brigades and the importance of the Spanish Civil War within the context of a wider worldwide struggle between communism and fascism.

As the very name of the company implies, the Unity Theatre was closely tied to the Communist Party and its calls for a government of national unity to combat the rise of fascism. Unity also developed a close collaboration with Victor Gollancz's Left Book Club, generating a nationwide network of amateur theatre companies reporting to the Left Book Club Theatre Guild.[49] This network would send out recommendations of plays written for a left-leaning working-class audience, therefore offering a theatre programme completely distinct from the popular mainstream theatre of the era, which offered little comment and no leadership on the subject of Spain. The scale of Unity's effort cannot be sufficiently stressed: my research uncovered records of at least a dozen more Spanish Civil War plays, although I have not yet been able to track down these scripts.

The plays compiled in my book, *El Unity Theatre y la Guerra Civil Española* (Unity Theatre and the Spanish Civil War), were written by left-wing writers and

---

[48] Esta publicación se inscribe en el Proyecto de Investigación I+D Métodos de propaganda activa de la Guerra Civil. Parte II: estudio y edición de obras inéditas (Ministerio de Economía y Competitividad de España. Referencia FFI2016-74873-P).

[49] Editor's note: The Left Book Club was founded by Victor Gollancz in 1936 to bring together different left-wing tendencies, in large part due to the imperative to respond to the rise of fascism. A short history by Roger van Zwanenberg is available at: <https://www.plutobooks.com/blog/the-origins-of-the-left-book-club/> .

International Brigaders, some of whose names are now largely unknown.[50] Perhaps the most famous piece is Jack Lindsay's *On Guard for Spain!* (1937), which has enjoyed a long publication history, more often as a poem rather than a play. However, it was conceived as a piece of theatre, a 'mass declamation' as he termed it, to be performed by a chorus of voices: it was enormously popular in the early years of the war, becoming the most frequently performed play on the Spanish Civil War, staged many times by Unity companies all over the UK. However, it was not the first play on the subject: Randall Swingler's *Spain* (1937) was the earliest response, performed at the Unity Theatre's Britannia Street venue, and containing all the major hallmarks of these pieces: a preoccupation with explaining the nature of the conflict, connecting it to a wider global struggle, and offering a damning indictment of the Conservative government's policy of non-intervention. The collection's other plays include two sketches by Edgar Criddle for the Liverpool Unity Theatre, *Insurgent's Aid Committee* and *Before Guernica* (1937), both satirising the rebel forces and the complicity of the UK government in their atrocities.

Two further plays examine the International Brigades centrally: J.S. Frieze's *We Fight On* (1943) and Ted Willis' *All One Battle* (1945), both plays written after the conclusion of the Spanish Civil War, with the Second World War well underway, and designed to suggest that the fight against fascism had started with the Communist Party's leadership forming a working-class army in Spain. The propagandistic bias of these plays is evident, but it goes some way towards helping us understand the concerns of the British public and the efforts of the British Communist Party and the Comintern to present a particular narrative of the events from 1936 onwards.

Two plays remain, which we may slightly set apart from this purely propagandistic intent, although they both quite clearly display their leftist sympathies, as they attempt to show a more human side to the conflict rather than simply making broad political statements. The first is Carmel Haden-Guest and Robert Orchard's play *Madrileñas* (1937), which shows us the Red Aid offices in Madrid under siege. Haden-Guest's visits to Spain and her humanitarian efforts resonate clearly throughout a piece that attempts to show the suffering of Spanish civilians under intolerable circumstances. The second play is George Leeson's *This Trampled Earth* (1946), the only full-length play in the collection. With echoes of Lorca and Lope de Vega, the play presents a Spanish village attempting to resist its Falangist mayor, and seeks to generate a great deal of empathy with the repressed ordinary townsfolk depicted. Leeson was an International Brigader and one of the men captured at Jarama in Harry Fry's machine-gun company. At the time he was already translating Lorca and Alberti and he would later become the general manager of the Unity Theatre in London. The personal involvement of both Haden-Guest and Leeson in the conflict produced the two most naturalistic plays depicting ordinary Spaniards and the situation in Spain as directly witnessed, rather than the more dispassionate external perspective on the

---

[50] Simon Breden, *El Unity Theatre y la Guerra Civil Española* (Madrid: Guillermo Escolar, 2020).

conflict that the other playwrights in this collection had provided.

My book presents all these plays in English alongside my translations into Spanish. The introduction, also in Spanish, summarises the British literary responses to the war and seeks to place these rediscovered plays within the more familiar context of Spanish Civil War poetry and prose. They offer a valuable window into how resonant the conflict was at the time and how it polarised public opinion. Most importantly, it restores the Unity Theatre to a place of prominence at the forefront of literary responses to the war, demonstrating the extent of its engagement, through the creation of a variety of new plays in different registers, performed by hundreds of amateur companies around the country.

Simon Breden is an academic at the Universidad de Deusto in Bilbao, whose research focuses on Spanish theatre. His publications include *El Unity Theatre y la Guerra Civil española: propaganda literaria y teatral en el Reino Unido* (2020). This essay was published in issue 58 (September 2021) of *¡No Pasarán!*

For the happiness of the children of Spain

Ajmal Waqif

The International Brigades were to an extent defined by their political and social consciousness. Many among the cohort of volunteers who went to Spain were committed to the idea that they were defending the Spanish Republic and fighting alongside its people in their struggle for liberty and social progress. It was precisely these ideas which fascism sought to roll back. This commitment on the part of the International Brigades can be seen not only in their readiness to fight, and in many cases die, alongside the forces of the Spanish Republic, but also in their concern and support for the population.

Of particular concern were the children of Spain. Over 200,000 child refugees fled war zones as Franco's fascist rebels conquered more territory. The majority of displaced children received assistance from the Republic. They were placed with foster families and in residential schools in the east of the country, away from the front. The international effort which resettled around 25,000 Basque refugees, led by civilians across Europe and the governments of the Soviet Union and Mexico, is relatively well known. What is less known is that Brigaders and medical volunteers in Spain were active in providing aid for displaced and orphaned children.

The Comité Pro-Niños Españoles de las Brigadas Internacionales (International Brigade Committee for Children) came together on the first anniversary of the formation of the International Brigades, coordinating and funding homes for refugee children. The committee's activities were documented in a photo book titled *Los Niños Españoles y las Brigadas Internacionales* (*Spanish children and the International Brigades*) published in 1938. The book was compiled on the initiative of Luigi 'Gallo' Longo, inspector-general of the International Brigades. *Los Niños Españoles* features a collection of photographs from across Spain, as well as text and captions in five languages: Spanish, Czech, English, French and German. Its preface is clear about its purpose: 'We hope that this little book will win new friends for the Spanish cause and above all for the Spanish children.'

Separated into roughly two parts; the first half of the book provides an assortment of anecdotes and accounts placed alongside photos of the aftermath of war, children at the front and their interactions with Brigaders. Early in the first section is an interesting but unattributed letter dated 7 September 1937, supposedly from an International Brigader fighting on the southern front. Writing to his son back home, he emphasises the importance of education as a part of the anti-fascist struggle: 'As soon as we Internationals come to a new place where there are no schools we help at once to organise them. If you think it over you will understand how important this is. For we lead this war not only with cannons. You also, dear, must learn as much as possible.'

This part also presents a few anecdotes: a Chinese volunteer speaks to a group of children who express concern about fellow children in China, a German volunteer attends a Christmas celebration at a children's home in Madrid and an unspecified Brigade unit throws a party for children in a village, pulling together what meagre resources they had. Photo sets titled 'Bombardment' and 'Evacuation' have grim photos of children killed from fascist bombing raids or being evacuated from battle zones. 'In every region, wherever the fascists attack, the people flee. They come with the remains of their belongings on foot, with mule carts, on trucks, with countless children,' states the caption.

The second half of the book highlights several residences established for refugee and orphaned children. It details the activities run for the children in a home operating in the requisitioned castle of Moraleja near Madrid. Further along it discusses the town of Benisa, south of Valencia, where anarchist workers and convalescing International Brigaders worked together to set up a home and school for refugee children, naming the building 'Solidaridad'. The International Brigades also had a hospital in the beachside resort of Benicasim, with one large country house set aside for orphans from Madrid and Asturias. Wounded Brigaders spent their time in recovery entertaining and playing with the Spanish children: photos show volunteers making toys and an anecdote tells of a Canadian Brigader on crutches at the beach, talking about wooden planes with the children.

The concluding pages urge the reader to send goods and raise funds for the provision of further support for the refugee children — in Spain and back at home. Returning once more to the letter in the opening pages of the book, the Brigader expresses his hope for a peaceful future for all: 'Tomorrow we shall have a party for the children of this place. We love the Spanish children . . . we do not only fight for the freedom of Spain and for the happiness of those splendid Spanish children, but for the freedom of our own country and your future as well.'[51]

Ajmal Waqif has been the editor of *¡No Pasarán!* since 2020. This text appeared in issue 60 (May 2022) of *¡No Pasarán!*

---

[51] Editor's note: This topic is explored in more depth in a recent academic article by the author of one of our other chapters, Adrian Pole, "Soldiers of Culture' and their 'Little Comrades': The International Brigades and the Children of Civil War Spain, 1936-1939', *Contemporary European History* (2022). <https://doi.org/10.1017/ S0960777322000388>.

Aftermath

Syd Harris, the Leeds-born Lincoln Battalion veteran who survived shooting and imprisonment, pictured at a post-war anti-fascist rally in Chicago. Courtesy of the Harris family.

The struggle never stopped

Bill Alexander

Sam Wild set the scene in December 1938 when, with the arrival in Britain of the main group, he said: 'We have changed the front but our fight continues.'[52] The welcome meetings, packed and enthusiastic, were mobilising meetings. The Spanish people fought on for another three months while the British Tory government extended its criminal appeasement policies — so-called 'non-intervention' — recognising Franco one month before his military victory. Brigaders went out on exhausting tours of meetings rousing opposition to the government and urging support for the Spanish Republic.

We and the Lincolns were lucky and could return home to comparative safety. But the Germans, Italians and Brigaders from reactionary states were interned in savage conditions in French concentration camps. Efforts to ease their conditions and to get some out began at once, with Winifred Bates and Lon Elliott organising help. Thousands of Spanish families had fled over the Pyrenees, thinking better the bare sands of the French camps than a fascist bullet. When Mexico offered them visas, Wogan Philipps chartered a ship. Nan Green fed the babies of 5,000, on their way to freedom but exile.

Of course we found time to be united with our families, get married, find jobs. But it was in this background of activity for Spain that the International Brigade Association was set up at the very end of February 1939. A number of far-sighted, wise decisions were made. The name International Brigade Association had no connotation of military organisation and gave a welcoming place to all who had served in Spain, no matter their nationality or birthplace. The agreed sole aim of the association was to 'fight in our own country to help the Spanish people in their struggle to restore liberty and democracy in Spain.' This provided unity of purpose while the volunteers, as individuals, were free to take part in other activity.

There is no record of the number who linked up with the association; it must have been under 1,500. Today there are 114 members, only two under 70 years, members of all political parties, many of none. We are united only in our common pride that at a turning point in history we stood together to fight for civilisation, freedom and peace. The long, proud record of the association must be seen against this picture of ageing and falling membership.

It was accepted that we had to integrate once again in the popular, progressive class organisations from which we came. The Dependants' Aid Fund was wound up,

---

[52] Editor's note: Sam Wild was the last commander of the British Battalion, replacing Bill Alexander after the latter was wounded in early 1938. He led the Battalion at the Ebro, for which he received the Republic's highest decoration for bravery.

with all possible help being given to our disabled, grants to widows and jobs and apprenticeships for children. A proposal that we should campaign for International Brigade pensions was turned down, so that today Brigaders are prominent fighters at local and national level for adequate pensions for all. There was to be no special social club, so the local pub or workingmen's club was used. Above all, as our members got jobs, they worked in their factories and trade unions, not only for the general interests of all, but to use them to keep up the fight against Franco fascism. The efforts to black work for Franco, the resolution at nearly every TUC and Labour Party conference, usually had their origin in the activity and initiative of our members.

With the outbreak of World War II, which we tried to prevent, there were some difficulties. Was it a continuation of the war against fascism, or was the discrimination against International Brigaders a sign of the continuation of 'non-intervention' and appeasement? But soon there was acceptance that there could be no freedom for the Spanish people without defeat of the main pillars of fascism — Hitler and Mussolini. Spain had gone off the front pages of the papers. Members were in the forces or working 12 hours a day, every day, in the war industry. But Jack Brent, despite severe wounds from Jarama which kept him in lasting pain, kept the campaign of the association to the fore. He was the first of the group of outstanding leaders of the IBA: Nan Green, Alec Digges, Alan Gilchrist, Lon Elliott, Jim Ruskin and others, who never forgot their pledge to aid Spain.

Our paper, *The Volunteer for Liberty*, carried articles on how to fight the war, some written by Hans Kahle, commander of the XI Brigade. Campaigns were waged to save Luigi Longo, Rau and others from death at the hands of the fascists. Great efforts were made to secure the release of Frank Ryan, Tom Jones and Jim Cameron, still in Franco's prisons. Despite problems of contact, funds were got to International Brigade prisoners still in Miranda de Ebro. With the Allied advances in Europe and North Africa, Spanish Republicans and Brigaders managed to get to London and the IBA helped many to find their place with their 'free government.' In 1944 the IBA members decided to turn their main efforts to make sure the imminent defeat of Hitler and Mussolini was followed by the defeat of Franco. Our journal, renamed *Spain Today*, campaigned for economic sanctions, no trade or aid for Franco. But, despite the election of a Labour government and a big campaign, the arguments of the Cold War prevailed.

Franco carried on for another 30 years his reign of terror against the Spanish people, against all who resisted in any way his savage dictatorial power. He was supported by economic and military aid from the US and British governments. We kept up a continuous campaign trying to change this, exposing the treatment of Spanish democrats and the threat to peace and freedom everywhere while Franco's infection centre remained. For 39 years, until Franco's unlamented death, the Association acted as a catalyst, inspiring the Aid Spain movement, the trade unions and Labour Party, Appeal for Amnesty in Spain, Youth Aid for Spain and other organisations, and also helped the organisations of Spanish workers in Britain, exiles, immigrants and the grown-up 'Basque children.'

Franco's reign of terror continued — indeed, there were executions for political 'crimes' until 1975 — arrests, torture, near summary trials in a military court, execution or long terms of prison. We tried to help all — communists, socialists, anarchists, freemasons, students. There was almost a pattern — news of an important trial, approach to an MP, lawyer or prominent individual, frantic efforts to raise the fare, then a campaign of exposure, leaflets, meetings and protests. These efforts gave hope, as a socialist put it to an observer from Britain: 'We know we are not forgotten.' Will Paynter went to find out about Camacho and the Carabanchel Ten, imprisoned for building the illegal workers' commissions. When we met Camacho in 1981 he told us of the added strength they derived from his visit.

Things were difficult for the IBA in the Cold War period. Spain was not in the limelight. Members and friends became involved in other urgent campaigns and organisations. Reactionaries and the right-wing were emboldened to attack and denigrate the fight in Spain and the Association. Old slanders were dusted off: the effect of the *vino*; the military incompetence; the dupes of Stalin and so on. Money was very short, the office and full-time secretary had to go, *Spain Today* went bimonthly and then had to close. Alec Digges, determined to send a lawyer to a trial, borrowed the fare on his personal guarantee. But even so, activity was kept up. Money was collected to help Republicans still in France; funds were smuggled out to help the underground trade unions in Spain. Franco was never accepted by the British people. Manuel Fraga Iribarne, Minister of Information, was chased all round London when he tried to justify the execution of Julián Grimau.

With Franco's death and the quite firm steps towards democracy in Spain, the Spanish people will now be able to sort out their own problems — there are plenty — by their own forces, experiences and organisations. The contribution of the British Volunteers for Liberty fighting in Spain and the campaign of aid and international solidarity with the Spanish people is part of the history of democratic, progressive struggles of our peoples. The ruling class still attempts to denigrate our role and 'write us out of history.' But the successful campaign of meetings, exhibitions and demonstrations, the 34 local memorials — statues, plaques and buildings — for their 'own' Brigaders show that the International Brigade has deep roots among the people.[53] There is still great interest in our experiences and their impact on events at home and in the world. As individuals our members continue to play their part in widely differing organisations of their choice. After 50 years the International Brigade Association can say with pride, tempered with humility, we have done our best to fulfill our pledge to help the Spanish people achieve democracy. We have made a contribution to bring peace and freedom to people.

---

[53] Editor's note: As of August 2022, there are almost 200 International Brigade memorials around Britain and Ireland of many different shapes and sizes. A database with information and photographs can be found at <https://international-brigades.org.uk/memorials/>.

Bill Alexander was commander of the British Battalion at the Battle of Teruel early in 1938. Later in life he wrote *British Volunteers for Liberty: Spain 1936-39* (1982) and *No to Franco: The Struggle Never Stopped 1939-1975* (1992), and was secretary of the International Brigade Association from 1984 until his death in 2000. This chapter featured in issue 47 (January 2018) of *¡No Pasarán!*, reprinted from the March 1989 newsletter of the IBA, now held in the Marx Memorial Library, Spain Collection, Papers of the International Brigade Association, SC/IBA/6/1/39. Reproduced with kind permission of the Marx Memorial Library and Bill Alexander's son, Keith Alexander.

From the Ebro to the Battle of Britain

Geoff Cowling

Some time ago I stumbled upon the following reference in the Imperial War Museum archive to a Luftwaffe propaganda film of August 1940 describing a 'Stuka attack on England . . . escorted by Bf109Es, including one with Spanish Civil War markings "Arriba de Campo" and crossed swords, before peeling away to attack "ports, industrial installations and airfields". Oil storage tanks blaze below.' This fascinated me because I have long thought there might be direct photographic evidence linking the Luftwaffe Condor Legion's activities in the Spanish Civil War with the aerial conflict which took place in the skies over Britain during the Second World War. We know from accounts written by RAF Battle of Britain pilots that they were taken aback by the sophisticated 'finger-four schwarm' combat tactics used by the Luftwaffe's pilots, who developed their considerable combat skills in the skies of Spain. Our inexperienced pilots suffered heavy casualties in the first phases of the Battle of Britain until the RAF stopped flying in their traditional parade ground 'vic' formations and adopted the far more flexible German aerial battle tactics.

Would the Luftwaffe film actually show the very same Messerschmitts that first appeared in the skies of Catalonia above the Ebro battlefield, flying over southern England? I asked the Imperial War Museum if I could see the film, but they told me that it was in a precarious condition and had never been viewed since it was catalogued shortly after the Second World War. It could only be renovated at considerable cost. I persisted and to their eternal credit the museum renovated the film and I collected a copy from their archivist, Matthew Lee.

In fact, the DVD showed the aircraft to be factory-fresh Messerschmitt 109Es and not the 109D which operated in Spain just two years earlier. And the markings themselves raised as many questions as answers. One 109E carries the slogan '*Arriba el Campo*' along the engine nose. Above the slogan is a symbol of crossed daggers. This aircraft and another in the background are also painted with a 'top hat' symbol on the fuselage. Gerald Howson, the renowned expert on Spanish Civil War aviation and author of the definitive *Arms for Spain*, confirms that the 'top hat' symbol was carried by the 2/88 Group of the Condor Legion. The slogan '*Arriba el Campo*' ("Up the Countryside") has no meaning on its own. Howson believes it may have its origins in a poem of that name by the Falangist poet Dionisio Ridruejo which could have been adopted as a battle slogan by one of the Condor Legion squadrons, but we have no evidence to prove this is true. The crossed dagger symbol too remains a mystery. Historian Paul Preston points to a passing similarity to the Carlist emblem, the Burgundian Cross, but a check of images on Google shows significant differences. And its similarity to the symbol of the Falange (Spanish fascist party) is only passing.

As I said, this exercise has raised as many questions as answers. Whatever the origins of these symbols, it does show that the Luftwaffe pilots gazing at us from these photos honed their fighting skills in the skies of Spain — which they then went on to use in the Battle of Poland, the Battle of France, and the Battle of Britain. For them the Second World War did not begin in September 1939, but in 1936 when the Luftwaffe first appeared in the skies of Spain. This three-minute film demonstrates just how right and far-sighted were the members of the International Brigades to volunteer and sacrifice their lives in the fight against the rise of fascism in Europe when they did. It's a pity that others were not listening and the world had to endure the devastating consequences which followed.

> Geoff Cowling was HM Consul General in Barcelona from 2002 to 2005, and an IBMT trustee from 2006 to 2008. This article first appeared in issue 23 (June 2009) of the *IBMT Newsletter*.

A still taken from a Luftwaffe propaganda film of an attack on England; the crossed daggers symbol with 'Arriba el Campo' slogan is visible on the engine nose of the plane closest to the camera. Courtesy of the Imperial War Museum.

Forgotten heroine of Spain and France

Angela Jackson

Volunteers from all over the world, concerned about the rise of fascism in Europe, went to Spain to join the International Brigades and help the Spanish Republic. Women were able to volunteer as nurses, often serving in improvised hospitals with poor sanitation and short supplies. One such nurse was Madge Addy, from the Chorlton-cum-Hardy area of Manchester. She arrived in Spain in 1937 and became head nurse at a hospital in an old monastery at Uclés in Castile. Like some of the other British nurses, she was also involved with the fund-raising campaigns back home. Madge would write detailed letters about the work in the 'Manchester Ward' at the hospital in Uclés to the chairman of the North Manchester Spanish Medical Aid Committee.

Her appeals were given national coverage by the *Daily Worker*, with the dramatic headline 'Nurse gave her blood to save men of Madrid,' together with a picture of her in a direct arm to arm transfusion with a wounded soldier. This rather haphazard but often effective method for saving lives was to lead to the development of new, improved techniques for the mass collection and preservation of blood by the doctors in the Republican medical services. Their work was to save countless lives in the Second World War. Meanwhile, as the battles raged on, Madge wrote to say she had become 'very much attached' to a Mr Holst, who held an important position at the hospital, and that they intended to marry. 'In the meantime,' she wrote, 'Spain and the hospital come first. I have pledged myself to both for a year, then I am hoping to be able to turn my thoughts seriously to some kind of happy future . . .'

As the war progressed, conditions worsened and shortages became more acute. One of Madge's letters explained:

> . . . the Committee sent out a gross of Izal toilet rolls, but they cannot be used for the purpose they were intended for. The director said to me, 'Madge, we were very glad indeed for the paper.' I said, 'What paper?' and he said, 'Well it was really toilet paper, but we are using it in the office, come and see.'

Her pleas became desperate as supplies could not always get through. Hundreds of sick and wounded men were arriving from the front. The few clothes they had were infested with lice and had to be burned, and they had often been fighting in bare feet. 'You probably wonder where the things go to,' wrote Madge, 'but you cannot take the shirt, pants and vests off them when they are discharged.' She told the committee in Manchester that the last group had arrived with next to nothing and would have to be discharged 'practically nude' as there were no more clothes to give them. Her patients were dying from lack of food and there was only one syringe in the hospital which she 'guarded with her life.' Her requests were simple: '. . . please ask Manchester to do its utmost to send money so that you can buy stuff necessary. Don't send anything for me, devote every penny to the hospital.'

Madge Addy was the last British nurse to leave Spain. She stayed on at the hospital for as long as she could, not returning to England till June 1939 after the Spanish Medical Aid Committee had intervened with the British Foreign Office to secure her a visa. What happened after that did not come to light until recently. Madge married the Norwegian she had written about from Spain, Wilhelm Holst, and was with him in Paris carrying out relief work when the Germans broke through in 1940. After moving to Marseilles, she met Thorkild Hansen, a Danish national who served in Special Operations Executive's 'DF' escape section. Madge was soon involved in secret operations and went on to play a vital role in setting up the famous 'Garrow-Pat O'Leary' escape line, working with MI9. She was awarded the OBE for her work in France. Her bravery included travelling as a Norwegian subject on German civil flights, carrying secret messages sewn into the lining of her fur coat, 'cool as a cucumber.' As an English woman operating in enemy occupied territory, she would have known what the penalty would be if caught.

After the war, she married Hansen and her bravery was recognised in letters of thanks from the British and Dutch authorities for her assistance with Allied escape lines. Madge Addy died in 1970 before I had the chance to interview her, but, in the course of my research, I was lucky enough to get to know some of the other women who had worked as nurses in Spain. Their fascinating experiences not only led me to write several books on the history of their work in the civil war but also inspired me to write a novel, *Warm Earth*, to reveal the true extent of the fortitude and passion that had filled their lives.[54]

Angela Jackson is a historian and writer whose publications include *British Women and the Spanish Civil War* (2002, republished in 2020 by *The Clapton Press*) and the Spanish Civil War novel *Warm Earth* (2007) based on the first-hand testimony collected during her research. This appeared as 'Madge Addy: Forgotten heroine of the wars in Spain and France' in issue 43 (September 2016) of the *IBMT Newsletter*.

---

[54] Editor's note: After reading this article in the *IBMT Newsletter*, the writer Christopher Hall (whose essay about the Independent Labour Party during the Spanish Civil War appears in this volume) campaigned successfully to have a plaque installed at Madge Addy's old home in Manchester and later wrote a biography of her: *The Nurse Who Became a Spy: Madge Addy's War Against Fascism* (Barnsley: Pen & Sword History, 2021).

Reluctantly finding a home in Britain

Herminio Martínez

1939 and 1940 were crucial years for us. The Spanish Civil War ended in April 1939 and the Second World War started in September. By early 1940, most of the nearly 4,000 *niños vascos* (Basque children) had been repatriated. The British government never wanted us and did its utmost to get rid of us. But some 470 of us remained in the UK to live through the duration of the war. At the end of the civil war other exiles arrived. Some managed to come as diplomatic exiles because of their positions in the Spanish Republic's government. Others were brought out of the concentration camps on the beaches of southern France by Quakers such as Alec Wainman, who had to guarantee their keep because these exiles were not allowed to work. Others arrived via Gibraltar, joining those citizens evacuated to Britain. Some made their way here via the French Foreign Legion. The British government did not want any of us. We were classified as 'aliens' and we had to observe many restrictions. Life could be difficult. Some of these older exiles helped out in the colonies ('*colonias*' or residential homes) for Basque children and did excellent work among us.

There was little cohesion amongst these diverse *Republicanos* having to survive in a foreign country. The Basque refugees had the common unifying experience of having lived together in the *colonias* scattered throughout the UK. Those living in the Midlands tended to meet up at the home of Molly Garrett in Birmingham. They organised a football team. Those living in the London area started to publish a regular bulletin, *Amistad*, with contributions from around the UK. Much of the work was done at the offices of the Basque Children's Committee at 39 Victoria Street, London. The *colonias* gradually closed till there was only The Culvers in Carshalton, which housed the younger children. Theatre director Pepe Estruch, who had been a friend of Federico Garcia Lorca and was one of those taken out of the French concentration camps by Alec Wainman, ran the *colonia* and several other adults helped out. The Culvers became a meeting place not only for the Basque refugees but also for some of the older *Republicanos*. *Fiestas* were organised there and some cultural activities, such as a theatre group.

Dr Juan Negrín, the Republican Prime Minister, who had sought exile in Paris, came to London when Nazi Germany invaded France. Other politicians, such as Álvarez del Vayo, the Foreign Minister, Pablo Azcárate, the Republican ambassador, sought asylum in London. Negrín was very supportive of the Republican exiles. He would visit the children at The Culvers and Barnet *colonias* and helped with funding. He made sure there was money for the Juan Luis Vives scholarships that allowed many exiles and refugees to study. In October 1941 Negrín took on the lease of a large house at 22 Inverness Terrace in Bayswater, west London, which became the 'Hogar Español' (Spanish Home) or simply El Hogar.

El Hogar became a social, cultural and political centre for all the *Republicanos*.

Other anti-fascists also met and socialised there. Jack Brent, the International Brigader, was often at the entrance giving out literature. Nan Green, another volunteer in Spain, was to be seen there with friends. The Brigaders also used the Hogar for some of their meetings. Suddenly, all the pent-up energies of the diverse groups of *Republicanos* were released. *Amistad* now had a centre from which to operate. Dances were held at weekends. Gradually, many of the exiles and refugees tended to move to London. They now had a 'home.' Deep friendships and comradeship were forged. Apart from the socialising and political campaigning, there were some wonderful cultural activities. A mixed choir was formed under the direction of Manolo Lazareno, who had been a professional musicologist in Spain. It was wonderful to see such a diverse set of young exiles taking so well to this work. A theatre group was set up under the direction of Pepe Estruch and a folk-dancing group was run by several other individuals. Also, an excellent football team was established.[55]

I have always likened the cultural activities at El Hogar to the work done in Spain with the *Misiones Culturales* (Cultural Missions) of the Spanish Republic — artistic exhibitions and performances which toured remote parts of Spain. For many of us who missed out on living our early life in Spain, it was a priceless opportunity to encounter the richness of Spanish culture. Pepe Estruch directed the *grupo de teatro* at the Hogar. It tended to stage works by the classical dramatists of Spain's Golden Age: Calderón, Lope de Vega and Cervantes. But the group also produced works by modern dramatists such as Lorca. Not being an actor in any way, I was the prompter. We were fortunate enough to get to know Spanish theatre at its best. Pepe eventually returned to Madrid and transformed the moribund Spanish theatre scene. He was awarded the Premio Nacional (National Prize) in 1990 for his work. The refugees and exiles came from all the corners of Spain. Hence, the performances of the folk-dancing group represented many of the regions. I especially loved the *Toledana* (from Toledo). I still have in my mind these beautiful dances and regional costumes.

As for the political activities at the Hogar, I am afraid that the dissensions and divisions that had plagued the Spanish left during the short period of the Second Republic affected the politics of the Hogar. There was a dreadful lack of unity.

At the end of the war in 1945 we were all expecting the Allies to end Europe's last remaining fascist dictatorship. At The Culvers we lit a great bonfire to celebrate the end of the war and our forthcoming return to Spain. It was not to be. The Cold War set in and the Americans wanted the bases that Franco was prepared to provide. Ernest Bevin, the British Foreign Minister, made welcoming overtures to Franco. The disillusionment was horrific. Some of the refugees found their families in France, Chile or Mexico and joined them. The Hogar closed in 1947. Negrín and other politicians had gone to Mexico. Franco's fascist regime was well established. We maintained some of the activities started at the Hogar in various places. Every Saturday evening there was

---

[55] Editor's note: Some of the Basque *niños* would enjoy illustrious footballing careers. See Daniel Gray's chapter, 'From refugee boys to professional players.'

a dance at the Fox School in Notting Hill. The folk-dancing and choir also continued, as did the theatre group, staging plays at the 20th Century Theatre in Notting Hill and other venues. We always kept hope alive, but it would be many years before changes in Spain permitted us to return.

> Herminio Martínez was one of the Basque child refugees who arrived in Southampton in May 1937. This essay was originally featured in issue 42 (May 2016) of the *IBMT Newsletter*, appearing as 'Reluctantly finding a home in Britain: Spanish Republican refugees and exiles in the 1940s'. Re-published with kind permission of the Martínez family.

Herminio Martínez in 2017, holding a photo of the Habana, the ship which brought him and nearly 4,000 other Basque child refugees to Britain. Jubilee Gardens, London. The historian Paul Preston is visible in the background. Courtesy of the photographer, Andrew Wiard.

Dad's Army: the Spanish connection

Peter Frost

In 2016, the classic television sitcom *Dad's Army* returned as a feature film. Directed by Oliver Parker, it stars Catherine Zeta-Jones, Toby Jones, Bill Nighy, Tom Courtenay, Bill Paterson and Michael Gambon. Today we treat the Home Guard as a bit of a laugh. Dad's Army, as it is usually known, has been the butt of many jokes and the subject of the hilarious TV programme and now the film.

In fact, the Home Guard was a serious attempt at building an organised resistance that would fight a guerilla war if Hitler's plan to invade Britain came to pass. It would be the final defence to stop our country falling under the Nazi jackboot. No joke really. Civilians trained in guerilla warfare and classic resistance techniques like street fighting, sabotage and civil disobedience would be the last bastion against the Nazi invaders and the British traitors, some of them members of the aristocracy, press barons and even the royal family who would have undoubtedly thrown their lot in with the Nazis.

The man who dreamed up this fighting group, officially known as the Local Defence Volunteers, was Tom Wintringham, long-time communist and Marxist, military theoretician and historian who had fought in the trenches in the First World War. Wintringham learnt about guerilla warfare commanding the British Battalion during the Spanish Civil War. When he wasn't fighting he was a noted journalist and writer, particularly on politics, military affairs and military history. Wintringham was born in 1898 in Grimsby. In 1915 he won a scholarship to study history at Balliol College, Oxford, but left university to join the Royal Flying Corps. Poor eyesight stopped him flying, so he worked as a mechanic and motorcycle despatch rider.

At the end of the First World War he was involved in a mutiny before going back to Oxford. Already sympathetic to communist ideas, he spent his first long summer holiday in Moscow. Back in England he assembled a group of students aiming to establish a British section of the Third International. This grouping would be one part of what would eventually become the Communist Party. Wintringham graduated from Oxford and moved to London, ostensibly to study for the bar at the Temple, but in fact to work full-time in left-wing politics. By 1923 he had joined the newly formed Communist Party of Great Britain (CPGB) and in 1925 he was one of the 12 CPGB leaders jailed for seditious libel and incitement to mutiny.

In 1930 he helped to found the *Daily Worker*, the predecessor of the *Morning Star*, where his name became well-known. At the same time in pamphlets and articles in other communist publications he established his reputation as the party's military expert. Even before Nazi planes bombed the Basque town of Guernica — a rehearsal for later Blitz bombing — he called for air raid precautions. The CPGB took up this campaign and even shaped government policy.

At the start of the Spanish Civil War, Wintringham went to Barcelona, initially as a journalist for the *Daily Worker*. He soon swapped his pen for a rifle, joining and eventually commanding the British Battalion of the International Brigade. While in Spain he met and started a romance with left-wing US journalist Kitty Bowler, who was reporting on the Republican cause. Later Kitty would become his second wife.

In February 1937 he was wounded in the Battle of Jarama. While injured in Spain he became friends with Ernest Hemingway, who based one of his characters on Tom. Following a second injury in action, this time on the Aragón front, a seriously infected wound saw him near death. Kitty visited him in military hospital and discovered he was suffering from typhoid and septicaemia. Patience Darton, a nurse with the International Brigades, saved his life: 'I poked around with a pair of scissors and found he had a lot of pus in his wounds, which had been sewn up too tightly. And that was it; he got better very quickly.' He was repatriated, and wrote a book, *English Captain*, based on his time in Spain. Kitty came to England with him but in 1938 the CPGB accused her of being a Trotskyist and a spy. Tom refused to leave her and was expelled from the party.

He found a job at *Picture Post* magazine. He also started to campaign for an armed civilian guard to repel any fascist invasion. As early as 1938 he was calling for what would become the Home Guard. In *Picture Post*, the *Daily Mirror*, *Tribune* and the *New Statesman* he wrote articles calling for all-out war against the Nazis. The Communist Party was deeply divided. Wintringham strongly condemned the comrades who wanted to stay out of the war. He was even stronger in his criticisms of Prime Minister Neville Chamberlain. He regarded the Tories as Nazi sympathisers and campaigned for them to be removed from office.

In May 1940, after Dunkirk, Wintringham began to campaign for the founding of squads of Local Defence Volunteers, the forerunner of the Home Guard. He started his own military training school at Osterley Park, London. There he taught volunteers the guerilla warfare techniques he had learnt in Spain. Along with other ex-International Brigade comrades he taught street fighting, anti-tank warfare, sabotage and demolition — all the skills in fact that would be essential to resist a Nazi invasion. He wrote many articles putting forward his views under the slogan 'a people's war for a people's peace.'

The Colonel Blimps of the army did not trust Wintringham because of his communist past. After September 1940 the army began to take charge of the Home Guard training in Osterley and Wintringham and his comrades were gradually sidelined. Wintringham resigned in April 1941. Despite his role in founding it, he was never allowed to join the Home Guard because of a rule barring membership to communists and fascists. He helped to found the briefly popular socialist Common Wealth Party. Later he and Kitty joined the Labour Party. In his later years he worked mainly in radio and film. He continued to write about military history, opposing atomic weapons and championing China and Tito's Yugoslavia. Tom Wintringham died on 16 August 1949, aged 51.

See the film, have a good laugh, but never forget what Dad's Army really stood for: a civilian guerrilla resistance movement that could have stood between us and the horrors of a Nazi occupation.

Peter Frost is a journalist for the *Morning Star* and a contributor to *Culture Matters*. This story was published in issue 41 (January 2016) of the *IBMT Newsletter*, after previously appearing in the *Morning Star* on 14 October 2015.

Ramona: the militiawoman who settled in England

Marshall Mateer

A newspaper cutting[56] from *La Dona Catalana* — a Barcelona women's magazine — dated September 1936 has come to light in the Working Class Movement Library (WCML) in Salford. Printed in sepia, it shows a young woman, head and shoulders, smiling in her militia cap and overalls with the caption in Catalan saying: 'A beautiful and brave militiawoman ready to go to the [Aragón] front.' Her name is Ramona Siles García, a nurse who joined the militias and whom we have known until now simply as 'Ramona,' the one woman in the iconic Tom Mann Centuria photograph taken at the Karl Marx Barracks in Barcelona in September 1936.

Ramona met Londoner Nat Cohen under fire on the beaches of Mallorca in August 1936 as they were strafed and bombed by Italian aircraft during the militia's disorderly retreat from the island. Siles and Cohen, who after eight years in South America[57] was a fluent Spanish speaker, remained together from that day until Ramona died in London 28 years later in August 1965. Ramona and Nat were married, and after Nat Cohen was wounded — his knee-cap blown away on the Aragón front — they crossed the Spanish border and made their way to England via Paris.

Nat returned to London on 9 April 1937 and the *Daily Mirror* of the following day reported that 'he limped home on crutches . . . and was given a conqueror's reception by the Communist Party and a guard of anti-Fascist ex-Servicemen wearing their medals jumped to attention on Victoria platform, but he was a sad man. His pretty wife Ramona . . . was detained in Paris by passport difficulties.' However, Ramona arrived in London a few days later and, as advertised in the *Daily Worker* on 17 April, 'Romona [sic] (Nat's wife, 1st Spanish militiawoman)', was to be on the platform with Nat at the Whitechapel Gallery for the 'grand wind-up' of an Aid for Spain parade, which would begin that Sunday in Stepney with 'Decorated Lorries, Ambulances, 20-foot foodship, Militiamen, Nurses and Sailors' and would hear 'the final and magnificent total collected in Stepney's Spain week.' Ramona also spoke at other meetings and, according to a *Daily Worker* small ad, offered 'Spanish lessons.'

After a period of evacuation from Stepney to Hertfordshire to avoid the

---

[56] Photographs and newspaper cuttings referred to in this article form part of the Working Class Movement Library's Spanish Civil War collection — parts of which can be viewed online at <www.wcml.org.uk>.

[57] Editor's note: Cohen had been an active communist union leader in Argentina, resulting in his expulsion in 1932 in the wake of General José Uriburu's right-wing *coup d'état*. A brief account of this part of his life appeared in issue 31 (January 2012) of the *IBMT Newsletter*, written by Argentine historian Jerónimo E. Boragina.

bombing during the Second World War, the couple moved to the St Helier estate in Morden, South London. The Cohens were amongst those who helped the Basque children's colony at Carshalton, near where they lived. In 1944 in South London a local newspaper reporter attended a 'Christmas Treat for 250 Children.' Someone points out the 'Organiser, Mrs Ramona Cohen' and says something along the lines of: 'You see that woman; she fought in the Spanish Civil War.' Ramona then explained to the eager reporter, in one of the very few records we have of her talking: 'I fought on two fronts Mallorca and Aragón. There were quite a number of women in the Spanish army for they were short of men. We wore trousers, our battle-dresses being something like a boiler-maker's overalls.' She continued:

> Yes, I used to carry a gun, and use it too. Whether I killed any of Franco's soldiers I don't know, but I did my best to do so in the battles in which I took part. I think I must have done. I shall never forget that I am a Spaniard and fought for my beloved country.

The report ends with a quotidian flourish: '. . . and then she went on cutting sandwiches.'

You can see Ramona smiling in the much replicated Tom Mann Centuria photograph. In the captions to the photograph the names of the men are always given in full: Sid Avner, Jack Barry, Nat Cohen, David Marshall, Giorgio Trioli and Tom Wintringham. But the single woman is given only her forename, Ramona, or sometimes she is referred to as 'later Nat Cohen's wife' — never Ramona Siles García. In England she used the short form Ramona Siles in official documents. It is to be hoped that in future, in respect of the photograph's captions, she will be given her full name and stand alongside the men on equal terms, just as she did on that day in the Karl Marx Barracks in September 1936 and just as she did in her commitment to fight for the Republic and against fascism.[58]

>Marshall Mateer is the IBMT's Film Coordinator and was an IBMT trustee from 2015 to 2018. This essay appeared in issue 39 (May 2015) of the *IBMT Newsletter*.

---

[58] The author would like to thank the Working Class Movement Library and their archive volunteer Stuart Walsh for help with this work.

An image of Ramona Siles García in her militiawoman's uniform, published in a Catalan women's magazine during the war. The caption, in Catalan, reads: 'A beautiful and brave militiawoman ready to go to the front.' Courtesy of the Working Class Movement Library, Salford.

Shunned for their politics?

Fraser Raeburn

As the train from Newhaven pulled into London's Victoria Station on the evening of 7 December 1938, hundreds of returning volunteers arrived home from Spain to a rapturous crowd and an uncertain future. The story of what they had achieved in Spain as part of the International Brigades is well known and has been celebrated ever since. Yet what came next for the veterans of Spain is often much less clear. Their relationship with the British state was already strained, having fought for a foreign government in a conflict that Britain did its best to wash its hands of. Above all, their close association with the Communist Party of Great Britain (CPGB) and their clear willingness to fight and die for their beliefs marked their loyalties out as suspect in the eyes of the political establishment.

This question was thrown into sharp relief by the outbreak of war against Germany less than a year later: to what extent would the British state trust the Spanish veterans to participate in the war effort? Unlike their service in Spain, we know far less about what happened to the volunteers during the Second World War. Broadly speaking, there are two settled-upon narratives of what happened. The first reflects continuity — those who had recognised the dangers of fascism the earliest gearing up for a new phase in the struggle, swapping the battlefields of Spain for those in France, North Africa and elsewhere. There are numerous individuals, such as Roderick MacFarquhar or Bill Alexander, whose talents were recognised through commissions, or Tommy McGuire, who was killed while serving as a paratrooper, whose wartime service conforms to this picture. They are not the focus of this essay, however, which is concerned with the darker narrative: one of exclusion, victimisation and waste. Despite the volunteers' recent experience of modern warfare and their demonstrable commitment to opposing fascism, they were shunned by the British state and prevented from participating in the war effort. These, in the parlance of the American volunteers, were the 'premature anti-fascists,' a label adopted out of ironic pride in the face of official absurdity.

Historians of the British Battalion have long been aware that the ex-volunteers faced highly variable treatment at the hands of the state during the Second World War, but have struggled to explain exactly what was going on. Clearly, the boundaries to participation were not absolute, otherwise many ex-volunteers' distinguished wartime service would have been impossible. Equally, there are many cases where individuals faced obvious or implied discrimination. This problem is compounded by the absence of wartime records or testimony from the bulk of ex-volunteers, which makes building an overall picture very challenging.

As part of my research into Scottish volunteers, I sought to understand and explain why the International Brigade veterans faced such variable treatment. The picture that emerged from MI5 records was mixed — on one hand, there was plenty of confirmation that many veterans were subject to surveillance, discharged unfairly or otherwise had their participation in the war effort monitored or curtailed. Yet it also became clear that this treatment was rarely the result of their service in Spain. In the records of investigations I found, outcomes were rarely connected to the International Brigades. In some cases, punitive action was straightforwardly non-political, such as for Glaswegian Robert Middleton, who was arrested for desertion and assault in 1941, and who had run afoul of battalion authorities in Spain as well. William Gilmour, originally from Blairgowrie in Scotland, is an interesting exception. He was one of relatively few Scottish volunteers discriminated against by MI5 for explicitly political reasons — his application to join the Home Guard was refused in 1942. Yet his file revealed that it was not his time in Spain that sealed Gilmour's fate. Rather, it was a report from the City of Glasgow Police, which noted that he had been dismissed from a factory in May 1941 for carrying out 'abnormal communistic activity in his place of employment.' In fact, Gilmour's service in Spain had been declared as prior military experience on his application to join the Home Guard. If this sufficed to bar him from enlisting, no investigation would have been required in the first place.

This needs to be understood within the context of wartime anti-communist policy. While MI5 in particular always held that the CPGB represented a dangerous enemy to be countered at every turn, they were canny enough to realise that disproportionate persecution would only strengthen the communists' case. Instead, they advocated only targeting communists who had demonstrated the capacity and willingness to undertake subversive activity in wartime. This last point was crucial — MI5 was aware of ruptures within the CPGB following the decision in September 1939 to oppose the war with Germany. They judged that most party members, while not enthusiastic about the war effort, would not go so far as to actively undermine it. They were therefore to be treated as individuals, and their participation in the war effort managed according to their specific threat. As a result, by early 1941 — before the invasion of the Soviet Union — only about 30 British communists had actually been prevented outright from joining the armed forces.

This, however, does not seem to tally with what we know from the International Brigaders themselves, more than 30 of whom faced discrimination during the war. Upon further investigation, it became clear that the answer to this — and the broader question of why the volunteers were treated so variably — lay in the limitations of MI5 itself. Far from the omnipotent organisation depicted in popular culture, it had little capacity to monitor over 1,000 returned volunteers across the country amid many other more pressing duties. Especially outside of London, they were reliant almost entirely on local police to actually keep tabs on persons of interest, and I found that a lot of the variation in volunteers' experiences could be explained by geography — places with a history of militancy and a large, well-resourced police force were much better at monitoring. For Glaswegian veterans such as James McFarlane, it was the anti-communist obsessions of local police rather than MI5 or the armed forces that kept them on the security services' radar.

Moreover, MI5 had only limited influence in actually enforcing its recommendations. Sometimes, this meant that obvious security threats slipped through — such as when communist James Klugmann was employed by the SOE (Special Operations Executive) over their protests — but this could also work the other way. It appears that the procedures were rarely followed to the letter (or at all). Instead of liaising with MI5 as they were supposed to, local British military authorities often seemed to take it upon themselves to decide what to do with potential 'subversives' in the ranks. While MI5 had spent 20 years trying to understand and evaluate the CPGB, the British military had far less knowledge and understanding of British communism. This meant that the kind of nuanced judgements envisaged by MI5 when it came to the Spanish veterans were circumvented by the whims of local commanders. Some lost little time in getting rid of 'reds' using whatever excuse they could find, such as when Frank McCusker was discharged days after his old Spanish wound was discovered by an army doctor. Others kept them under close watch, although some ex-volunteers such as Bob Cooney were able to subvert their efforts neatly. Yet many British officers, perhaps most, came to the view that it mattered little what a soldier's political opinions were, so long as they did their jobs. Equally, many veterans of Spain — despite their radical reputations — were happy enough to do just that, a small price to pay for another chance to fight fascism.

>Fraser Raeburn is a historian based at the University of Sheffield and author of *Scots and the Spanish Civil War: Solidarity, Activism and Humanitarianism* (2020). This essay was first published in issue 50 (January 2019) of *¡No Pasarán!*

From refugee boys to professional players

Daniel Gray

In October 1938, La Pasionaria described departing International Brigaders as examples of 'the universality of democracy.' Six Basque refugee children in Britain who went on to be footballers represent the universality of football: an internationalist game for an internationalist cause. By the early spring of 1937, Spain's Basque Country was, perhaps, Franco's deepest irritation. Hitler's Condor Legion and the Italian Legionary Airforce were laden with bombs and advanced on the Basque Country. What happened next was a heinously brutal chapter in a war full of them. For the first time, civilian targets were bombed from above and modern methods of atrocity were born. In all of this, of course, children, or those that survived, had to carry on. They had to find their joy, kick stones among ruins, play hide-and-seek in the rubble. Our six footballers were among them; most came from Durango and Guernica.

In May 1937, an evacuation programme for Basque children began. Thirty-three thousand children were shipped off to Belgium, Denmark, Mexico, the USSR and Switzerland. At first, Prime Minister Baldwin held the British non-intervention line — no children would be taken, and in his words, 'the climate wouldn't suit them.' But public pressure could not be ignored. Though no government aid would be given, a ship carrying 4,000 children would be permitted into Britain, and each permitted to stay for three months. Most stayed for longer; some made their homes here. The ship carrying them to the UK was a cruise liner, the *Habana*, adapted to carry ten times its normal capacity of 400. It docked in Bilbao on 20 May 1937, preparing to set sail for Southampton. It is a difficult scene to try and imagine. No-one really understood where they were going; Britain was left to the imagination.

Clasping a few belongings wrapped in paper and tied with string, each child queued to climb aboard the *Habana*. Every girl and boy had an identification number, written on a tag worn around their neck. Among those children were: Emilio Aldecoa, Sabino Barinaga, José Bilbao, Antonio Gallego, José Gallego and Raimundo Pérez Lezama. Each one of these boys would grow into a professional footballer. On 23 May, they arrived at Southampton to a splendid, heartfelt welcome from locals and those from elsewhere who had been part of a magnificent fundraising campaign for the Basque children. All children were given a medical, fed and put into a camp consisting of hundreds of bright white tents. Football soon erupted — balls scrounged from somewhere and dribbled among guy ropes and campfires. Then, the children were dispersed to homes or 'colonies' across Britain.

As there would be no state aid for the refugee kids, everything provided would have to come from charity: fundraising, donations, appeals, events. Everything ran on goodwill, too — churches, wealthy people and educational establishments gave up entire houses that were hastily converted into Basque children's homes. The example I know best is Mall Park in Montrose, 30 miles north of Dundee. Its creation and existence were typical of the many places our footballers and the other thousands found home. Its funding came from a typically diverse set of people: The Bakers' Union, the Blind Institution, the Dundee Breakfast Club and the Women's Liberal Association donated generously. Dockers took on a team of locally-berthed Spanish seamen at football and raised a hefty sum on the gate and from donations, while the Dundee School of Music staged a concert in Caird Hall. The first residents arrived in late September 1937. Though distraught with homesickness and worry for their families in Spain, the children did find great contentment. Bene González, 15 years old on the day she arrived at Mall Park, recalled in 1985 that the children had lived 'immensely happily, and joyfully.' It is important to point out that the Basque children also raised money for themselves. They performed dance routines and organised football matches. It was in these matches that some of our six first showed their remarkable talents.

This brings us to one such boy, Emilio Aldecoa. Emilio was 14 when he boarded the *Habana*, one of the older refugees. From Southampton, he was sent to live in a Basque colony in Stafford. His interest in football blossomed into love, and Emilio developed his tricky, wily left-foot not least in those fundraising games. Being old enough, instead of returning to Spain in 1938 or 39 when so many did, he decided to stay in England, despite the end of war in Spain and its beginning in Britain. Emilio took a job with English Electric and began playing for the works football team. His skill was obvious. He stood out. Wolverhampton Wanderers offered him a trial. This was war-time football, meaning that the normal league structure had been suspended, and regional fixtures organised in its place, all of them to take place in daylight on Saturdays. Guest players were needed, but few were more exotic than Emilio. In 1943 Emilio made his first-team debut against Crewe Alexandra. It made him the very first Spaniard to play a professional match in England. What a thing for a teenager who had seen and heard things that no-one should, a migrant who had sailed into the unknown. That 1943/44 season, Emilio was Wolves' top scorer. He was a dazzling footballer, full of vim and verve. Here was a technicolour footballer in a black and white world.

In 1945, Emilio moved on to Coventry City, scoring against Portsmouth on his Sky Blues debut. He married a local girl and stayed for two seasons. For a while, another Basque refugee *Habana* kid played alongside Emilio. By some strange fate or mere coincidence, José Bilbao wound up at rickety Highfield Road. José was an outside left, meaning that for his six Coventry games he played immediately next to inside left Emilio. Such an unlikely pairing so far from home; two young Basque men in the blue and white of Coventry City, tearing down the wing in their long shorts. 'City's attack proved that it was the best constituted for a long time,' said one match report in a local newspaper. 'The all-Spanish left-wing was a happy partnership.' Walking around Coventry must have been a chilling reminder of what they had left behind almost a decade before. After all, like their Basque homeland, the city had been pummelled by German planes, its cathedral violently sacked.

Yet both had played football just as it was being reborn after the horror of war. A footballing boom was on the way, one tenet of quietly emerging optimism in the country. It is hard to think of a more intriguing time for the Basques to have been plying their beloved trade in middle England. José Bilbao slipped from view like many war-time footballers; we don't even know if he stayed or went home. Emilio Aldecoa returned to Spain and played for Athletic Bilbao, Valladolid and Barcelona. But perhaps Emilio's greatest achievement came after his playing career. A dedicated, precise and sagacious student of the game, he compiled a lengthy blueprint document for youth development and scouting, setting out how Barcelona could become the greatest club in the world. Emilio was not finished with England, and from 1960 undertook a coaching and scouting role at Birmingham City, implementing systems for finding and developing players way ahead of their time.

Before Emilio Aldecoa and José Bilbao had begun their professional careers, two Basque refugee boys had used England as a starting point for theirs. Both would become greats of the Spanish game. Sabino Barinaga and Raimundo Pérez Lezama were also among the 4,000 on the *Habana*. Sabino was leaving behind the debris of the bombed town of Durango, while Raimundo came from Baracaldo, just outside Bilbao. At the time of the sailing, Sabino was 14 and Raimundo 16. By some cosmic coincidence, these two young people who would become Spanish football stars were housed together. Neither was forced to leave Southampton, a place of fond memories for young Basques after the welcome they had received. The two teenagers were instead given lodgings in Nazareth House, a city orphanage run by nuns. Outside, in the safety of this refuge's gardens, both began to play football in every spare moment they had. Raimundo went further, studying textbooks about the game and its rules in his bunk bed. That adoration of football was again blossoming for young Basques in England.

Their enthusiasm was matched by ability. It seems that both-footed forward Sabino impressed Saints first team manager Tom Parker. 'Sabino is one of the most brilliant youngsters I have ever seen,' he noted. Goalkeeper Raimundo was soon scouted too, or possibly concurrently; one telling of the story goes that the two were spotted kicking a ball around in the car park outside The Dell, Southampton's dear old home. Both soon began playing for the Southampton youth team. In 1938/39, their performances in the local youth leagues were astonishing, even if at a level clearly already beneath them. The team played 33 games, winning 31, scoring 277 and conceding just 17. In the 13 games he played in, Sabino scored 62 times. Raimundo eventually played three games for the first team. Southampton wanted to make them first team players, but their Home Office licences to remain were not extended. Besides, Britain was now at war where peace, albeit buttressed by violence and suppression, existed in Franco's Spain.

The two travelled home in March 1940. In three years they had grown into young men, fought the psychological traumas of fascist invasion and become two of the most promising footballers in Europe. Back in Spain, they pursued what family they had left. Being Basque in Franco's Spain was difficult enough; being Basque and probably the sons of dreaded Reds was even worse. Maybe it was football that spared them the repression of so many thousands of others: Spain needed players; it needed to rebuild its teams and league. Despite an offer to stay in Bilbao and play for Athletic (now renamed Atlético under Franco's orders), Sabino understandably took the greater offer of Real Madrid money. Seeing the poverty of his family must have made that a fairly simple decision. Raimundo signed at first for a lesser Basque side, Arenas, but after three months was spotted and scooped up by Atlético Bilbao. He was to stay for 16 years. Raimundo's playing style made him both a marvel and a novelty. With Atlético Bilbao, the bunk-bed boy of Nazareth House won two La Ligas and six cup medals. Sabino, meanwhile, set Madrid alight. The strapping Basque scored four goals in an 11-1 mauling of Barcelona in 1943. Then in 1947 he became the first man to score at the brand new Bernabeu Stadium. Perhaps, in quiet moments, he allowed himself a bittersweet grin: the son of a Basque communist, now the hero of what some regarded as Franco's team.

Raimundo and Sabino's paths must have crossed regularly in league fixtures, but in 1943 the Nazareth boys clashed in the Spanish Cup Final. Atlético Bilbao defeated Real Madrid 1-0; some said that Raimundo Lezama won the match. What joy to have seen Franco's face that day. While Raimundo was a one-club man, Sabino played for Real Sociedad and Real Betis after the Bernabeu. He then became a manager, holding the reigns at more than a dozen club and international sides, in Spain and across the world. Sabino died in 1988, aged 66, while Raimundo lived on until 2007, passing away aged 84. Both retained a lifelong love of Southampton, and of the England that gave them everything, including football. While at times the relationship between Sabino and Raimundo could appear to be that of adopted brothers, our last two *Habana* refugee footballers were blood brothers.

Antonio and José Gallego came from Errentería in the far north-east of the Basque region. In April 1937, their father had been killed at Guernica. Defying the heartbreak it would bring, the boys' mother insisted they board the *Habana* with their three sisters for safety in England. Twelve-year-old Antonio, 14-year-old José and their sisters were given beds at first in Eastleigh, and then Cambridge. They stayed in a home for 30 Basque children, owned by Jesus College, Cambridge. Soon, like Sabino and Raimundo on the lawns of Nazareth House, and Emilio Aldecoa with his fundraising games, the Gallego brothers set up football teams and matches. In 2012, by then in his late 80s, Antonio told the *El País* newspaper:

> Football was all we thought about. As long as we had football we were happy. It meant everything to us; it was the only thing we knew about. We got attached to Cambridge and made a lot of friends there through playing football. If it hadn't been for football, we would have lived a very different life.

Though never scaling the heights of Sabino, Raimundo or Emilio, both Gallegos had talent in abundance. They may have daydreamed that, had they gone home to Spain like those three, their careers could have taken off. But England, particularly Cambridge, had become home to the Gallegos. In the mid-1940s, José, a left-winger, and Antonio, a goalkeeper, were signed up by local non-league side Cambridge Town. Scouts flocked to see the exotic Basque boys in this most unlikely of settings. José was signed by Brentford, and Antonio by Norwich City. Things did not work out for Antonio, and he was freed in 1947, returning to Cambridge Town. José played six times for the Griffins, before a 1948 move to that home-from-home for Basques, Southampton.

Football, while clearly a second heartbeat for the Gallegos, must often have faded into the background as the five siblings wondered what had happened to their mum. That year of 1947 marked a decade since they had last seen her at the harbour in Bilbao as the Habana set sail. Then, a breakthrough: mother and beloved children were reunited after the Red Cross helped her locate them. Soon, she too settled in Cambridge. A family reunited 10 years after those vile bombs had fallen on their homelands. The Gallego brothers, meanwhile, played football into their 50s — the game was under their skin. Antonio married, started a family and stayed here for the rest of his days, until he died in 2015. The story of the Basque refugee footballers is an incredible one. Six young people, from the jaws of hell, arriving in a country where people defied their cowardly government to open their arms and rooms. All six were united by the misery they had left behind, and the miracles they became.

Daniel Gray is a researcher, writer, and lecturer. His multiple books include *Homage to Caledonia: Scotland and the Spanish Civil War* (2008). This edited version of the author's 2019 Len Crome Memorial Conference lecture was published in issue 59 (January 2022) of *¡No Pasarán!*

Chris (right) and Betty Birch protesting outside the Spanish Embassy in London in 1952. In the centre is Alec Digges, a veteran of the British Battalion and former secretary of the International Brigade Association and the Friends of Republic Spain. The photograph was taken by Sid Kaufman at a protest for Gregorio López Raimundo, a Spanish communist who was tortured and jailed by the Francoist regime after returning from exile in 1947 to undertake clandestine resistance. Courtesy of the IBMT.

I was spied on for being an anti-fascist

Chris Birch

My wife Betty and I had always assumed that our mail was read and our telephone calls listened to by MI5 and the Special Branch as we had been active Communist Party members, albeit at a very lowly level, since our time at Bristol University. When we moved to London we were both very active in our local party branch. The fact that our letters were being intercepted and read by the Security Services was dramatically proved in the 1950s when we lived in the same west London street, but on the opposite side of the road, as Bert Baker, the editor of the Communist Party's weekly bulletin, *World News and Views*. One morning, I opened an envelope addressed to me only to find a letter for Bert inside while, on the other side of the road, Bert found my letter inside his envelope. Obviously, Homer had nodded off and after having read our letters replaced them in the wrong envelopes.

Nevertheless, it was a considerable shock to sit in the Document Reading Room at the National Archives at Kew recently and to read some of the mass of material with our names in it that had been accumulated by MI5 and the Metropolitan Police's Special Branch in the two years 1952 and 1953.[59] At that time my wife and I were heavily involved in the Aid to Spanish Youth Committee, which was campaigning, with some notable successes, on behalf of the young political prisoners in Franco's jails and in particular the Spanish youth leader López Raimundo and his 33 companions.

There is a four-page typed report headed 'Metropolitan Police Special Branch. Subject: Anti-Franco Meeting,' dated 27 March 1952, and signed by an inspector, a chief inspector and a chief superintendent. It begins ploddishly:

> Accompanied by other Special Branch officers, I was present at 7.30pm today at Connaught Place, London W2 in connection with a proposed torchlight procession to the Spanish Embassy, 24 Belgrave Square, London SW1, organised by the International Brigade Association, Friends of Republican Spain and the Aid to Spanish Youth Committee, to protest against the sentences passed by the Spanish courts on Spanish workers and to demand the release of those at present awaiting trial.

The policeman reports there were about 150 people, some of them with stick-torches or flares, and a large number with placards demanding the release of the Spanish strikers, and gives a lengthy account of the speech I made and had long forgotten. Headed by a drum and pipe band, the procession proceeded via Park Lane and

---

[59] Editor's note: This visit had been prompted by an article by Daniel Ahern in the previous issue of the *IBMT Newsletter*, which described finding several folders of MI5 documents (KV5/46-58) in the National Archives detailing the surveillance of International Brigade Association activities during the 1940s and 1950s.

Piccadilly to Headfort Place, where it was stopped by the police, although a deputation of three, including myself, was allowed to take a petition to the embassy while the rest of the marchers 'were passing the time by singing revolutionary songs.' According to the police report: 'The whole demonstration from start to finish was carried out in a peaceful way, and nothing suggesting of disorder occurred during the proceedings.' It was, perhaps, reasonable to send a couple of coppers to make sure we didn't use our torches to burn down the embassy, but what a waste of notebook and pencil writing down everything I said!

Another report, headed 'Secret' although there was nothing secret about it, lists the names, including Betty's, of the newly elected members of the IBA's executive committee. The secret report says that its 'source was extremely well placed to obtain the above information.' So far, so silly. What is more sinister is the evidence of the interception of letters and phone calls and the bugging of rooms. There is a very long list of the names and addresses including mine, divided into London and outside London, of individuals and organisations who had written to the Spanish ambassador expressing their concerns about political prisoners in Spain. And there are photographs (this was before the advent of photocopiers) of minutes of the Aid to Spanish Youth Committee, typed on my old Olympia portable, and letters I wrote together with extensive transcripts of private conversations in the office at Communist Party headquarters of Peter Kerrigan, who had fought with the British Battalion of the International Brigades in Spain. All this was in the files kept on the IBA and the Aid to Spanish Youth Committee. There were apparently separate files on Betty and myself, numbered PF76717 and PF402/51/1064 respectively, but these have been retained by MI5 under section 3(4) of the Public Records Act (1958) and are exempt from disclosure under the Freedom of Information Act (2000). So that's all right then. It's all nice and legal.

Chris Birch was a journalist, dedicated anti-Franco activist and former treasurer of the International Brigade Memorial Appeal. This report appeared in issue 20 (June 2008) of the *IBMT Newsletter*. Reproduced here with kind permission of Chris Birch's wife Betty and their daughter Harriet.

The publisher who took on Franco

Adrian Pole

In the early hours of 14 October 1975, a bomb exploded in the heart of Paris's Latin Quarter. The blast, which could be heard throughout the Left Bank, smashed several windows and damaged over 30 cars. The target was the premises of the Spanish publishing firm Éditions Ruedo Ibérico, notorious for its bold investigations — banned in Spain — into the dictatorship of Francisco Franco and the Spanish Civil War which had brought him to power. A squad of Francoist ultras soon claimed responsibility for the attack, leading the firm's founder, José Martínez Guerricabeitia, to conclude that the supporters of the regime were finally going on the offensive.

Martínez, an exiled anarchist from Valencia, had a simple objective: to weaponise the printed word against the myths and distortions propagated by the Franco dictatorship. Given the poor output of historians in Spain, it was left to foreign writers to undertake the challenge of researching the civil war in a scholarly and objective manner. Works by the likes of Hugh Thomas and Herbert Southworth helped launch a historiographical tradition which modern scholars have inherited. Ruedo Ibérico's legacy hasn't been limited to the footnotes of academic articles, either. The contraband books — translated into Spanish and smuggled into the peninsula from the Canary Islands or France — were sold from under the counter to Spaniards still living under the shadow of dictatorship. They were the very first examples of civil war history not written by the victors, and they exposed no end of inconvenient truths. Small sales did not necessarily mean a small readership, with writer Alfons Cerva assuring us that Ruedo Ibérico books 'were the most stolen from our homes by our own friends.'

Today, the firm has slipped into obscurity. Ian Gibson, whose breakthrough came when José Martínez published his book on the wartime assassination of poet Federico García Lorca, doubts that younger Spaniards have ever heard of it. It comes as no surprise that, despite his countless interviews on Spanish radio and television, the topic 'hardly ever comes up.' Its legacy, as Gibson himself argues, deserves to be better understood.

Éditions Ruedo Ibérico was founded in March 1961 by five Spanish exiles living in Paris, two of whom had to sell their cars to get the project off the ground. The driving force from beginning to end was José Martínez, whose libertarian family had sided with the Republic when the military rebelled in July 1936. With the victory of Franco's Nationalists in 1939 came spells in a reformatory, prison and military service. Undeterred, the obstinate anarchist soon got back to distributing illegal literature throughout his local area before deciding to join the growing ranks of Spaniards seeking political refuge in France. He arrived, on foot, in 1948, and immediately encountered the same problems of finding work, lodgings and documentation which had been faced by his predecessors. One of his friends at the time reminds us that: 'In '48 life in Paris was still hard for the French, but for young Spaniards it was impossible.

I remember his [Martínez's] anguish when he broke his only pair of glasses and spent a few days in jail for problems with documentation.'

France could already boast a sizeable community of exiled Spaniards by the time its newest arrival crossed the border; Paris was well on its way to becoming a centre of intellectual opposition to the Franco regime. The founding of the Union of Spanish Intellectuals in 1944 was followed by a string of other institutions devoted to Spanish politics and culture. Martínez himself participated in the activities of the Spanish Students' Federation before realising longer-term goals were needed if the exiled opposition were to pose a meaningful threat to the dictatorship. With the Americans feting Spain as a Cold War front against communism, Franco seemed stronger than ever and sporadic protest no longer seemed sufficient. Without ever renouncing his anarchism, Martínez desperately wanted to overcome the factionalism of the left in order to create a cohesive counter-narrative to that propagated by the victors of the Spanish Civil War. In doing so, he thought it essential to give to the democratic opposition within Spain a voice of its own. The founders of Ruedo Ibérico in faraway Paris assumed there must be sheaves of unpublished manuscripts in the desk-drawers of Spaniards still stuck on the wrong side of the Pyrenees.

While Martínez was busy formulating his ideas in Paris, Spanish society was undergoing momentous changes. Government technocrats in Madrid had finally abandoned Franco's ill-advised drive for self-sufficiency and had set Spain on a course of economic integration with the rest of Europe. The country was hurtling towards industrialisation on an unprecedented scale, surpassed only by Japan, and suddenly found itself a country of consumers. Many Spaniards — especially those born after the war — began to expect more from their government. Workers went on illegal strikes, dissatisfied with the absence of independent unions, while university students demanded the same political freedoms enjoyed by the German and Swedish tourists now flocking to the Spanish costas. Born after the war, these were precisely the people who, in the words of José Martínez, wanted to 'respond to a series of whys, to recover their own identity . . . to know the causes of the war, the consequences of the trauma, the configuration of Francoism.' The consequence, according to historian Aránzazu Sarría Buil, 'was a period from the end of the '60s to the end of the '70s when the book became a weapon of political struggle.' The state could censor, but it was struggling to convince.

The mountains of unpublished material Martínez had hoped for never materialised. Fortunately, an English historian by the name of Hugh Thomas had recently taken on the suggestion of a literary agent and embarked on writing a history of the Spanish Civil War. He admitted years later that, as a young academic searching for an interesting topic, he might just as easily have written about the Turkish Revolution had it been proposed to him. As it was, his book on Spain — entitled, quite simply, *The Spanish Civil War* — was published to positive reviews in the US before catching the eye of Martínez, who commissioned a Spanish translation as Ruedo Ibérico's first title. Published in 1961, it was the first attempt at an objective, comprehensive account of the war. The 5,000 copies smuggled into Spain soon sold out. Though few in number, copies were constantly passed around and discussed. Officials betrayed their deep anxiety by sentencing Octavio Jordá, a 31-year-old smuggler caught at the border with two suitcases packed full of the book, to two years' imprisonment for 'spreading communism.'

A lecture in military history delivered at the University of Zaragoza in the same year the book appeared gives a good indication as to how the war was 'officially' represented in Spain at the time. The minutes don't refer to a civil war at all, but rather a 'War for National Liberation,' parroting the official line that Franco had 'liberated' Spain from godless anarchy by leading a three-year crusade for the country's Catholic redemption. Hugh Thomas had fundamentally challenged this narrative, leaving readers with little doubt that the conflict had begun as a premeditated military *coup* against a democratically elected government. Most shocking of all were the details of mass killings in Franco's rebel zone. When asked about this, Franco responded with the absurd claim that he had commuted various death sentences during the civil war — something for which there is simply no evidence.

Ruedo Ibérico's second title was a translation of Gerald Brenan's 1943 classic, *The Spanish Labyrinth*. Whereas Hugh Thomas had concentrated on great men and high politics, Brenan's left-wing sympathies impelled him to take into account Spanish class structures and their influence on the coming catastrophe of war. At the time he decided to write the book, Spanish historiography, whatever the period in question, was still dominated by old-fashioned political accounts. Having lived in Spain himself, and having fled soon after the outbreak of war, Brenan was more interested in explaining why Spanish history had taken the disastrous course it had. Supplementing his own experiences with extensive research, he managed to produce an extraordinarily vivid portrait of Spanish society on the brink of war; a portrait in which the landless labourer figured every bit as prominently as the cabinet minister, and in which regional variations in rainfall mattered just as much as election results. Nothing at the time could compare to the sheer analytical scope of the book. Raymond Carr described it as a 'revelation.' When the Spanish translation was smuggled into Spain in the 1960s, he writes, it became 'the sacred text for the democratic opposition to Franco.'

Nor did Spain forget about Brenan in the years after Franco's death. In 1984 the townspeople of Alhaurín el Grande launched a successful campaign to bring '*Don Gerardo*' back to Spain after it was discovered he was living in a retirement home in London. In 1987 Brenan died in the country he loved so much, aged 92. Today, Alhaurín is home to some 5,600 books donated from the author's personal library. Brenan returned for a three-month trip around Franco's Spain over a decade after the end of the civil war. Perhaps the defining — and certainly the most moving — part of his journey came when he visited the city of Granada. It was there that the poet Federico García Lorca had been shot during the first days of the uprising. Brenan decided to lay a wreath at the poet's grave, only to discover that such a place didn't exist — and still doesn't. The exact circumstances of Lorca's death would remain obscure for years. The embarrassed dictatorship eventually settled into blaming the assassination on rogue elements with private motives, thereby acquitting itself of any responsibility.

In the summer of 1965, Ian Gibson, an Irish doctoral student with a passion for Lorca's poetry, settled in Granada to write his thesis on the poet. After discussions with various locals he decided instead to focus on the taboo topic of his murder. 'It was a wild, romantic thing to do,' Gibson writes, 'shelving the thesis and changing direction the way I did during that year off, but I was powerless to resist the urge.' The lengths he went to in order to obtain information about wartime Granada were truly extraordinary, and help explain why Graham Greene found the subsequent book to be 'as interesting as a detective story.' Posing as an English teacher, turning up unannounced to ask for interviews and secretly taping conversations with those he held responsible for the poet's assassination were all part of his investigative arsenal. He also got to know various people who had known Lorca who were still living in Granada in the 1960s.

Despite people's terrible fear of discussing the repression and the consequent difficulty of obtaining accurate information, Gibson completed the book — only to have it repeatedly rejected by publishers. He was, by his own admission, a 'complete beginner,' with no contacts in the publishing world. Then someone suggested Ruedo Ibérico. 'At that time,' recalls Gibson, 'all I knew about Martínez was that he published Hugh Thomas and Gerald Brenan.' He wrote to the historian Herbert Southworth, whose own *El mito de la cruzada de Franco* had been published by the firm a few years previously, causing a sensation for its systematic dismantling of the concept of the war as a 'crusade.' Southworth must have been impressed by Gibson's book, as he now acted as the go-between and encouraged José Martínez to take it on. In 1971, the definitive account of Lorca's assassination — written in English in the hope that it might eventually be translated into Spanish — appeared under the title of *La represión nacionalista de Granada en 1936 y la muerte de Federico García Lorca*. The small but revelatory book placed responsibility for the murder squarely on the shoulders of local reactionaries and demolished persistent claims that Lorca was some kind of unfortunate collateral damage caught up in the chaos of war. Lorca, Gibson made absolutely clear, was not 'apolitical,' as some would have it, but rather had powerful enemies in the town in which he was murdered.

Some of the first copies to undertake the crossing into Spain did so in the author's own car. Distributing them to friends was a thrilling, subversive experience, but the regime was relatively slow to catch on to its existence, only realising the seriousness of the situation when the book won a major prize in France in the following year. By then, Francoist ministers had no choice but to ban it. The book, which exposed the horrific scale of terror in wartime Granada, was unacceptable to officials and deeply shocked readers. Gibson was particularly moved by the impact it had on Spanish poet Luis García Montero, professor of literature at the University of Granada: 'The testimony to the effect of the book on young Spaniards that most affects me is Luis

García Montero's, who has said that reading it shocked him and changed his attitude to his native Granada, where nobody had told him about the scale of the repression and Lorca's death was ascribed to personal motives, homosexual jealousy or whatever.'

Published in France and smuggled into Spain, the banned books of Ruedo Ibérico constituted a challenge beyond the control of the Juntas de Censura. If anything, government censorship helped shape the thematic priorities of Ruedo Ibérico, which José Martínez came to regard as an 'anti-ministry.' Despite their inability to prosecute authors due to their tactical use of pseudonyms, ministers were made aware of the urgent need to update their approach to official historiography. This became increasingly urgent as Spain entered the 1960s with an eye to shoring up its international reputation. The Centre for Civil War Studies was accordingly established under the auspices of the Ministry of Information. Its director, Ricardo de la Cierva, himself the author of numerous books in defence of Francoism, was charged with launching the dictatorship's intellectual counter-attack against Ruedo Ibérico. That it felt the need to do so demonstrates, in the opinion of Sarría Buil, 'the importance that the regime granted to the writing of history, and its obsession to control it.'

One of Ricardo de la Cierva's most ambitious attempts to reclaim the regime's intellectual credibility was an enormous Spanish Civil War bibliography, published in 1968. The result — more propaganda than scholarship — was a disaster. It listed hundreds of authors that didn't exist and several books that had never been written. Herbert Southworth wrote scathingly that it was an 'intellectual scandal.' As the owner of the world's largest collection of books about the Spanish Civil War, he was well-placed to make such a judgement. The erudition and precision Southworth had demonstrated in *El mito de la cruzada de Franco* was something Ricardo de la Cierva could never compete with. Moreover, by financing the publication of *El mito* himself, Southworth had saved Ruedo Ibérico from economic collapse. Unsurprisingly, he and Cierva would remain irreconcilable enemies until the end.

In November 1975, with Ruedo Ibérico still stubbornly undefeated, Spanish television announced the death of Franco. An amnesty for Francoist criminals and a 'pact of forgetting' between the new political parties smoothed the delicate transition to democracy, but left little room for José Martínez's lifelong project of recovering Spain's uncomfortable past. Meanwhile, his greatest opponent, Ricardo de la Cierva, went on to become a senator, government adviser, and Minister of Culture in the new democratic Spain. Struggling to find its place in the new order, Ruedo Ibérico finally closed in 1982. There is no question that the books it published, many of them not mentioned here, represent a remarkable contribution to our understanding of Spain.

The group of writers brought together under the banner of Ruedo Ibérico was truly extraordinary. Brenan, Southworth and Gibson were not typical, academic historians. They wrote their pioneering works of history because of a deep-seated desire to take on the systematic lying of the Franco regime, which still, in the words of Paul Preston, receives a 'relatively good press.' Some of them are household names in Spain, more famous there than in their own countries. This remarkable legacy was never assured. As José Martínez himself asked: '. . . which Spanish distributor or bookseller in his right mind would accept to distribute and sell our books at the risk of going to jail or being heavily fined for it? And let's not talk about the readers, who, in case of police registration, ran similar risks.' Incredibly, the readers were willing to take those risks. Like them, anyone at all interested in the history and culture of Spain owes Ruedo Ibérico an extraordinary debt.

> Adrian Pole is a PhD student at the University of Edinburgh, researching cross-cultural encounters between Spaniards and international volunteers during the Spanish Civil War. This essay appeared in issue 51 (May 2019) of *iNo Pasarán!*

British Battalion veteran David Lomon lifting the Spanish Republican flag to unveil the plaque for the International Brigade memorial in Jubilee Gardens, London. The unveiling took place in 2012 when the main memorial sculpture by Ian Walters was moved to its current location, and by his side is David's son, Irving. Courtesy of the photographer, Andrew Wiard.

Brigaders' Reunion

Connie Fraser

These frail old men are young and strong today,
Bearing the banner upright as they stand
Steadied with sticks or helped by caring hand
Protective as the stone arms round their dead.

Yet once these same legs climbed the Pyrenees
By smugglers' paths in sheltering of night,
With spirits high and blistered urban feet
They came to aid the Spanish people's fight.

So long ago and yet so close at hand,
The weary blur of battle on strange ground,
The heat and cold, the hunger and the thirst,
Persistence when the odds were all against.

Now a new speaker tells the old brave tale,
Putting some sort of pattern to the whole,
The song that always follows sounds again
Ragged at first — 'Jarama' — then the pain
And pride swell out to fill their shrinking world.

And we who were not there join in, aware
Their fading eyes show what we cannot hear,
The ageless guilt which all survivors feel
That they live on when friends and comrades fell.
For them — and us — and brothers not yet born,
We raise clenched fists and shout '¡No pasarán!'

> Connie Fraser was married to International Brigader Harry Fraser and was a founding member of the IBMT, as well as an Open University tutor and a poet and playwright. This poem, originally written in summer 1998, was published in issue 57 (May 2021) of *¡No Pasarán!*

Reflections

This stained-glass window tribute to the International Brigades was created by Alpha Stained Glass of Derry and unveiled at Belfast City Hall in November 2015. Located alongside the stained-glass tribute to James 'Big Jim' Larkin and the 1907 dockers strike, it commemorates the men from all the city's communities who went to fight against fascism in Spain. It uses the red, yellow, and purple of the Spanish Republican tricolour, and includes an image of 'La Pasionaria', the three-pointed red star of the International Brigades, and the names of all the battles where Belfast Brigaders were involved. Courtesy of the photographer, Marshall Mateer.

An inspiring spirit of humanity

Michael D. Higgins

The International Brigades were formally established by a decree of the Spanish Republic on 18 October 1936. Around 40,000 international volunteers from more than 50 countries joined the brigades. Amongst them were two hundred Irish-born volunteers moved by the plight of the working classes of Spain and who, deeply concerned by the threat to democracy and the lengthening shadow of fascism that was spreading across Europe, decided to volunteer for the International Brigade. Over 60 of these Irish internationalists would never come home.

The International Brigades were drawn from a wide range of social strata and occupations. Some of their number, like the novelist George Orwell,[60] the poet W.H. Auden,[61] or the former Church of Ireland minister Robert Hilliard, were intellectuals drawn from the middle classes, but most historical studies now agree that the vast majority of the Irish and British who joined the International Brigades were manual workers, workers with an extraordinary sense of social and political justice and the importance of defending workers' rights wherever they were at stake. As the research of Angela Jackson, among others, has shown, women — many of whom worked in medical units or relief organisations — for that reason played an important role in the International Brigades.

The carnage of the working class in the trenches of World War One in what was above all a contest of empires, was for them a fresh memory. The authoritarianism at its source, the culture of absolutionist power that was fascism, was already thick in the air. Not just historians, but all of us, owe a debt of gratitude to the International Brigade Memorial Trust, who continue to keep alive the memory of the Irish and British men and women who so bravely fought to defend democracy and fight fascism in Spain. The death in January 2009 of Bob Doyle — whom I had the pleasure of meeting on a number of occasions with Michael O'Riordan and his colleagues — marked the passing of the last veteran of the Connolly Column; reminding us of the role the Trust and all who support it play as important custodians of the history which had such an important influence on the society in which we now live. We must be

---

[60] Editor's note: Rather than the official International Brigades, Orwell served with a militia of the revolutionary Marxists in the Workers' Party of Marxist Unification (POUM).

[61] Editor's note: Auden's desire to join the International Brigades went unfulfilled. Upon arriving in Spain he decided that instead of fighting he intended to drive an ambulance, but in the end was put onto propaganda work, which he found deeply dissatisfying and soon abandoned. He left Spain with rather ambivalent feelings about the realities of the anti-fascist coalition. Described in Edward Mendelson, *Early Auden* (New York: Viking Press, 1981), pp. 195-8.

grateful to the Memorial Trust for their untiring work in ensuring that the task of striving to achieve a full and ethical interpretation of that most controversial of conflicts that was the Spanish Civil War, and its place within the history of modern Europe continues. It is appropriate, too, that we recall how long the consequences would last in Spain, the cruelty of the extrajudicial killings, the incarcerations, and the long wait for parliamentary democracy that would ensue. Engaging with the past may be a difficult and complex process, but it is ethically unavoidable. The *Pacto del Olvido*, imposed by political elites in Spain after the fall of Franco signifies the fears that so often exist around any deep or honest reflection on a history that, in the case of the abusing elites, has much to hide.[62]

If we are to stand back and take in a longer historical perspective of the events leading up to the Spanish Civil War, our gaze might initially fall on the rise of liberalism across Europe during the 19th century, and the opposing voices of authoritarianism that emerged and saw, in the demand for democratic participation, a threat from the new voices that were challenging the previous unassailability of Monarchy, Nobility and Church. We can perceive how such growing democratic demands and political agitation and related organisation gave birth by way of response to the curious relationship between monarchy and dictatorship which existed throughout Europe in the 1920s. We can also observe the strain on fragile democracies across the continent, as they sought to deal with the weight of class confrontation in conditions of change and the conflict between the left and right political forces, and the often differences within each. Those with fascist sympathies offered support in the name of order to dictatorship as it promised strong actions to solve the consequences for their nations of a worldwide economic crisis; a crisis that would claim lives and livelihoods all over the world. The politics of fear meant that an opportunity had emerged for the seizure of powers.

It would be simplistic, however, to claim that the war that broke out in Spain on 17th July 1936 was *ab initio* a straightforward clash between forces calling themselves democratic and fascist. As with all major wars, the Spanish Civil War was the outcome of observable social forces; an impoverished and disenfranchised workforce, landholding patterns of the rich that were almost feudal, an elite intent upon maintaining their wealth and privilege, strong regional autonomy movements, and a Church newly committed to corporatism, drawing on such documents as

---

[62] Editor's note: The *Pacto del Olvido* ('Pact of Forgetting') refers to a political consensus in Spain in which the topic of the civil war and Francoism is not confronted directly. It was a key element of the Spanish transition to democracy which occurred after Franco's death in 1975, and was institutionalised with the 1977 Amnesty Law, which freed political prisoners but also granted immunity to the dictatorship and its supporters for their role in decades of repression. The *pacto* has been a source of controversy for historians and has come under pressure in recent years, with legislative efforts at de-Francoisation and the promotion of 'democratic memory': a more overt official condemnation of the Francoist *coup* and dictatorship alongside public rehabilitation and commemoration of its victims.

Quadragesimo Anna, which recalled Rerum Novarum of 40 years earlier, which had condemned what it generalised as Marxism and Communism. Hitler's rise to power, which had culminated two years before with his achievement of absolute command of Germany — together with his alliance with Mussolini and his concern to distract western powers from his Central European Strategy — resulted in Nationalist rebels receiving support from Nazi Germany and Fascist Italy.

As to the position of other countries, despite the signing by 27 countries — including Britain, France, Germany, Italy and the Soviet Union — of a non-intervention pact in September 1936, it was a war that was soon to take on an international dimension. Stalin, worried by the rise of fascism in Europe and the threat it presented to the Soviet Union, moved to prevent the Nationalists from taking power by providing military assistance to the Republicans. Ireland's reaction to the civil war was probably unique across Europe. It was a war which provoked a divided response, with volunteers going to Spain to support both Nationalists and Republicans. It is difficult for some even today, given the high regard in which the Irish International Brigaders are now held in this country, to understand how the great majority of Irishmen who fought in the Spanish Civil War did so in support of General Franco.

We must remember, however, that support for Franco in Ireland was sourced in the conservative institutional forces dominated by a brand of clericalism far more authoritarian than spiritual and imposed through fear, and many of those who decided to join the International Brigades faced public opprobrium at home. Rather than being seen as a struggle between democracy and fascism, the Spanish Civil War was widely presented in Ireland as a conflict between Catholicism and Communism. Yet both Catholic and non-Catholic clergymen in Northern Ireland would support the Spanish Republic. The Catholic hierarchy's pastoral warning against the spread of left-wing ideas in Ireland, issued some years before, had clearly stated that the two beliefs, Catholicism and Communism were completely incompatible.

Meanwhile the influence of the movement that would come to be known as the Blueshirts continued to spread under the leadership of Eoin O'Duffy, who was an admirer of European fascism and not committed to democratic politics if it included workers entitled to agitate for their rights. Described by Diarmuid Ferriter as 'a mirror to the Ireland of the Twenties and Thirties,' O'Duffy's 700-strong Irish Brigade was supported by the Catholic Church, the Dean of Cashel sending them on their way with the blessing of such words as: 'The Irish Brigade have gone to fight the battle of Christianity against Communism.' Throughout the country the church gate collection for 'ambulances for Franco' was the largest since the time of Daniel O'Connell's campaign for Catholic Emancipation in the previous century.

Meanwhile, like the tens of thousands of foreigners who had decided to come to the Republic's aid in Spain, many Irish men and women were moved by the distress of the democratically-elected Spanish government, and the suffering of civilians. They were courageous and determined. They had to be as for many of them, getting to Spain involved great difficulty and hardship, as described by the late Michael O'Riordan who recalls his own illegal and clandestine journey through London and Paris as a 'difficult and long road.' Most of the volunteers were smuggled in over the Pyrenees, where they received a sadly inadequate training for the war they were about to fight. They had, however, been left under no illusions upon recruitment about the bloody and brutal battle that lay before them. Michael O'Riordan remembers the 'authentic, realistic and honest' description they received of what they were likely to encounter in Spain, which had the effect of some volunteers stepping out and returning home.

Among the ranks of the International Brigades was the brilliant young poet, Charles Donnelly, whose final words were to become an almost iconic description of the Spanish Civil War, still remembered and quoted today many years after they were first uttered on the battlefields of Spain. Described by Eavan Boland as 'a dark star' who can 'haunt a generation,' Charles Donnelly was just 22 years of age when he decided to come to the aid of Republican Spain. Donnelly, with hundreds of men from the International Brigades, fought in one of the bloodiest confrontations between Republican and Nationalist forces — that of the Battle of Jarama, which took place just seven weeks after his arrival in Spain. It was here, during a lull in machine-gun fire and just moments before a bullet was shot into his temple, that Charles Donnelly plucked a bunch of olives from the dust and squeezing them spoke the five simple words that still echo poignantly across the decades: 'Even the olives are bleeding.'

At Jarama, a battle took place that, in the words of Cathal O'Shannon many years later, was to 'epitomise war in all its horror.' Here, the Irish and British battalions fought side by side, and suffered huge casualties, yet achieving one of their finest hours as they played their brave role in thwarting an attempt by Franco's forces to encircle Madrid. Ten days after his death, Charles Donnelly's body — 'face fresh, naive looking' — was buried beneath one of those olive trees in that foreign land far away from his native Tyrone; his family left unaware of his death for some time, his distressed father unable to talk about him for years.

Yet it is important to recall that support for the Spanish Republic drew alliances together between religions in Northern Ireland. The silence of the relatives of the lost is as moving now to recall as it was understandable in its time. Sadly, such silence was not unusual. Many of those who died so bravely for freedom, were marginalised back home in Ireland for many years. Many had their teaching posts taken from them. Communist Party spokesman Eugene McCartan, describing the anguish and despair of those who lost sons serving in anti-fascist forces in the Spanish Civil War, said: 'To be attached to someone who died was not safe in Ireland. The Catholic Church made a rallying cry for fascists and held collections to support Franco. It was no wonder families kept their heads down.'

However, while O'Duffy's Irish Brigade was comprised wholly of Roman Catholics, we must not forget that many committed Catholics fought with the International Brigade, seeing no conflict between their religious beliefs and the spirit of solidarity which drove them to fight, and in some cases sacrifice their lives, for democracy in Spain. Frank Ryan, leader of the Irish contingent of the Brigade, wrote when completing a questionnaire on his arrival at the concentration camp of San Pedro de Cardena, that he had come to Spain for two reasons; one to aid a democratic government, and the other because he believed that religion was not at stake in the Spanish War and he wanted to show that O'Duffy did not represent the Irish people. The Ireland of the 1930s that produced these opposing forces was an Ireland that experienced the extremes of authoritarianism imposed on the people, be it in relation to culture, dance, books, moral panics against communism and fear. The character of the Irish International Brigade, with its mix of socialists, idealists, communists, and men of all religions and none can perhaps be best summed up in the words of the late Paddy O'Daire, a leader of the International Brigade, who said: 'All causes are worldwide. Freedom is indivisible. If a man fights for freedom in one place, he is fighting for it everywhere.'

The urge to defend the Spanish Republic invoked internationalism and a shared humanism that was construed as a threat to the absolutism and the imposed certainties of the time. The response was vicious. It was to be a brave and bitter fight, culminating in an ungenerous defeat which saw thousands executed, a million people exiled or imprisoned, and a generation denied the right to live, grow and flourish in a democratic nation. Today, the people of Spain continue to grapple with transacting the legacy of a civil war that was undoubtedly the most important chapter of its 20th century history. It is a chapter which has left a profound legacy, with many citizens still engaged years later in a continuing search for contact with their past; a past, and as so often elsewhere, perhaps because of the pain or guilt, not discussed at home, and often left out of the history books studied in their classrooms.

Here in Ireland, as we engage with the ongoing Decade of Commemorations, we have been called to reflect on the challenge of remembering ethically.[63] Such remembrance must always aspire to respect complexity and to seek to understand, as they construed it, the integrity and the motivations of the men and women from the past. That is not an easy task. Such ethical remembering remains a challenge for Spain, as for us and for many nations around the globe, if just and enduring peace is to be achieved. As the world continues to face conflict, poverty and abuse of power, we are called upon to continue to show moral courage and be willing in our words and policies to demonstrate a sense of internationalism. If we are to overcome together the forces of greed, intolerance and oppression which deny so many of our fellow global citizens their right to justice and freedom it can only be with alarm that, 80 years after the beginning of the Spanish Civil War, we see xenophobic, nationalistic and inward-looking movements gaining traction again in mainstream politics right across Europe. If we are to tackle the growing divisions within the international community it is

---

[63] Editor's Note: The Irish Government designated the 2012-2022 period the 'Decade of Commemorations' or 'Decade of Centenaries', a hundred years on from many key events in modern Irish history, including the Easter Rising, the Irish War of Independence, and the partition of Ireland, with the aim of considering ways to remember potentially divisive events with sensitivity and respect.

important that we focus our efforts anew on building social cohesion and solidarity. In the centenary year of the republican uprising of 1916, and the 80th anniversary of fascism's attack on the Spanish Republic, we should recall the origins and aims of true republicanism, and strive to continue to show the strength of conviction, moral courage and generosity that was shared among those who fought in the International Brigades.

The inspiring spirit of humanity that defined the International Brigades has never, perhaps, been more movingly articulated than in the farewell speech of the great Spanish Republican, Dolores Ibárruri — or La Pasionaria, as she is better known. Addressing them at the final parade in Barcelona in October 1938 she told them that

> From all peoples, from all races, you came to us like brothers, like sons of immortal Spain; and in the hardest days of the war, when the capital of the Spanish Republic was threatened, it was you, gallant comrades of the International Brigades, who helped save the city with your fighting enthusiasm, your heroism and your spirit of sacrifice.

The volunteers who joined the Brigades from across Europe and beyond, set an example of international solidarity and global citizenship which today continues to inspire those who bravely march alongside the downtrodden, the excluded and the marginalised; and who battle against inequality in all its forms, fighting for justice and freedom in communities and societies across the globe, those who work to give meaning and greater democracy for all. As a nation we can be very proud of the brave Irish men and women who joined the International Brigade in 1936. May I commend you, therefore, for the work you do in keeping alive the memory and the values of all those who bravely fought for 'freedom everywhere' on the battlefields of Spain almost 80 years ago.

¡Viva la Quince Brigada!

> Michael D. Higgins has served as President of Ireland since 2011. This transcript of President Higgins's address to the IBMT annual general meeting in Dublin in October 2016 was published in issue 44 (January 2017) of the *IBMT Magazine*.

New perspectives on Orwell's memoir

Jim Jump

In her introduction to the 2021 republication of George Orwell's *Homage to Catalonia*, leading Spanish Civil War historian Helen Graham notes that the memoir has led 'a long and fraught afterlife.' It has often been misused and misunderstood by 'purblind political commentators determined to prove that the immensely complicated world of wartime Republican Spain could be reduced to a Cold War parable of "Communist control", or even more ahistorically, to "Soviet control of the Spanish Republic".' Given that it is probably the most widely read book in English about the Spanish Civil War, Orwell's account presents problems for historians of the war, says Graham. It lends itself to misinterpretation 'by what he left out or was silent on, as well as by what he simply could not have been expected to know or understand.'

Helen Graham is the author of several books on Spain's civil war, including *The Spanish Civil War: A Very Short Introduction* and *Interrogating Francoism: History and Dictatorship in Twentieth-Century Spain*. She is currently working on a history of Franco's prison system. In her introduction to Orwell's memoir she explains how the author served in the militia of the POUM Marxist workers' unity party in Aragón and was also a witness to the bloody street battles in Barcelona in May 1937[64]. These were between the POUM and anarchists on one side and, on the other, government forces wanting to take charge of official buildings such as the central telephone exchange.

The government prevailed after five days of fighting and those in the POUM in Barcelona who had opposed the government were charged and imprisoned. The Spanish Republican government's actions, taken with the full backing of the communists, formed part of efforts to assert control over Catalonia's factories and Aragón's food production in order to maximise the war effort. This meant dismantling the anarchist-led collectivist revolution that had taken place in both regions after the

---

[64] Editor's note: The 'May Days' fighting in Barcelona, which exploded against a backdrop of rising social tensions over food supplies in a city filled with refugees, almost led to a total breakdown of the anti-Franco coalition. Both at the time and in the years since the war, it has been a source of bitter controversy — interpreted as a minor political squabble, as a shameful attempt to undermine the Republican government and derail the war effort, or as a last-ditch attempt to defend a revolution which had given workers and peasants the impetus to resist Franco, depending on who you asked. Helen Graham is also author of an important academic essay about the different political and social factors which shaped the 'May Days': Helen Graham, "Against the State': A Genealogy of the Barcelona May Days (1937)', *European History Quarterly* 29. 4 (1999), 485-542. A recent academic article offers another perspective more sympathetic to the revolutionary argument: Danny Evans, 'In and Against the State: The Making and Unmaking of the Barcelona May Days (1937)', *European History Quarterly* 52. 3 (2022), 485-505.

July 1936 military uprising. In sympathy with the underdogs, Orwell turned his memoir, writes Graham, into 'an elegy to a lost revolution.' He was also angry at what he saw as the dishonest depiction in the communist press of the POUM as pro-Franco fifth columnists.

Orwell's writing has much to commend it, particularly its 'unadorned style', 'compelling immediacy' and the 'luminous humanity radiating through its pages.' Examples are the memorable despatches from the trenches in Aragón, describing the smell of excrement and decaying food, the ubiquitous lice and the tedium and terror of war. Then there is the author's powerful evocation of an unknown Italian militiaman he shook hands with when he arrived in Barcelona in December 1936. Confronted with the volunteer's shabby uniform and 'fierce, pathetic, innocent face,' Orwell saw clearly that there was no doubt as to who was in the right in Spain's conflict.

Missing, however, from the people and events described by Orwell is the wider war, with Hitler and Mussolini arming Franco to the hilt and Britain preventing the Republic from buying arms to defend itself. Graham writes: 'In narrating the May Days in *Homage to Catalonia* he narrows the focus greatly and sticks entirely with his own "street view" of events . . . as if they were exclusively about a sectarian political conflict of the Left.' Orwell wrote his memoir immediately after returning to Britain in June 1937. His view of the broader military and diplomatic context of the war had to wait another five years, until the essay 'Looking Back on the Spanish Civil War', which is included in the Macmillan Collector's Library volume. Here, he finally acknowledges that the outcome of the war was settled not in Spain but in London, Paris, Rome and Berlin. Yet, as Graham points out, the author, who died of tuberculosis in January 1950, never revised the text of *Homage to Catalonia* to reflect that conclusion.

> Jim Jump is the current IBMT chair and was the editor of the IBMT's magazine from 2008-2019. He has written and edited various publications about the Spanish Civil War and the International Brigades, including *Poems from Spain: British and Irish International Brigaders on the Spanish Civil War* (2006) and *Antifascistas: British & Irish volunteers in the Spanish Civil War* (with Richard Baxell and Angela Jackson, 2010). This essay appeared in issue 60 (May 2022) of *¡No Pasarán!*

Blinded by anti-communism?

Helen Graham

Weighing in at over 900 pages, military historian Antony Beevor's general history of the Spanish Civil War is a bestseller in Spain. The English-language edition, published in June 2006, has also received much media attention and at a relatively more manageable 526 pages, it too established itself as a market-leader.[65] After the author's previous blockbusting success with *Stalingrad* (1998) and *Berlin: the Downfall* (2002), there is, one might say, an identifiable Beevor 'product' which has a ready-made appeal to a very large general audience. The product is highly readable — for Beevor writes very well — and combines an original, archive-based take on the military dimension with an intelligent synthesis of the rest, culled from the publications of specialist academic historians whose work would rarely otherwise reach the general reader, even in its country of origin.

The Battle for Spain follows this formula and in many respects the resulting work of synthesis fulfils a useful function in giving a non-Spanish reading audience with an interest in the civil war access to the findings of recent specialist research. This is particularly noteworthy in the case of Beevor's treatment of the murderous Francoist repression of the 1930s and 40s on which a huge leading edge bibliography has been produced by Spaniards over the last 25 years but almost none of which has been translated into English. In terms of Beevor's analysis of the war itself, he is, as one might expect, most thought-provoking on the military detail. There are many nice observations which bring alive the problems ordinary soldiers faced.

Much more controversial is his negative assessment of Republican chief of staff, Vicente Rojo, considered by many commentators — including other military historians — to be the outstanding strategist of the war. Beevor is critical of his military leadership, and considers him irresponsible to have engaged in 'prestige operations,' as the author describes the Republic's major diversionary attacks at Brunete, Belchite, Teruel and the Ebro. Certainly these proved costly to the Republic in men and material. But such actions were vital to projecting an image of military vitality and political will. Without them the Republic's foremost political leaders knew they stood absolutely no chance of breaking the international diplomatic deadlock that, in perpetuating Non-Intervention, was killing the Republic. Indeed even Beevor's technical criticisms of the 'prestige operations' often ignore the profound and lasting effects of the arms shortages inflicted by Non-Intervention.

But Beevor is much less interested in the devastation wrought by Non Intervention than he is in Russian involvement with the Republic. He assumes rather

---

[65] Antony Beevor, *The Battle for Spain: The Spanish Civil War 1936-1939* (London: Weidenfeld & Nicolson, 2006).

than demonstrates that Republican military resistance was run by Soviet advisers. Moreover, he sees the Second Spanish Republic at war as virtually a Soviet satellite. But again, this is not a view sustained by his own substantial mining of newly available Soviet sources. Rather it is an article of faith, much as it has always been for Cold War historians, from Burnett Bolloten to Ronald Radosh, and to whose school Beevor clearly belongs. As with his predecessors, Beevor's anti-communism at times blinds him to the evidence of his own material. Many of the reports filed by the Republic's Soviet advisors indicate their utter powerlessness to affect military outcomes given material shortages and the huge organisational and personnel problems they confronted. They were equally bewildered by the complexity and diversity of the Republican political scene which neither they nor their Soviet masters ever really properly understood let alone controlled.

In the end, of course, the Cold War view of the Spanish Republic at war is an imperialist one: 'Spain' was a blank canvas until written upon by agendas of the great powers. The history of Republican Spain and the agency of its protagonists are entirely written out of the script. Without any apparent sense of the absurdity of the proposition, Beevor tells us that in August 1936 in Spain 'the communists' were interested in building an army only because they judged that, compared to the militia, it would be easier to dominate. But in the apocalyptic conditions of summer 1936, all of the Republic's frontline defenders were interested in building an army to fight Franco. For all had the most immediate and pressing of matters on their minds. Whether in Mérida or Madrid, communists, socialists, anarchists and republicans were absorbed body and soul by present danger: how might they conceivably offer a halfway effective resistance to the onslaught of the Army of Africa's seasoned troops? Quite simply, how might they stay alive?

Nor is the sociological complexity of Spain's wartime mass communism ever really explored. Beevor makes passing reference to the movement's social and cultural hybridity but never draws any conclusions from this in terms of its political trajectory during the war, nor to its manifest and obvious weakness when faced with the Casado *coup* that capsized Republican resistance in March 1939. For a movement that purportedly controlled everything in Republican Spain, the jobbing historian is increasingly awash with evidence (much of it courtesy of the Soviet archives) that indicates quite the opposite. Ultimately the problem with Beevor's quite relentless anti-communism is the problem of all conspiracy views of history: they can never do justice to the complexity of how and why things happen. No doubt many communists at the time believed their party-movement's rhetoric: that 'history' was on their side, that theirs was the grand design. But that belief is an historical phenomenon, while Beevor seems to mistake it for a methodology.

Much counterfactuality also creeps into Beevor's assessment, in spite of this being the historian's cardinal sin. If Francoism was bad, he insists that a victorious Republic, post-victory, would have engaged in just as bloody a repression. Once again, this isn't so much argued, as stated and assumed — indeed there isn't even a passing reference to the evidence/arguments to the contrary available in several of the specialist texts the author cites in his own bibliography. Taken together, the implicit message of Beevor's intense ideological anti-communism combined with his equally vehement criticism of Francoist barbarity would seem to be 'a plague on both your houses.' This is not so very far removed from views explicitly expressed by some elite British opinion formers at the time. But for a widely read professional historian to be implying the same in the 21st century is myopic and more than unfortunate, ignoring as it does the quite fundamental differences between the Francoist and Republican political projects. No doubt the author would say that this is simply the current reviewer's own 'article of faith.' But in fact these differences are pretty much empirically verifiable if one compares the judicial, social and economic practices of the Republican state at war (warts and all) with the practices of Franco's (emergent) new order.

Ideological blind spots notwithstanding, Antony Beevor's book is worth reading for its broad synthesising coverage — although the reader should beware of minor errors and gremlins that have inevitably crept in, given the scale of the author's endeavour. The book's real value, however, lies in Beevor's thought-provoking military analysis. For even if one disagrees with his conclusions, and there are plenty of grounds for doing so, his assessments will contribute to and stimulate wider interest in the complex ongoing debate over Republican military strategy and its political and material constraints. And that is no bad thing.

Helen Graham is one of the UK's foremost historians of modern Spain, with a focus on the Spanish Civil War and Francoism. She is an IBMT patron. Now Emeritus Professor of Modern European History at the Royal Holloway, University of London, her books include *The Spanish Republic at War 1936-1939* (2002) and *The War and its Shadow: Spain's Civil War in Europe's Long Twentieth Century* (2012). This originally appeared as a book review in issue 18 (September 2007) of the *IBMT Newsletter*.

A sketch and a song return from the past

Jim Jump

After nearly 75 years, International Brigade veteran David Lomon laid eyes on a portrait of him sketched in the prisoner-of-war camp in Palencia, northern Spain. The drawing was by the artist and poet Clive Branson, who like David was captured by Italian troops near Calaceite in the spring of 1938 when the British Battalion was forced to retreat through Aragón in the face of a massive offensive by the fascists. Dated 7 August [1938], the sketch is one of several portraits and other drawings that Branson produced as a prisoner at Palencia and also the prison camp at San Pedro de Cardeña. All his original sketches and poems were donated in 2011 by daughter Rosa Branson to the Marx Memorial Library in London, where they join an extensive International Brigade archive.

Now aged 93, David Lomon always remembered being sketched while at Palencia, but never thought that his portrait might have survived after all these years — until he found out about the existence of Branson's original sketches. The IBMT arranged a visit to the library in April 2012 to see if he could identify his portrait as a young man. 'It was amazing to see the drawing,' said David. 'It brought back memories of how most days we would all sit around talking or playing chess and then Clive would say "I want to sketch you today" and whoever it was would have to keep still for a while.' Turning to his son, Irving, who accompanied him on the visit to the library, he asked: 'Do you think it looks like me? I certainly had more hair then.'

Looking at Clive Branson's prison camp sketches — and listening to Billy Bragg's new recording of 'Jarama Valley' — have also brought back memories of songs that the captured International Brigade volunteers used to sing. At the Palencia prison, says David, they sang a variant of the 'Jarama Valley' song (to the tune of 'Red River Valley') that was originally penned by Glaswegian volunteer Alex McDade and then anonymously rewritten to become the unofficial song of the British Battalion. These are the words sung by the prisoners, as recalled by David:

> There's a prison in Spain called Palencia
> 'Tis a place we know all too well
> It was there that we gave of our manhood
> And spent months of misery and hell.
>
> Surrounded one day by Italians
> Who with guns bought by Chamberlain's gold
> Blown to hell by artillery and avion
> That's how our brave comrades were sold.

Several paintings by Clive Branson, who was killed, aged 36, while serving with the British Army in Burma in 1944, are in the collection held by the Tate Britain gallery in London. In 2011, the Marx Memorial Library organised an exhibition of paintings alongside a large mural-style painting by daughter Rosa, also an artist, paying tribute to the International Brigades.

> Jim Jump was the editor of the IBMT's magazine from 2008 to 2020. This article appeared in issue 32 (June 2012) of the *IBMT Newsletter* under the headings 'A sketch returns from the past' and 'Prison song lyrics resurface too'.

Sketch by Clive Branson of his fellow Brigader and co-inmate David Lomon, drawn in August 1938 while both were prisoners of war in Palencia prison. Courtesy of the Marx Memorial Library.

Fighting fascism then and now

John Pilger

16 July 2005: It was International Brigades' Memorial Day in Jubilee Gardens beside the Thames in London. It was a hot day with no breeze, 'a Spanish day,' one of the Brigaders said. Like the others, all in their 80s and older, he took shelter in the shade and rested on his walking stick. Twenty yards away, tourists waiting to board the London Eye, the great ferris wheel built for the Millennium, looked bemused at the elderly men in their berets, and the rest of us, not knowing who we were, what the men had done and why we were celebrating them.

Between 1936 and 1939, the International Brigade fought in Spain on the side of the Republican government against the fascist forces of General Franco. They were very young and all volunteers, determined to stop fascism in its tracks. They made a difference. Although the government eventually fell, in February 1937, the 600-strong British Battalion of the XVth International Brigade stopped Franco's advance on Madrid. Four hundred were killed, wounded or captured in four days' bloody battle, Madrid was spared. There were many battles like that. Sam Russell, a Brigader, described eloquently how on the Sierra de Pandols, 'there was not enough soil to bury the dead, so we covered them with stones.' The poet Martin Green who had written of his father, George Green, stood at the edge of the crowd. George was killed when Martin was four years old. For his father, he wrote:

> You had no funeral nor hearse
> No grave except the place you fell
> No dirge but a soldier's curse
> And an explosion tolled your knell
> ...
> I was a boy too young
> To take the blow that felled
> The tree that was your man.

On this warm Saturday, 67 years on, we stood and sang a tribute to them. To the tune of 'Red River Valley,' we sang the song of their battle for Madrid. And we stood and remembered them.

Jack Jones, the president of the International Brigade Memorial Trust,[66] read out the names of his comrades who had died since their last reunion: Charlie Matthews (who had been reported killed on the battlefield in 1939 and whose obituary had appeared in his local paper) and Cyril Sexton, who was wounded at Jarama and went

---

[66] Editor's note: The IBMT co-founder, Jack Jones — trade union leader and veteran of the International Brigades, wounded in action at the Ebro — was life president of the organisation upon his death in April 2009.

on to fight at Aragón, Belchite, Gandesa and Ebro where he was wounded again.[67] Last April, he died at the age of 91.

I was given the honour of describing the meaning of the Brigaders' heroism today. I thanked David Marshall, an International Brigader who had put my name forward and whose poetry had been an inspiration for what I wanted to say. This is what I said...

I first understood the importance of the struggle in Spain from Martha Gellhorn. Martha was one of my oldest friends. She was one of the greatest war correspondents and is remembered for her dispatches from Spain during the civil war. In November 1938, she wrote this:

> In Barcelona, it was perfect bombing weather. The cafés along the Ramblas were crowded. There was nothing much to drink: a sweet fizzy poison called orangeade and a horrible liquid supposed to be sherry. There was, of course, nothing to eat. Everyone was out, enjoying the cold afternoon sunlight. No bombers had come for at least two hours. The flower stalls look bright and pretty along the promenade. 'The flowers are all sold, señores. For the funerals of those killed in the 11 o'clock bombing, poor souls.' It had been a clear and cold day all yesterday ... 'What beautiful weather,' a woman said and she stood, holding her shawl around her, staring at the sky. 'And the nights are as fine as the days. A catastrophe,' she said.
> ... everyone listened for the sirens all the time, and when we saw the bombers, they were like tiny silver bullets, moving over, up, across the sky.

How familiar that sounds. Barcelona. Guernica. Hiroshima. Vietnam. Cambodia. Palestine. Afghanistan. Iraq. Martha never tired of explaining why people fought for the Republic, the *causa*, and why going to Spain was so important. She wrote of the International Brigade: 'Whatever their nationality, whether they were communists, anarchists, socialists, poets, plumbers, middle-class professional men, or the one Abyssinian prince ... they were fighting for us all in Spain.'

The enemy then was fascism, out-and-out fascism. Armband-wearing, strutting, ranting fascism. The enemy then was a great world power, rapacious, with plans of domination, of capturing the world's natural resources: the oil fields of the Caspian and the Middle East, the mineral riches of Africa. They seemed invincible. The enemy then was also lies. Deceit. News dressed up as propaganda. Appeasement. A large section of the British establishment saw fascism as its friend. Their voice was a section of the British press: *The Times*, the *Daily Mail*. To them, the real threat was from ordinary people, who were dreamers, many of them, who imagined a new world in which the dignity of ordinary life was respected and celebrated. Some were wise dreamers and some were foolish dreamers, but they understood the nature of fascism, and they saw through the lies and the deceit and the appeasement.

---

[67] Editor's note: Cyril Sexton's first-hand account of battle is included in his volume — see 'Panic at Brunete'.

They also knew that the true enemy didn't always wear arm bands, and didn't always strut, or command great rallies, but were impeccable English gentlemen who supported ruthless power behind a smokescreen of propaganda that appropriated noble concepts like 'democracy' and 'freedom' and 'our way of life' and 'our values.' Does all this sound familiar? I ask that question, because when I read the aims of the International Brigade Memorial Trust, I was struck by a reference to 'the historical legacy of the men and women who fought with the International Brigades against fascism . . .' The 'historical legacy' of the International Brigade, as Martha Gellhorn wrote, is that they were fighting for us all.

For me, that means a legacy of truth — a way of seeing through the smokescreen of propaganda, including and especially the propaganda of our own governments: a legacy of confronting great and rapacious power in whatever form. That legacy is needed today more than ever. Impeccable gentlemen now invade defenceless countries in our name. They speak of freedom and democracy, and our way of life and our values. They don't wear armbands and they don't strut. They are different from fascists. But their goals are not different. Conquest, domination, the control of vital resources. When the judges at Nuremberg laid down the ground rules of international law following the Second World War, they described an unprovoked, violent invasion of a defenceless country as 'a crime against humanity, the paramount war crime.'

The world is a very different place from Barcelona in 1938, and from the Sierra de Pandols, and the Valley of Jarama, but the legacy of those who confronted fascism then endures as a warning to us all today. It is a warning about sinister power behind democratic facades that uses the battle cries of democracy. It is a warning about messianic politicians, apparently touched by God, and about appeasement and truth. It is about moral courage: about speaking out, breaking a silence. I salute those International Brigaders who are here today, who did more than speak out. I thank you and your fallen comrades for what you did for us all, and for your legacy of truth and moral courage. *¡La lucha continúa!*

John Pilger is an award-winning journalist, author and documentary filmmaker. This text, following on from his speech at the IBMT annual commemoration 2005, first appeared in issue 12 (Oct 2005) of the *IBMT Newsletter*.

Little resemblance to history — or my own experience

John Dunlop

Land and Freedom is the title of the film which opened the Edinburgh International Film Festival on 13 August 1995, more than half a century after the events it purports to describe. Land and freedom were certainly what the war was really about. But what was the film about? It was really about boy meets girl in an exotic location (for the boy and most of the viewers); they fall in love, have temper-tantrums, make it up again and then the girl dies tragically in an unreal situation, all told by the boy's granddaughter 58 years later in flashbacks from her grandpa's letters home, with reams of photographs of him and his comrades.

As one who was there at the time of the supposed events depicted I can certify that it bore little resemblance to the realities of those days and the filmmakers made little attempt to get even the small details right. In Spain in 1937 Doc Marten boots had never been heard of, far less seen, yet they were there on the feet of the actors in the film. Blue jeans? Don't be silly! What about all those large photographs of the English boy and his comrades supposed to have been sent home by him? Photographers were few and far between, especially in the supposed locations of the film.

Back to clothing — in reality our trousers were baggy khaki-coloured denim or woollen, caught in at the ankles by buttons or a knitted woollen band to keep the dust from going up inside the trouser-leg. The woollen ones which flopped over my boots were my first trousers, with a short military-style woollen jacket. I was lucky to get a pair of boots to fit me — and I lost them after I was wounded. Thereafter I wore *alpargatas*, open canvas sandals with plaited grass soles held on by tapes round the ankles. The men in the villages also wore *alpargatas*, with baggy trousers made of hard-wearing black corduroy. Some of us had khaki dispatch rider type denims caught in below the knee. John Black, second in command of the XV Brigade's Anti-Tank Battery wore them with British Army puttees wound from his boots to his knees — the only man in Spain to do so. That was how his body was recognised after he was blown up by a shell.

Now for the storyline. At the time the young Liverpool communist left to go to Spain, we went in groups and not on our own. These groups were organised by the Communist Party and one of the group carried an introduction to the French Communist Party, who arranged for their transport and accommodation through France and over the border into Spain. By November 1936, all volunteers crossing the frontier were taken to a huge fort at Figueras from where they went in larger groups by train to Albacete, where they were documented and received into the International Brigades. So the naïve depiction of how the young Liverpool Communist Party member was persuaded by complete strangers to join the POUM militia was a virtual impossibility. In any case no enthusiastic young communist of those days would have been taken in in such a way. Whoever thought up that story line displays a singular lack of knowledge of the communists of those days.

Now here let it be said that when the International Brigade Association was told that a film was to be made by Ken Loach about the war in Spain they offered their services, but the offer was rejected. So the makers of the film bear full responsibility for all the wild inaccuracies and anachronisms that the film depicts. One wonders why the offer was refused. Let it also be made clear that the Spanish Communist Party took the realist view that the war was not about achieving a communist state in Spain but about the defence of the democratic constitution established in 1931. This was a left-liberal constitution which contained provisions for much needed land reform and universal education that preceding governments had failed to implement. In this aim they were supported by the international communist movement as expressed by the formation of the International Brigades. To attempt a workers' revolution at a time when international opposition to communism was at its height would have been suicidal.

Communists regarded the war as one against international fascism, against three fascist dictators whose declared aim was the destruction of Western liberal democratic institutions and the creation of new empires. Italy, in spite of being a member of the League of Nations, was already engaged in wars of imperial conquest in Africa.[68] I spent the last few days in France in the company of three Italians home on leave from the war in Africa who had arrived in their home village in the north of Italy to hear of the war in Spain and had promptly crossed the frontier into France to join the International Brigades. In Germany democratic institutions had been destroyed by Hitler, whose declared aim was to spread Nazi power through Europe and recover all Germany's imperial possessions lost to it after the Great War of 1914-18. The Italian dictator Mussolini was trying to recreate the ancient Roman Empire and to this end the Berlin-Rome-Tokyo Axis had been created along with the Japanese war lords who were waging a war of conquest against China. In furtherance of these aims Hitler and Mussolini had formed an alliance with the revolting Spanish generals and were supplying them not only with arms and planes but also pilots and combat troops, without anything being done to effectively stop them by the Western democracies that were next on the list for destruction.

There is considerable controversy over what indeed the POUM (Partido Obrero de Unificación Marxista — Workers' Party of Marxist Unification) were up to in Spain. From their own literature it is clear that they considered the communist attitude a betrayal of their aim of world revolution. At that time the anti-Franco forces in Catalonia were not unified under the central command of the government but were composed of the volunteer anarchist or POUM militias, each acting as they saw fit. The

---

[68] Editor's note: In 1935, Italy commenced a bloody invasion of Ethiopia (then often referred to as Abyssinia) with fascist colonial designs. During the war, Italian forces killed hundreds of thousands of Ethiopian civilians, including by the deliberate use of chemical weapons such as mustard gas against civilian populations.

government, with the support of the communists, was determined to create a unified command. This was opposed by the anarchists and the POUM. George Orwell in his *Homage to Catalonia* portrays the POUM as the innocent victims of the struggle between the anarchists and the communists. The action taken by the Republican government on 3 May 1937 in occupying the telephone exchange in Barcelona was the flashpoint. The reaction to this by the anarchists, who had taken control of the exchange at the time of Franco's rebellion, was what sparked the fighting. The government responded by attacking all the buildings controlled by the militias and confiscating their arms. The crux of the difference between the three groups was the call of the communists for full support for the Republican government in its fight against the fascists and the calls by the POUM and some of the anarchists for a workers' revolution.

Strangely, ever since the publication of Orwell's book in 1938 the POUM have been portrayed as the 'goodies' in this fight and this has coloured all reports of the war since then. But for a participant looking back, it is significant that on the very day, 26 April 1937, that Nazi German planes manned by German pilots launched the fiercely destructive raids on Guernica, the POUM withdrew their forces from the front line in Aragón on the flank of the Carlos Marx Division, leaving a gaping hole in the Republic's defences. At the time these events were going on in Catalonia, the British Battalion, with other units of the International Brigades, had been holding a defensive position on the banks of the Jarama river just south of Madrid. Our lines were only half a mile from the Madrid-Valencia highway and were established at the end of a furious battle in February in which we lost two-thirds of our men, killed, captured or wounded defending this vital road against constant fascist attacks. Not surprisingly we in the International Brigades had little sympathy with the attitude of the POUM.

By the middle of May 1937 when I crossed the Pyrenees into Spain the POUM had been suppressed and their and the anarchist militias were being enrolled in the ranks of the Republican Army. The fortress of Figueras was packed with them when I arrived there. They had given up their firearms but were still armed with huge knives. We got on fine with them, being greeted as brothers and later, when Spanish troops were being taken into the International Brigades, we had some of these anarchists in the machine-gun company of the British Battalion. So much for the historical accuracy of Ken Loach's film. I can think of at least six real heroes, four of them Scots, known to me personally about whom he could have made a better film. One wonders why he did not do so while there are still some of us around to give him the details. As far as the viewers of the film were concerned, most of them had hardly heard of the war in Spain and cared even less about it. The film did little to enlighten them.

> John Dunlop was an International Brigades veteran who was wounded at Brunete in July 1937 but went on to see further action at Fuentes del Ebro, Teruel and the Battle of the Ebro. This essay was published in issue 55 (September 2020) of *¡No Pasarán!* Republished with kind permission of the Dunlop family.

Necessary lessons for the left

Ken Loach

The volunteers from across the world who went to Spain in the 1930s to fight fascism and defend the Republic will always remain in our collective memory for their courage and simple class loyalty. They were the flower of their generation. They saw people like themselves, from ordinary working class backgrounds, who had achieved a measure of political power democratically and were determined to use it to make life better for everyone. That meant structural changes in society, and questioning who owned and controlled the land and the major industries. Then they saw those hopes being attacked by a fascist elite, led by General Franco, and backed by the military, the Church and the old establishment. The ruling class would not hand over its power without a fight. Then, as now, democracy was only acceptable to them if it produced the result they wanted. Germany and Italy intervened to support the fascists. Russia and Mexico backed the Republicans and Russia sold them arms. Britain, France and the US stayed silent in public, but gave discreet support to Franco. In that febrile atmosphere, the courage and political commitment of the volunteers is all the more remarkable.

There are so many stories to be told about Spain's civil war. In 1994, Jim Allen, the writer, Rebecca O'Brien, the producer, and I had the privilege to make a film, *Land and Freedom*, that told just one such story. It is the struggle for leadership between different factions on the Republican side. This disastrous conflict revealed necessary lessons for the left that we have to re-learn time after time. Various political groups and factions came together to fight Franco, all with their own traditions, perspectives and tactics — a familiar pattern for those experienced in the politics of the left. Social democrats, communists, anarchists, revolutionary socialists and citizens with no prior political allegiance would all play their part. Inevitably there was a struggle for leadership.

This conflict at the heart of the Republican forces seemed to Jim and me the story that had to be told. It raised questions that are always central to issues that socialists and radical movements face. This conflict was expressed in many ways: how to organise militarily, how to transform a citizens' militia into an efficient army, what political changes to implement where the left held power, and how would these decisions affect the Republicans' capacity to win the war? To us, the starting point of the story was critical. Jim suggested that our main character should be a working class man from the industrial north of England, who goes to Spain at the outset of the war, before the International Brigades were fully organised. He would join the POUM, the revolutionary socialist group, small in number but significant in its political position. That would take us into the heart of the conflict over the question of leadership.

The central question confronting the militia was this: do we win the war by implementing a revolutionary programme, taking ownership of industries and collectivising the land to transform society in the interests of the working class? Or do we put the revolution on hold and concentrate solely on the war effort? Dramatically, we put this dilemma in a scene where a village had been liberated by the militia, and the inhabitants and the militia men and women hammer out the pros and cons of this issue. Trade unionists from the area, politically active in real life, joined the cast to clarify and sharpen this argument. Their passion was electrifying. The words were mainly as written by Jim, but the scene had an element of improvisation. The decision was to collectivise — but strong arguments were put on both sides.

As the war developed, the citizens' militias were transformed into a more traditional army, with the hierarchy of rank that it involved. It was a reorganisation led by the Communist Party. More conflicts arose — the role of women, for example. Were they front-line fighters, as in the militias, or doing traditional women's work like cooking? We met a woman in the market in Barcelona who had fought in the war and who was still furious that she had been denied the chance to shoot fascists. That was typical of our experiences. At the outset we were told no one would speak about the war, it was too painful. But once people started to talk, the floodgates opened. The anger, the outrage, the bitterness at what had been lost and the ensuing brutal oppression by Franco's government were very close to the surface.

Then the other part of the story, the split on the left became violent, the militia were disbanded, the POUM was named an enemy of the Spanish people and declared illegal. Its senior members were arrested and Andreu Nin, its leader, murdered. The *Daily Worker* declared the POUM to be Franco's fifth column. Remember, these were the years of the Moscow Trials and the removal by Stalin of many of the Bolsheviks who had led the October Revolution. Sadly, the two sides turned their rifles on each other in Barcelona in May 1937. Our part of the story ends with the company of militia fighting, and losing an engagement with fascist troops. The militia are then confronted by a detachment of the newly formed Republican Army, communist-led, which disarms the militia fighters at gunpoint and the captain in charge is arrested. The scene was based on the experiences of Juan Rocabert, a veteran who had fought with the POUM, had lived his life in exile in France, and had only recently returned to Spain. As the events of the day unfolded, he stood silently watching, and the tears rolled down his face.

There will be many interpretations of these events, and they will be fiercely contested. Motives will be challenged, consequences evaluated and memories will be at odds with each other. But the big questions are always with us and we have to confront them day by day in our present struggles: How do we win the socialist revolution? When do we lay aside our revolutionary programme and when can it be the engine of our success? When, if ever, should one struggle be made subordinate to another? How do we develop class consciousness? What is the role for socialists who see the need for revolutionary change? What are the essential tasks of political leadership? Before we answer these questions, we must know what happened in Spain. But even before we do that, we must pay tribute to the brave and principled young men and women, some of whom did not return, who left the safety of their homes to fight for the people of Spain.

Ken Loach is a director, twice recipient of the Palme d'Or, whose films include *Kes* (1969), *Raining Stones* (1993), *The Wind That Shakes the Barley* (2006), and *I, Daniel Blake* (2016). This essay featured in issue 55 (September 2020) of *¡No Pasarán!* as 'Necessary lessons for the left from the Republic's infighting'.

Director Ken Loach on the set of Land and Freedom (1995). Courtesy of Sixteen Films.

My friend, the Scottish anarchist who wanted to kill Franco

Paul Preston

Stuart Christie was a close friend, a warm and funny man who was famous for his involvement in, and later imprisonment for, an ill-fated operation to assassinate Franco. We met in the 1970s in the Centro Ibérico in London, a rather ramshackle affair where people interested in the Spanish Civil War, particularly from an anarchist point of view, used to meet. Among the regulars was Miguel García, fresh (or perhaps wilted) from 25 years in Franco's prisons and author of *Franco's Prisoner*. Another was Pepe Martín-Artajo, son of Franco's one-time Minister of Foreign Affairs, Alberto Martín-Artajo. Pepe had been obliged by his father to leave Spain because of his left-wing views.

One thing that most of the obituaries have missed is that Stuart was a learned man. In the early 80s, he secured admission to Queen Mary College in the University of London where I was then teaching. He did a degree in History and Politics. During his time at QMC, I'm sure that I and my colleagues learned as much, if not more, from him as he did from us. Not long after, he began a series of publishing ventures which led to the appearance in English of many important works about the anarchist role in the Spanish Civil War and in the opposition to Franco. These included Chris Ealham's important annotated English edition of the great classic by José Peirats, *La CNT en la revolución española*.[69]

He also wrote several of his own books including his memoirs. The commercial publication *My Granny Made Me An Anarchist* (Scribner, 2004) was an abbreviation of three earlier volumes published by Stuart's own outfit: *Vol. 1 My Granny Made Me an Anarchist. The Christie File: Part 1, 1946-1964* (Christie Books, 2002) was about his childhood in Glasgow; *Vol. 2 General Franco Made Me a "Terrorist". The Christie File: Part 2, 1964-1967* (Christie Books, 2003) about the bungled attempt on Franco's life; and *Vol. 3 Edward Heath Made Me Angry. The Christie File: Part 3, 1967-1975* (Christie Books, 2004) about the period of Edward Heath's Conservative government when Stuart was accused of belonging to the urban guerrilla group known as the Angry Brigade. They were a relatively feeble part of the anti-Vietnam War movement and one erstwhile member later described it as 'the slightly cross brigade.' After 18 months in prison awaiting trial, Stuart was acquitted.

---

[69] Editor's note: Published in English as *The CNT in the Spanish Revolution*. The CNT (Confederación Nacional del Trabajo / National Confederation of Labour) is an anarcho-syndicalist trade union federation in Spain. It was founded in 1910 and played a significant role in the Spanish Civil War as one of the main groups opposed to the generals' rebellion and in the revolutionary changes that accompanied the outbreak of the conflict.

Among his other books are *We, the Anarchists! A Study of the Iberian Anarchist Federation (FAI) 1927-1937)* (AK Press, 2008) and a superb trilogy about a fictional Scottish anarchist involved in the Spanish Civil War, *¡Pistoleros! The Chronicles of Farquar McHarg* (Christie Books, 2009-2012). Both funny and full of insight about the Spanish anarchist movement, we were embarrassed after the appearance of the third volume when I received a request from a student who wanted to do a PhD on McHarg whom she had assumed to be real. Looking at my copies of the three Farquar McHarg memoirs, I can see why. The second volume contains numerous endorsements from British journalists and academics from across Stuart's wide circle of friends, among them the actress Julie Christie and myself. Rereading them makes it clear why the student might have thought that it was a genuine memoir. Julie Christie wrote:

> When I was in Spain making Doctor Zhivago I well remember a strikingly dashing and charismatic Scot who was working as an extra. His name was Farquar and one night after shooting we talked for hours in the bar. He said that he had been in love with a woman called Lara. I recall that he had had a remarkable life and I told him that he should one day write it down. What a thrill to find out that he did so.

I wrote:

> Having known Farquhar McHarg in his prime, and despaired of him ever putting down on paper his extraordinary experiences, I am delighted that he has finally done so. Glasgow's answer to Victor Serge has produced a document of remarkable value, so grippingly written that one might almost think it was a novel.

As might be imagined, we laboured for some time on how best to let the student down gently.

Although the dominant anarchist theorist in the UK, Stuart was remarkably open-minded. His publishing ventures never made much money and he augmented his income by editing some periodicals that might have seemed at a distance from his ideological beliefs. These included *House Magazine*, the journal of both Houses of Parliament, and *Pravda Digest*. In the case of the latter, he added a 'Soviet Observatory' section with a series of critical articles by Sovietologists. For my sins, I was the music critic on both magazines. I have the most wonderful memories of Stuart, a witty and generous man, with many friends and deeply loved by his wife Brenda, who died last year, and his daughter Branwen and her two daughters.[70]

Professor Sir Paul Preston is the IBMT's founding chair. This obituary for Stuart Christie was published in issue 56 (January 2021) of *¡No Pasarán!*

---

[70] Editor's note: Stuart Christie died in August 2020, aged 74.

Saluting the Brigaders' internationalism

Ronan Burtenshaw

Without the Spanish Civil War, without the International Brigades, there is no *Tribune*. It was born on the same day in 1937 as something called the Unity Campaign, which was to bring together a broad front of socialists and communists. The opening letter called for a united working-class effort against fascism in Europe and was inspired by the battles that were going on in Spain. *Tribune* was a mouthpiece for this campaign and that effort to build unity on the left against fascism.

Throughout the 1930s *Tribune* carried eyewitness reports from Spain, including one by Clement Attlee which highlighted the scandal of Britain's attitude to the situation in Spain. In 1938, *Tribune*'s front page and its May Day rally was in support of Spain and freedom. And over the years I'd like to think Tribune has kept that memory and that tradition alive.

We've had many International Brigaders who have written for us. I think of Geoffrey Bing, an Irishman from County Down, who was a journalist with the International Brigades, went on to be a Labour MP and who wrote for *Tribune* for many years. I think of Jimmy Jump who wrote for *Tribune* on numerous occasions, including a commemoration of his comrade George Jackson, which was one part of a regular pattern of commemorations of Brigaders that have featured in the publication over the years.[71]

This is a story of the threads that run through history. We think of those who went to fight in Spain on behalf of the Spanish Republic, we think of the names of the battalions they formed. They talked about Abraham Lincoln and the struggle against slavery in the United States and they talked about Tom Mann and the struggle of the British labour movement here. They talked about Ernst Thälmann and the struggle against Nazism in Germany and they talked about Jarosław Dąbrowski, who was one of the last commanders of the Paris Commune, his name borne by the Polish battalion in Spain.

Those threads wove for us a wonderful tapestry, a flag that represents a universal struggle for working-class liberation at every corner of the earth. And that is what was passed to us by all of those who went and fought and died or were injured. Something wonderful that was given to us from terrible conditions, from incredible

---

[71] Editor's note: James 'Jimmy' Jump was a reporter involved with anti-fascist activism in Britain when, in the summer of 1937, he met and fell in love with Cayetana Lozano Díaz, one of the Spanish *señoritas* who had arrived in Southampton in spring of that year accompanying Basque refugee children. He went on to join the International Brigades and was mentioned in despatches for bravery during the Ebro offensive. James Jump's recollection of Spain, *The Fighter Fell in Love: A Spanish Civil War Memoir* (London: Clapton Press, 2021), includes some of his wartime and postwar poetry.

difficulties. I'm very happy to be able to speak on behalf of that cause today. I say long live the cause of the International Brigades, and in the Spanish that was their slogan: '*por vuestra libertad y la nuestra*'.

Ronan Burtenshaw is editor of *Tribune* and has also written for outlets including *The Guardian* and the *Irish Times*. This is the text of a speech given at the IBMT annual commemoration on 3 July 2021 at Jubilee Gardens in London. It was published in issue 58 (September 2021) of *¡No Pasarán!* under the heading 'Commemoration salutes the Brigaders' internationalism.'

Poster for the Teatre del Raval (Barcelona) performance of Goodbye Barcelona. The design features the International Brigade flag: the Spanish Republic tricolour with the three-pointed red star of the Brigades. Courtesy of K.S. Lewkowicz.

The Brigades in theatre

Marlene Sidaway

January 2012
This inspirational production of Judith Johnson and Karl Lewkowicz's *Goodbye Barcelona* was rapturously received by regularly full houses at London's Arcola Theatre — and rightly so! The songs are a good mixture of rousing choruses, tender love songs, and amusingly cynical takes on the political situation in Spain. The story takes us smoothly from the struggle against the Blackshirts in Cable Street, through to the volunteers' difficult journey and arrival in Spain, the adjustment to an unfamiliar country, climate and diet and the difficulties of actually fighting a war with inadequate arms and forces. Woven through all of this are the two love stories of the young Sammy who volunteered, aged 18, and the Spanish girl Pilar whom he meets in Barcelona (Tom Gill and Katie Bernstein) and Sammy's mother Rebecca, who follows him to Spain as a nurse, and the anarchist Ernesto (Lucy Bradshaw and John Killoran).

Sammy's enthusiastic idealism provokes some lively debate with his fellow Brigaders, the cynical First World War veteran Jack and the dedicated communist George (Mark Meadows and Jack Shalloo). Laura Tebbutt's wonderful voice makes the words of La Pasionaria come to life, and other ensemble members of the cast give enthusiastic and tuneful support. The musicians, under the direction of Mark Smith, deserve a special mention too, and I'm sure I wasn't the only one wanting to join in with some of the rousing verses of 'The Internationale' and 'Jarama Valley' with such a wonderful accompaniment. The director, Karen Rabinowitz, and the whole of the design team have created a backdrop that evokes the times and passions of the 1930s, which the book and music of Judith Johnson and Karl Lewkowicz bring out so well.

Judith and Karl have been working on this project for six years, having been inspired originally by *The Guardian*'s supplement about the Brigaders in November 2000. They then interviewed volunteers Penny Feiwel, Jack Jones, Lou Kenton, Sam Lesser and Alun Menai Williams — and their inspiration for the project is acknowledged in Judith and Karl's programme notes. I congratulate them on a fantastic achievement, which does great credit to the Brigaders and all who supported the Spanish Republic. This is an ambitious work, combining love stories with the fate of the International Brigades and the doomed Republic. It eschews the usual clichés that the volunteers were communist dupes or that their idealism was betrayed by Stalin. Instead, we hear that they went to Spain without regrets and, in the words of poet Cecil Day Lewis that are sung in *Goodbye Barcelona*, because their 'open eyes could see no other way'.

January 2017
Performed brilliantly by the two actors, David Heywood as Clem 'Dare Devil' Beckett and Neil Gore as Christopher Caudwell (his real name was Christopher St John Sprigg,

or 'John Sprigg' in Spain), *Dare Devil Rides to Jarama* is a must-see play. The performances have warmth and humour and, with a poetic script, foot-tapping music and enthusiastic audience participation, it all makes for a lively and enjoyable evening. Louise Townsend's direction keeps the play whizzing along, shifting easily between humour, agitprop and tragedy. Poems by Caudwell and others are woven into the drama, among them Jack Lindsay's powerful 'On Guard for Spain', and David Kirkpatrick's songs are guaranteed to stay in the head for many days to come; all this, and at the same time it's a lesson to those unfamiliar with the story of the anti-fascist war in Spain — a seminal event in the history of the 20th century. David Heywood captures Beckett's dash and glamour, while Neil Gore not only plays Caudwell but also wrote the play himself and gives impressive and truthful portraits of many other characters who feature in the story — everyone from Blackshirt leader Sir Oswald Mosley to Communist Party general secretary Harry Pollitt!

Beckett and Caudwell, so different in background and personality, form a bond of purpose that typified so many of those who volunteered to fight in the International Brigades during the Spanish Civil War. They had also been drawn to communism, as many other such unlikely bedfellows were during the terrible depression years of the 1930s and the social inequality that they produced. The first act gives us glimpses of that inequality, with conflicts involving privileged bosses and landowners, such as the 1932 mass trespass on Kinder Scoutfor the right to roam in open countryside, as well as efforts to form a trade union and demand better and safer working conditions.[72] Clem Beckett's politics were shaped by these struggles. We follow his personal journey from a blacksmith saved from unemployment by his unique skills to a champion speedway motorcyclist and rider on the 'Wall of Death.' Angered by the growing exploitation in the sport, including the rising death toll among untrained youngsters entering it, he forms a union for speedway riders. He is blacklisted as a result and takes his skills to the continent, including Germany, where he witnesses the rise of fascism.

The second act sees these two 'unlikely warriors' in Spain, united in the anti-fascist war and with each using their complementary skills: Beckett the fearless rider, mechanic and leader of men; Caudwell the wordsmith, inventor and technician. Together they go through training — with the frustrations of inappropriate armaments and ammunition — and endure boredom, hunger, exhaustion, triumph — and the ultimate sacrifice at Jarama in February 1937. The IBMT is proud to have commissioned this dazzling new play as part of our commemorations for the 80th anniversary of the formation of the International Brigades. The production has also been supported by many trade unions and other organisations and will surely bring the story of the International Brigades to new audiences. It has justly received rave reviews: 'quite simply the best political theatre produced for a long, long time,' said the *Morning Star*. *Dare Devil Rides to Jarama* will be touring again all over the country early in 2017. Make sure you see it.[73]

---

[72] Editor's note: See Mike Wild's chapter 'Rambling to Spain' in this volume.

[73] Editor's note: An audio play of *Dare Devil Rides to Jarama* has subsequently been

Marlene Sidaway is an actress and the president of the IBMT. She was the long-time partner of the late IB veteran and poet, David Marshall. The review of *Goodbye Barcelona* appeared in issue 31 (January 2012) of the *IBMT Newsletter*, while the review of *Dare Devil Rides to Jarama* appeared in issue 44 (January 2017) of the *IBMT Magazine*.

Actor David Heywood as Clem 'Dare Devil' Beckett in Dare Devil Rides to Jarama. Courtesy of Townsend Theatre Productions.

---

released by the Townsend Theatre Productions, available online.

Making history: an interview with Paul Preston

Professor Paul Preston was interviewed by Jim Jump on 8 March 2018 at the LSE.

You've never shied away from taking a partisan view of the Spanish Civil War and make no secret of your support for the Spanish Republic. Has that fundamental view changed at all over more than 40 years of scholarship?

First of all I would dispute that thinking the Spanish Republic was in the right and the Francoists were in the wrong is partisan. No-one, for example, would dream of accusing anyone of being partisan for writing in a way that was critical of Hitler. Yet, amazingly, to be critical of Franco can still invite accusations of bias. The reasons are obvious. They are about the way his reputation was enhanced during the Cold War. This meant he always enjoyed a good press, obviously in Spain, but also in Britain. But there is nothing much that has altered my view of Franco over all those years.

 In terms of the origins of the war, I can see more clearly now that the Republican politicians made mistakes. That was to be expected. They came into power facing horrendous problems, with no experience whatsoever. As for the internal politics of the Republic, there are all kinds of nuances that have shifted on my part. The idea that the POUM [Partido Obrero de Unificación Marxista] were hard-done-by victims doesn't last very long the more you read. While I'm deeply aware of the way that the POUM were smeared, I'm also aware that they did things that could very easily be construed as sabotage: pulling troops back from the front and so on. Last week I had an amazing three hours with a young Spaniard who is doing research on the Fifth Column of Franco supporters in the Republican zone, and the information he has on links between the POUM and the Fifth Column is just hair-raising. I'm looking forward to his PhD. I've also become much more critical of the anarchists and specifically of the *chequistas* who carried out extra-judicial executions, torture and imprisonment. They did immense damage to the Republic in terms of its possibility of securing foreign aid. Obviously the anarchists' view that they should be allowed to make their revolution is nuts. Short of being able to say to Franco: 'Can you just hold on for another five to six years until we've made the revolution and then we will go back to war?', it was just utterly unrealistic; ditto for the POUM.

 As far as certain individuals are concerned, if you take my book '*¡Comrades!*', which has portraits of various people, the person who comes out best is the socialist Indalecio Prieto. But now I've arrived at a different conclusion. Prieto was wonderful for the Republic until he got the hump for being excluded from the government in April 1938 when Prime Minister Juan Negrín took the not unreasonable view that he could not have a defeatist as his Minister of War. Prieto never forgave Negrín and accused him of being a puppet of the communists and so on. I've come to see that what Prieto was doing was preparing for a future following a Franco victory when you were never going to be able to survive in exile if you were known to be pro-communist. It didn't take me very long to reach the conclusion that Negrín's predecessor, Largo Caballero, was a total disaster, that he was an appallingly bad war leader. By contrast, over time my admiration for Juan Negrín has just grown and grown.

So, within the Republic, my views are now much more nuanced, much more critical, especially regarding the atrocities, even though these crimes are often unfairly pinned on the Republican authorities. No, they took place within the Republican zone where law and order had broken down. The idea that they were countenanced let alone encouraged by the Republican authorities is absolute nonsense.

Overall, looking at both sides in the war, I'm also much more ready to see good and bad on both sides. Not everyone on the Republican side was an angel; nor was everyone on the Francoist side a villain.

What about the International Brigades? When they came back from Spain they were denigrated and regarded with great suspicion. Now they're generally admired. Do you think historians like yourself have had any role in that transformation?

I would take no credit for any of that. I think that Richard Baxell is the person who should be taking credit, or Angela Jackson, Linda Palfreeman and other people who have done hard research. I have to say also that I'm amazed and full of admiration for what the IBMT has achieved. My *A Concise History of the Spanish Civil War* is dedicated to the International Brigades and that goes back to my friendship with people like Bill Alexander and Dave Marshall. I knew lots of them and had a wide-eyed, fan-like admiration for them. I always thought the whole idea of the International Brigades and their sacrifices and so on were just amazing, and of course I've tried to express that in my books.

There's still an awful lack of understanding of the Brigades as well. I'm thinking of people who want to say: 'They're just like the foreign jihadis.' Rubbish like that, along with some of the American research about the 'Comintern Army', has to be combated. I'm not a military historian, but the Brigades seem to have been used like shock troops that could be easily sacrificed, in much the same way as the Francoists used the Moors. As the war went on it became more difficult to rotate troops. But the International Brigades were harder done by than almost any other unit — taken out after a month in the field, told they'd have a week off and then two hours later they're back, that kind of thing. It makes me wonder what exactly was the attitude of the general staff of the Republic to them. I can't get a clear view of that, though they were clearly seen as dependable and politically committed.

What drew you to becoming a historian and to take a special interest in Spain and 20th century history?

I think it goes back to the fact that I was born in 1946 in Liverpool, which had been a

Paul Preston (second from left) listens to the general secretary of the Spanish Socialist Workers' Party, Felipe González (foreground), who would go on to serve as Spain's Prime Minister from 1982 to 1996 — the first Socialist to lead the country following Franco's death in 1975 and the subsequent transition to democracy. The photograph is from the launch of one of Preston's books in 1978 and was taken by a member of the publishing house. The other individuals are the historian Joaquín Romero Maura (far left) and the publisher Manuel Arroyo-Stephens (second from right). Courtesy of Paul Preston.

target during the Blitz. The surrounding areas had been badly bombed, including the house that I was brought up in by my grandparents. Luckily no-one was killed — it just so happened to be one night when they were all in an air-raid shelter. Growing up in the late 40s, the Blitz and the Second World War were on everybody's lips. As kids our games would be British versus Germans and we would all be running up and down the street being Spitfires and Messerschmitts.

When I was about 10 or 11, I began making Airfix aeroplane model kits. I got really hooked on the Second World War and started to read quite serious books about it. Then I was lucky enough to get a scholarship to Oxford. Being a scum of the earth working-class Scouser in Oxford wasn't very common in those days and it was actually a horrible experience. There are lots of wonderful things about Oxford. It's a lovely place to be, and the libraries are mind-boggling. You could go to lectures by some pretty amazing people — Isaiah Berlin was absolutely fantastic. But the teaching overall was diabolical. Also, there was hardly any contemporary history taught. There was enormous stress on Anglo-Saxon, medieval and British history and very little 20th century or European history. The nearest to what I wanted to do, which would have been the origins of the Second World War, was the origins of the First World War.

How did you begin studying the Spanish Civil War in particular?

After Oxford I did an MA at Reading University. It comprised two options. I did left-wing literature of the interwar period and the Spanish Civil War. The left-wing literature part was a doddle for me, because it was basically about books that I had been devouring for years. I was manically obsessed with the likes of John Steinbeck and his contemporaries. The Spanish Civil War was taught by Hugh Thomas, who in 1961 had written *The Spanish Civil War*. I'd read a couple of books, but didn't really understand anything. Thomas was, in his way, a brilliant teacher. He didn't really give a hoot, but was eccentric and amusing and there were only four of us on the course. It was a great experience, not least because of all the people Thomas knew and brought into the classes to talk to us. Thomas encouraged us especially to read the left-wing books. We were pushed into answering the basic question on the left — war or revolution. The book that had the biggest impact on me was Gerald Brenan's *The Spanish Labyrinth*, which I still think is a fabulous book. Subsequent research has questioned much of it, but it remains amazingly perceptive. Thomas' book too has many qualities. There are things in it that I would dispute. But every time I take it off the shelf I'm always tickled by the way he writes — it's very colourful — and I still think, despite the fact that much of it is from an English middle-class perspective, that it's a great book.

There was never any question about which side to be on, the Spanish Republic versus Franco — it was obvious who were the goodies and the baddies. That was not a question, even for Thomas. But there was an issue about whether the goodies were the anarchists and the Trotskyists and the baddies were the communists. That was the standard view at the time. So I read Gaston Leval and a whole pile of stuff on anarchists, collectivism, quite a lot on the POUM and so on. *The Grand Camouflage* by Burnett Bolloten was a big influence.

Is this when you realised that researching and writing about the Spanish Civil War might become your life's work?

There came a point, probably after about a term at Reading when I thought, this is great. I'd spent ages in Oxford thinking what the hell to do next, what to choose. But with the Spanish Civil War you don't have to choose. You get everything: Stalinism, Trotskyism, fascism, communism, Hitler, Mussolini. It's fabulous — and here I am nearly 50 years on and I still think that.

At Reading I also realised that I had to learn Spanish and I set about doing it in the daftest way possible, which was to read a book that I had to read, an unspeakable book, by Santiago Galindo, very pro-Franco. I read it with a dictionary and of course learnt a lot of Spanish along the way; not how to pronounce it, but I combined that with going out drinking with Colombian students in the bar and bit by bit I began to speak a few words. Then in 1969, I think it was the Easter holidays, I went to Spain for the first time, to a village called Arroyo de la Miel. By then I was hooked. My friends would go into Torremolinos for a rave, and I would go into the local village. In those days it was rare for a foreigner to learn Spanish, so a crowd would gather, and I would be trying to order things and saying '*tengo sed*' [I'm thirsty] and I'd go back to the bar the next day for a coffee and by then I could say '*tengo hambre*' [I'm hungry].

I decided I wanted to do a PhD and I went back to Oxford, supposedly to be supervised by Raymond Carr. I had read Carr's *Spain 1808–1939*, which I found very hard going and even now find pretty knotty. But he was in America most of the time. Carr let me down in many ways. I had this awful *contretemps* with him because I wanted to work on the direct origins of the civil war. I saw him before he went off and he told me: 'No, you can't do that.' He always got his students to study what he was interested in, and at the time he wanted someone to work on the Primo de Rivera dictatorship, which I started. I went to Madrid and began doing research, but I never got the hang of it. Funnily enough it's a topic that I'm now writing about, but there is a lot of material available now that wasn't then. I decided that what I wanted to write about were the right-wing conspirators, the people behind the conspiracy that led to the civil war. I did some quite useful work on them and then Carr came back and, in a very insensitive manner, says: 'You can't do that, find something else.' So I began looking at a group called the *mauristas*, the followers of Antonio Maura, who were key to the Primo de Rivera dictatorship. But I couldn't find my way around the archives. Then in 1971 there came a point, away from Carr, when I thought, to hell with this, I'm going to do what I want to do and started to study the Second Republic and that became my thesis and my first book.

By now I was way behind in my PhD and my grant had run out. I was having to earn a living in Madrid, but absolutely loving it. I was doing all kinds of things. I was a film extra in *Nicholas and Alexandra* and taught American students. In 1973 Hugh Thomas went on sabbatical and I had two years as a temporary lecturer at Reading as his replacement. Then in 1975 I was lucky enough to get a lectureship at Queen Mary College, University of London, on condition that I finished my PhD within a year. It was published as *The Coming of the Spanish Civil War* in 1978 and got a rave review by Carr in *The Observer*, which, I don't know, might even have been an apology of sorts.

One of the books you must have read early on in your studies is George Orwell's Homage to Catalonia, *which takes the side of 'revolution' over 'war', as you put it, and paints the Spanish Civil War as a conflict between two unappealing extremes who between them crush a noble people's revolution. Do you think Orwell's views, which tend to remove the Spanish Civil War from the context of the wider world war against fascism, are a factor in why the war in Spain is so rarely or poorly taught in schools?*

I don't think that is much to do with Orwell. The dominant figures in the historiography of the interwar period tend to be either British, American or German scholars and there is this notion that what's important is a line that goes from London to Paris with a bit of a dip to Rome and then to Berlin and Moscow. Spain doesn't even come into it. That is partly because these people aren't specialists. Just to cope with the hard detail of British foreign policy, German foreign policy, French, Italian, Russian foreign policy is a monumental task. Yet the Spanish Civil War is effectively the first battle in the Second World War, and appalling mistakes were made in British foreign policy at the time.

As I put it in *A Concise History of the Spanish Civil War*, the British ruling classes put their class prejudices ahead of their strategic interests. It was Churchill who went from class prejudice to strategic interests. He kept changing his mind and ended up, from having been a fervent Franco supporter to being a supporter of the Republic. That failure on the part of the ruling classes might explain something about how British historians see the war in Spain. But for the most part they're not really that interested. You need to be a historian of Spain to start seeing it and particularly to be a historian of the international dimension of the Spanish Civil War. For instance, the conventional wisdom is that the Germans and Italians intervened in Spain because of ideological solidarity and in order to try out weaponry. I don't think that's true. What they were doing is seeing how far they could challenge British and French hegemony and change the international balance of power. This comes out at a meeting early in the war between Franco, Göring and Mussolini, when Göring effectively says to Mussolini: 'Come on, we've got to hurry up. There is no way the British and French are going to carry on letting us do this.'

You've recently published a couple of very strong critiques of Homage to Catalonia.[74] *What's the reason for this?*

One of my constant beefs is that people read one book, usually *Homage to Catalonia*, and think they have the right to pontificate about the Spanish Civil War. Yet Orwell is only in Spain for six months. The idea that he's totally honest isn't sustained by a detailed reading of his book. He says himself that his Spanish was appalling and his Catalan was non-existent, yet he relates in detail conversations that he could only have had in Catalan. What he actually witnessed and describes, the excrement in the trenches, the rusty cans, the lack of food, the wasted bread, the mud in your boots, all of that is brilliant, absolutely superb reporting. What it was actually like to be on the streets of Barcelona during the May Days is also great.

The political interpretation, however, is utterly inappropriate in many ways. Orwell leaves Spain in June 1937 and his book is published the following year. In it he's saying things which are taken by readers to explain why the Republic loses the war nearly two years after Orwell left Spain. That's simply not valid. What I've discovered recently is that in 1940 Orwell, as a journalist, is introduced to Juan Negrín, who is in exile in London, and they have a long series of conversations. But Orwell doesn't mention his links with the POUM. He keeps that quiet and years later when Negrín

---

[74] Editor's note: See Paul Preston, 'Lights and Shadows in George Orwell's *Homage to Catalonia*', *Bulletin of Spanish Studies* (2017).

finds out he is shocked. Negrín is a very reasonable person, but he ends up saying that, if Orwell had been honest with him, their relations might have been different. However, in 1943 Orwell writes this long article, 'Looking Back on the Spanish Civil War,' which is actually very good — and very different to his book. It clearly reflects his conversations with Negrín.

Another discovery I've made is a letter in December 1938 from Orwell to Frank Jellinek, an Austrian sociologist who had been in Spain. Orwell confesses that most of what he wrote in *Homage to Catalonia* about the POUM he didn't believe. He thought they were wrong at the time and he thinks they are wrong now, but he felt he had to write what he did in the spirit of fair play. After the Second World War, Orwell becomes very anti-communist and he writes *Animal Farm* and *1984*. He also corrects *Homage to Catalonia*, but surprisingly, given what he has learnt from Negrín and what he really thinks about the POUM, he only makes relatively small changes. One of my conclusions is that, even though Orwell knows he was wrong about many things in *Homage to Catalonia*, he doesn't make the necessary corrections because those things he wrote in 1938 have by now aligned themselves with what his anti-communist readers are thinking during the Cold War.

Do you regard the film Land and Freedom *in much the same way as Orwell's memoir?*

If you know nothing about the Spanish Civil War, the Ken Loach film is a great movie. I can remember seeing it in Spain after it first came out in 1995 in a cinema full of Spaniards who were weeping with emotion. They don't tend to do this in Britain, but the audience stood up at the end and clapped for about 10 minutes. There are some wonderful scenes in the film, for instance when Loach gets real village smallholders to pretend what it would be like at the time and to act out the issues of land reform; that is absolutely brilliant cinema. The film captures something very important and the framing of it is stunning, with at the start the old man, who is this hero of humanity, dying in Thatcherite Britain and then at the end the Spanish earth being tossed on his coffin. But there are things that I'm not so sure about: the American who shows up in jackboots is shocking, even though I accept there were some International Brigaders used as internal police in the Republic's army; also, the depiction of the POUM volunteers as a group of really groovy, beautiful people. I wrote once, and this made some people upset, that this is Cliff Richard's 'We're all going on a summer holiday' meets the Spanish Civil War. But my main argument against the film, as well as with Orwell's book, is that, if you knew nothing about the Spanish war, you would come away from the film thinking the Republic was somehow defeated by Stalin and not by Franco, Hitler, Mussolini and the British establishment.

The Spanish Civil War continues to cast a long shadow over Spanish society. Yet other countries suffered a comparable collapse in the 20th century and all seem to have recovered better than Spain. What is it about the Spanish experience that is so different?

That's a really easy question to answer. In Germany, Italy, Japan and other countries the fascist or the extreme rightist experience is brought to an end by external defeat. In countries like France, once the occupation had come to an end, they could go back to the sort of democracy they had had before. In Germany there is a very serious government-sponsored process of denazification, overseen by the occupying powers. The same is true of Italy and Japan. That doesn't happen in Spain. Franco literally gets away with murder during and after the Second World War because the eyes of the world are on other things. Franco's links with the Axis are quietly forgotten. During the Cold War, when it's believed that Western Europe is at any minute about to be invaded by the Soviet Union, Franco becomes a better bet than wanting the Republic back. After all, the Republicans are allegedly the puppets of Moscow. This is done even though there is a degree of distaste on the part of much of the British establishment, and of course the Labour Party doesn't cover itself with glory vis-à-vis Franco, because Ernest Bevin as Foreign Secretary goes along with the establishment line.

Franco has, from 1937 in those areas where he's already in charge and from 1939 in all of Spain, total control of essentially a terrorist regime. There is a huge investment in terror, a viciously repressive state apparatus and total control of the education system and the media. Until his death there is a great national brainwashing. He dies in 1975 and there's a very complex process until elections in June 1977. In those 18 months, and even indeed for a long time after, no-one wants to rock the boat. There is fear of another civil war or another dictatorship. The left goes easy and doesn't push for historical memory and recognition of what went on under Franco. The October 1977 Amnesty Law prevents any judicial proceedings against the perpetrators. There is also the fact that over those 40 years of dictatorship there are nearly three generations of people who've been taught that Franco was a wonderful man, that he saved Spain from the bloodthirsty hordes of Moscow. That doesn't go away when Franco dies; nor does it go away when there are democratic elections that bring in a very conservative and limited democracy.

The transition is a miracle under the circumstances, but the new democracy and the early governments are made up of Francoists. They're not going to start a process of counter brain-washing; that never happens. To this day there are many Spaniards brought up thinking Franco was a good thing, that the Republic was responsible for the civil war and so on. In the mid-1970s there were still many people who remembered the war. The women whose husbands, fathers, brothers and sons died in the war or were murdered are not going to say anything because they have lived in terror. Their children have been brought up in silence and they are told: 'Whatever you do, don't mention that we were Republicans,' or 'Don't speak Catalan in school.'

What might be a bit more difficult to explain is why this has gone on for so long. I can remember being asked in the late 1980s by a Spanish journalist how long the hatred would continue and I said confidently that it was all a matter of time and that time would heal everything. It has taken a hell of a lot longer. Perhaps it's not as burning an issue as it was when the Law of Historical Memory, for all its huge limitations, was passed in 2007.[75] But I think part of that is because of the economic crisis that followed. It's not really until the end of the 20th century when the grandchildren start asking questions and you get the movement for the recovery of historical memory and the push to find where the bodies of Franco's victims are buried. But there are problems. People are dying out. DNA testing costs a fortune, as do the excavations, and the new law makes no provision for any of that. Many municipalities are opposed to it and say that in any case they can't afford it. With the economic crisis and massive unemployment, people have more immediate problems.

You've always been a defender of the transition to democracy, saying just now that it was a miracle under the circumstances. But do you think that el pacto del olvido *[the pact of forgetting] and other shortcomings you've just alluded to have anything to do with some of Spain's current problems — the constitutional crisis centred on Catalonia, the political corruption scandals and the ongoing memory wars?*

The way those three issues intertwine is very complicated. For instance, there are people on the left who would be fervent advocates of exposing more of the crimes of Franco, but who are equally strong supporters of Prime Minister Mariano Rajoy for his hard line over Catalonia. That's not about the Spanish Civil War. Why is that? First of all there is a historic anti-Catalanism which has been stoked up by the government and the extreme right over the past 10 years. Some of the things you hear people saying in this regard are truly appalling. The generating of anti-Catalan sentiment is partly about masking corruption, but it's a two-way street, because there has also been massive corruption in Catalonia.

Where does the corruption come from? That's one of the things I'm struggling with at the moment. Corruption in Spanish politics goes back centuries. There is a notion, which used to be the case in Britain — but is less so all the time — that you go into public service for the public good. But you've only got to read the novels of Pérez Galdós to see that in Spain there is a huge tradition of corruption, that you go into public service for private gain. It's one of the ways in which you can survive. The corruption under Franco was rampant and actually a lot of recent research has shown how Franco was personally involved. If you'd asked me about this when I was writing

---

[75] Editor's note: This law, introduced under the Socialist administration of Prime Minister José Luis Rodríguez Zapatero, among other provisions, declared: that the judgements of Francoist tribunals were unjust (although it did not go as far as to overturn them); that the state would provide greater support for victims of Francoist repression and their descendants; that the government would aid in the identification and exhumation of mass graves; that Francoist commemorative symbols and insignia should be removed from public spaces; and that Spanish nationality would be awarded to International Brigade veterans without (as had previously been the case) requiring them to renounce their existing citizenships. However, the Law attracted criticism and controversy from both right and left, and more recent administrations have introduced further legislation to address the issue of historical memory.

my biography of him I would have said: 'Well, overall, Franco wasn't corrupt,' although I would have added: 'He didn't need to steal, because he thought it was all his anyway.' But now we know he was stealing as well. There were also mistakes made by the post-Franco democratic regime. There are specific legal issues, such as the law that allows the status of land to be changed and the powers that local mayors have been given to do that — which can lead to backhanders.

Given what you've just said, and what we saw with the independence referendum in Catalonia last October and the very heavy-handed response from Madrid, do you think Spain can be regarded as a mature democracy?

I don't think it's easy to make comparisons. Just think about the antics of politicians in this country over Brexit. Don't get me wrong — I am absolutely appalled by the things that have gone on in Spain, but I am absolutely appalled too by the things that are going on here. I always used to say when talking to Spaniards that the difference between Spain and Britain was that we have this concept of being able to agree to disagree. That simply does not exist in Spain. Spaniards are Manichean: those who are not with me are against me. But that's true here now because of Brexit. I am an absolutely fervent remainer, but I could also rant and rave for some time about the faults of the European Union, which is a fat bureaucracy that doesn't listen to people, and that's part of the problem.

Paul Preston addresses the 2016 International Brigade annual commemoration at Jubilee Gardens in London. Courtesy of the photographer, Andrew Wiard.

I'm writing a book at the moment, which is supposedly a history of Spain from 1874 to the present day. I don't want simply to do a resumé of everything I've written, so, after much thought, I've come up with what I see as the three themes of Spanish history during that period. They are corruption, the incompetence of the political class, and the consequential breakdown in social cohesion. The title is *A People Betrayed*. I'm not half way through, but sometimes I feel I'm writing an editorial for *The Guardian*. It's exactly what we're living through here.⁷⁶

Just to go back to your question, if we start trying to compare Spain with other democracies within the European Union, then what about Bulgaria, Romania, Hungary or Poland? Spain has monumental problems, but name me a country that hasn't.

Finally, given that the Spanish Civil War saw the agonising defeat of the Spanish Republic, terrible repression and four decades of brutal dictatorship, has there been any emotional cost to you personally from your scholarship? Has it affected your view of humanity, or can you detach yourself from all of the horrors that you've studied?

That's a really good question. It's certainly the case, for instance, to think of an extreme case, when I was writing '*The Spanish Holocaust*', Gabrielle, my wife, on numerous occasions would come home and I would literally be weeping. I mean that book is horrific. How the hell can people do such things? I don't know how I wrote it. I do not know how people can read it. I only put stuff in the book that I could prove, as it were, but I had many people writing to me at the time. To take one example, a woman wrote to me and she said: 'When I was three, the Falangists came and they threw us all out of the house and then they put my parents and my older brother back and they set fire to the house and left me on the street to watch.' Can you imagine? When *The Spanish Holocaust* was shortlisted for the Samuel Johnson Prize and the papers were talking about which book was likely to win, the other book along with mine that was considered one of the favourites was one by Steven Pinker, arguing that humanity is just getting nicer and nicer and I'm thinking: 'How could you possibly think that?'

I still get very angry. I'm absolutely fierce on the mistakes of British foreign policy and I learnt a lot while writing *The Last Days of the Spanish Republic*. One of the things that I really can't get over is that any general book on the Spanish Civil War sees General Casado, who led the *coup* against Negrín at the end of war, as a good thing because he supposedly heroically stopped the communists from taking over. That's nonsense. The invariably cited source for this is Casado's memoirs, which are completely made up — just like the fake books of Walter Krivitsky and Alexander Orlov. As I tried to show, Casado's motivation was much more selfish. He was hoping to be

---

⁷⁶ Editor's note: This book was subsequently published as Paul Preston, *A People Betrayed: A History of Corruption, Political Incompetence and Social Division in Modern Spain 1874-2018* (London: William Collins, 2020)

able to stay in Spain, to keep his rank, keep his pension and so on. At the end of the war what happens is the anarchists, who are part of Casado's junta, do absolutely nothing to facilitate evacuations and save lives. But Casado and his friends all get away to England, including the anarchist *chequistas* who were responsible for murdering hundreds if not thousands of people in Madrid. The British government lets them in, though they didn't want Negrín, an internationally respected physiologist, a man who speaks eight languages, who is as cultured as it is possible to imagine. I've found documents from Foreign Secretary Lord Halifax basically saying: 'We don't want that hooligan Negrín here,' yet they allowed in these killers and set them up. One even gets a restaurant in Regent Street. It just leaves you frothing at the mouth with indignation.

So, has all this had an emotional impact? It's probably driven me into reading detective stories and watching sit-coms on TV. After the horrors of my work I don't have much emotional room for anything but light entertainment, so that's an impact. I've also learnt a lot about politics and about relationships, but as a historian your career should teach you about life.

Professor Sir Paul Preston is one of the best-known and most decorated historians of modern Spain, having authored over a dozen books on the Spanish Civil War, Francoism, and the transition to democracy, including *The Spanish Holocaust: Inquisition and Extermination in Twentieth Century Spain* (2011) and *A People Betrayed: A History of Corruption, Political Incompetence and Social Division in Modern Spain, 1874-2018* (2020). He is Professor emeritus at the LSE. This interview was published in issue 48 (May 2018) of *¡No Pasarán!*

My Pyrenees crossing inspired by Nat Cohen and Laurie Lee

Dan Carrier

They came out of the mist and were as surprised to find me as I was to run into them. I was 1,500 metres above sea level, on the cusp of a rocky outcrop. The Spanish border police fired rapid questions: I understood little, but my dishevelled state spoke volumes. After explaining why I was wandering through the Pyrenees, and after they had checked I was in a fit state to reach my destination, they pointed into the fog behind them and told me it would take around six hours walking.

I had set out on a week-long journey. My aim was to retrace the steps taken by the British volunteers who joined the Spanish Republican army to fight fascism during the country's civil war of 1936 to 1939. I had been inspired by my family's involvement — my great uncle Nat Cohen was one of the first of 40,000 volunteers who saw that the war was a precursor to the larger conflict that would soon engulf Europe. He left Stepney on a bicycle in June 1936 to take part in the Workers' Olympiad. Due to be held in Barcelona, it was an alternative competition for those who did not want to go to the Berlin Olympics. He arrived just a few days before General Franco's *coup*: instead of turning round and going home, he joined a workers' militia and was in a small group who tried to retake the island of Mallorca from Italian troops. He then helped set up an English-speaking unit, called the Tom Mann Centuria, which was to become a precursor to the International Brigades. He was shot in the knee and invalided home and, when he returned, the streets of the East End turned out. He was pictured in the *Daily Mirror* being greeted by hundreds of people, with his new Spanish wife Ramona.[77] Later, Arnold Wesker wrote about him in his seminal play *Chicken Soup with Barley*, which contains the line: 'That Nat Cohen is a terror.'

In the Pyrenees I was retracing the route taken by Laurie Lee, author of *Cider with Rosie* (1959), who had as a 23-year-old travelled through France to join in the fight. The British and the French governments had set up a non-intervention pact. It meant volunteers, such as Lee, had to sneak over the border. Lee describes his time in Spain in the book *A Moment Of War* (1991). Where the Spanish police stopped me was the same area Lee was taken to by French shepherds under the cover of night. I had been walking for three days, a similar length of time it took Lee to do the same stretch. I was following well-marked paths on a route map: Lee had tried, and failed, to find a guide. Instead, he writes: 'I knew I simply had to go up, over and south. Behind me, as I climbed the gentle slopes, the foothills fell away to Perpignan and the sea, while the steep bulk of the Pyrénées Orientales filled the sky with their sunlit peaks.'

His journey started on 5 December 1936 and was to face some bitter weather.

---

[77] See Marshall Mateer's essay 'Ramona: The militiawoman who settled in England.'

I walked out in June 2008 and my admiration of his achievement increased. Even in summer, the Pyrenees can be unforgiving to the single traveller. When I was greeted by the border guides, I had not seen a soul for 48 hours. I was cold, stricken by bouts of vertigo, and worried I had got hopelessly lost in the mists. I had taken one wrong turn when I was at the top of a peak. The map proved to be little help: the paths on the paper did not seem to marry those on the ground in front of me. I decided to turn back. I found the spot where I had taken a turning instead of heading upwards. My path sent me along the side of a mountain, through a beech wood, and as I came out the other side, I saw the town of Las Illas nestling in a valley, which was my first stop.

Las Illas is a tiny hamlet that saw nearly 500,000 refugees pour through it at the end of the war. I stayed in an inn that hosted the Catalan president during the Spanish Republic, Lluís Companys, as he fled. I reached the inn and crashed out, exhausted. Lee's first night was less comfortable. He slept outdoors, and he was caught out in a December blizzard. 'Looking down, the foothills had disappeared and been replaced by a blanket of swirling vapour,' he writes. 'The shining peak of Canigou began to switch on and off like a lighthouse . . . then the wind rose to a thin-edged wail, and I felt the first stinging bite of snow.' Lee stumbled, fortuitously, across a 'rough little stone built shelter. It was half in ruins, and there was nothing inside it but straw, but I suppose it may have saved my life.'

The last day on the mountains was tough. My knees were agony, and the weather, for the morning and much of the afternoon, atrocious. It was here I met the Spanish police and was given the fillip of knowing I was nearly there. Then, the wind got up more fiercely than before and the skies cleared. I was still a good three hours away, with a valley to scramble down, but I could see the sun shining on my destination. I took a train to Figueres and laid flowers at a memorial to the Brigaders who stayed there. Lee eventually made it to the Spanish border, but was greeted with suspicion. He too made it to Figueras, but it was not long before he was arrested. No one believed he had walked over the Pyrenees in winter carrying just a violin and a saucepan, as his memoirs suggest. After a 50-odd mile walk of my own, without having to dodge border guards, my respect for Lee and the sacrifice he and his comrades were willing to make for the progressive political philosophy they believed in was underlined.

Dan Carrier is a journalist for the *Camden New Journal* and the great-nephew of International Brigader Nat Cohen. This account was first published in issue 21 (September 2008) of the *IBMT Newsletter*.

We must remember them by building a better world

Owen Jones

They came from Dundee, Hull and Glasgow; from the mines of the South Wales valleys, from Northumberland and Dumfries: over 2,000 from Britain, Ireland and the Commonwealth. They left the comforts of peace, the love of their families and friends for the horror, tedium and carnage of war, because they knew that Spain's fight was Europe's fight and they knew it was humanity's fight as well.

The boot of fascism was stamping on the neck of democracy across our continent of Europe. In Italy, a decade before, Benito Mussolini's fascist bands had roamed the countryside, pouring castor oil down the necks of peasants who organised for justice and crushing trade unionists at the behest of big business, before finally seizing Rome. In Germany, three years before, the most powerful labour movement on earth had been crushed virtually overnight, Hitler's Nazis already unleashing a campaign of terror against Jews, socialists, communists and trade unionists. Two years before Spain erupted in civil war, the fascists had marched on France's national assembly and rioted, conspiring to overthrow democracy and freedom. The lights were going out across Europe — and then the generals rose against the democratically elected government of Spain.

Those who fought in Spain didn't just have courage, they had foresights as well. The contemptible appeasers of London and Paris wanted a deal with Hitler to drive the Nazis eastward to the Soviet Union. But these wise, courageous Brits knew that war was coming, and not just any war: a war of annihilation and destruction unprecedented in the history of humanity. While the appeasers did nothing, which paved the way to that murderous calamity, the Brigaders wanted to stop fascism while there was still time on the clock. But the Western democracies abandoned Spain to its fate. They let the fascist flames of Germany and Italy unleash terror against the people of Spain. They stood back as Guernica was razed to the ground.

While the British and French governments betrayed the Spanish people and the cause of democracy, these brave British people did not. They were there for Spain in its time of need, over 500 of them never returning to the families and lovers they had left behind. Those fallen heroes died not just for democracy and freedom. They died not just for those in Spain — but died for all of us. Like Alfred Lichfield from Gateshead who died at Gandesa, James Walsh from Liverpool killed at Jarama, James Bentley from Hull at Calaceite and Thomas Flynn from Glasgow at Chimorra — these young men never made it back. They remain heroes for all of us here today. The roar of those lions echoes through the generations. They are the giants on whose shoulders we all stand. And they are an example to us all today.

They teach that democracy and all the freedoms our ancestors fought for at such cost and at such sacrifice must never be taken away from us; that we must never give in to those who peddle hatred and those who tell us to hate and to despise. And whether it be the Kurds who defend Kobani from the terror of ISIS, whether it be the Greeks who confront the fascism of the Golden Dawn, the spirit of those young men lives on today.

It is our duty and responsibility not just to remember what they fought against but also what they fought for. We owe it to them to build a different world, a world free of the oppression, injustice and poverty that scar the world in which we live. We owe it to them to build a different sort of society based on equality and justice and free from these scourges. That should be the great legacy in part that they left behind, that they bequeathed to all of us. Let's keep that struggle alive. Let's keep the flame burning that they so proudly lit all those generations ago. In the words of W.H. Auden:

> What's your proposal? To build the just city? I will.
> I agree. Or is it just the suicide pact, the romantic
> Death? Very well, I accept, for
> I am your choice, your decision. Yes, I am Spain.

Solidarity. *¡No pasarán!*

> Owen Jones is a political commentator and campaigner. He is a regular contributor to *The Guardian* and the *New Statesman*. His books include *Chavs: The Demonization of the Working Class* (2011) and *This Land: The Struggle for the Left* (2020). This transcript of Owen Jones's 4 July 2015 speech to the IBMT annual commemoration in Jubilee Gardens, London, was published in issue 40 (September 2015) of the *IBMT Newsletter*.

Witness as Hero

Francesca Beard

i.
This is for you,
Who set down pints,
Gave notice,
Traded in guitar, bike, season tickets,
Five-a-side in the rain,
Friday night at the pictures with Annie, Sally, Jane,
For Spain.

For how to clean a gun,
Hola amigo, garlic,
Earth for a pillow,
Night sweats, broken thread,
The man you called brother,
Bleeding out, warm and wet,
On a bed of rough grass and sheep droppings,
The knowledge of what it is to be human
From the point of view of an animal.

This is for you,
Who came back,
Tried to get a job with your red score sheet,
Adios amigo.
Gammy leg put you in goal,
But you're not a safe pair of hands.
Can't stand the roar of the crowd from the stands.
See Janey on the street, pushing a pram,
But war movies don't do it for you anymore and
Though Sunday roast is still the same
You, you have changed.

This is for you, who gave your all,
Came back to find
Life goes on,
Truth's a moveable feast and
Honour, freedom, solidarity
Are words that can be used by anybody,
Passed around, bartered like currency.

This is for you, not ideal.
This is for you, witness to the real.

ii.
And on a day like other days,
Tea-warmed, toast-crumbed, hazy,
We shake open the newspaper,
Read the headlines, lazy.

And on a day like other days,
Hazy, toast-crumbed, tea-warmed,
We scroll down bbc.com,
Digest the facts and yawn,

And on a day like all the rest,
Tea-warmed, hazy, toast-crumbed,
We watch the war on breakfast news,
In comfort, safe and numb.
There was a day, another time,
Another world at war,
And in the word 'democracy',
A truth worth fighting for.

So you stood up to volunteer,
You left your ease behind,
You made your way across a sea
To stand upon a line.

You left behind your families
You left behind your homes
You left behind your safety-nets
And everything you'd known.

You went towards the furnaces
Of brutal, bloody war
You went because your open eyes
Could see, could not ignore.

And in the balances you placed
The sum of all your weight
One man can make the difference in
A tug of war with fate.
And some of you came back from Spain

And some of you could not
But everyone who went to Spain
You will not be forgot.

For everyone who hears the tale
Will hear it and be marked
And everyone who knows your tale
Will know it by their heart.

And hope, it is an ember
We breathe it into flame
And by that light remember
Your courage and your fame.

> Francesca Beard is a performance poet and educator. This poem was published in issue 33 (September 2012) of the *IBMT Newsletter* after Francesca recited it at the IBMT Jubilee Gardens commemoration in July 2012.

Index of Contributors

Bill Alexander 121
Peter Anderson 11
Mike Arnott 43
Paula Bartley 101
Richard Baxell 23
Bob Beagrie 69
Francesca Beard 205
Chris Birch 146
Simon Breden 114
Ronan Burtenshaw 183
Dan Carrier 201
Christopher Caudwell 46
Nathan Clark 72
Bob Cooney 74
Geoff Cowling 127
Graham Davies 33
Mark Derby 82
John Dunlop 175
Sheena Evans 111
Frank Farr 90
Connie Fraser 155
Peter Frost 132
Steve Fullarton 77
Helen Graham 167
Daniel Gray 141
Christopher Hall 104
Jerry Harris 79
Michael D Higgins 159
Angela Jackson 125
Owen Jones 203
Jim Jump 98, 165, 170, 190
Sam Lesser 61
Christine Lindey 107
Ken Loach 140
Sarah Lonsdale 95
David Lowe 82
Herminio Martínez 129
Marshall Mateer 57, 135
David Merin 88
Jimmy Moon 50
Joshua Newmark 14
Manus O'Riordan 38

Paul Philippou 47
John Pilger 172
Adrian Pole 149
Margaret Powell 86
Paul Preston 181, 190
Fraser Raeburn 138
Cyril Sexton 67
Marlene Sidaway 186
Ajmal Waqif 64, 117
Mike Wild 30

Select Index

Abyssinia *see* Ethiopia
Addy, Madge 16, 18, 127-128
Aid Spain 31, 43, 95, 96, 98, 104, 109, 122
Aid to Spanish Youth Committee 147-148
Albrighton, James 34
Aldecoa, Emilio 141-144
Alexander, Bill 17, 27, 36, 121, 124, 138, 191
Allen, Jim 178
Álvarez del Vayo, Julio 75, 129
Angus, John 26, 27
Appeal for Amnesty in Spain 122
Aragón 16, 53, 57-60, 69, 72, 82-83, 86-87, 91, 133, 135-136, 165-166, 170, 173, 177
Army of Africa 34, 65, 168
Arroyo-Stephens, Manuel 189
Artists' International Association 17, 107
Asociación de Amigos de las Brigadas Internacionales 44
Asturias 51, 101, 118
Attlee, Clement 61, 99, 101, 102, 183
Auden, W.H. 159, 204
Avgherinos, Costas 47
Avgherinos, Hercules 47
Avner, Sid 60, 136
Azcárate, Pablo 129
Balchowsky, Eddie 79
Baldwin, Stanley 96, 101, 141
Barcelona 29, 51, 57-60, 78, 84, 87, 92, 95, 103-105, 112, 126, 133, 135, 143-144, 164, 165-166, 173-174, 177, 179, 185, 186, 188, 195, 201
Barinaga, Sabino 141, 143
Barry, Jack 60, 136
Basch, Anna-Marie 83, 85
Basque Children's Committee 129
Basque *niños* 17-18, 95-97, 122, 129, 136, 141-142, 144
Bates, Ralph 60
Bates, Winifred 121
Baxell, Richard 15, 19, 23-29, 166, 191
Bebb, Cecil 33-34

Beckett, Clem 30, 31, 186-188
Beevor, Antony 19, 72, 167-169
Belchite 40, 55, 63, 69, 79, 167, 173
Belfast 38-41, 157
Bell, Julian 108, 112
Bell, Vanessa 111, 112
Bentley, E.C. 11
Bentley, James 203
Berlin, Isaiah 191
Bernstein, Katie 186
Bevin, Ernest 130, 196
Bilbao 17, 33, 80, 95-97, 105, 141, 143-145
Bilbao, José 141-143
Binder, Pearl 107
Bing, Geoffrey 183
Birchall, Frederick T. 11
Black, John 175
Blackshirts 31, 43, 104, 186
Boland, Eavan 162
Bolloten, Burnett 168, 193
Boswell, James 107
Bowler, Kitty 133
Boyd, Joe 39, 40
Bradshaw, Lucy 186
Branson, Clive 18, 107, 109, 170-171
Brenan, Gerald 151-153, 192
Brent, Jack 122, 130
Brewer, Jim 35
British Battalion 15-17, 21, 24-27, 35-36, 39, 44, 46, 47-48, 53, 61, 65, 67-68, 69-71, 76-77, 82, 91, 102, 105-106, 109, 121, 124, 132-133, 138, 146, 148, 155, 162, 170, 172, 177, 184
British Union of Fascists *see* Blackshirts
British Workers' Sports Federation 16, 30, 71
Brooksbank, Mary 44
Brown, Isabel 111, 112
Browne, Felicia 57, 59, 109
Brunete 16, 25, 34, 36, 44, 61, 63, 67-68, 167, 177
Bruzzichesi, Ave 21
Buhle, Paul 48
Burke, Edward 61

Burns, Robert 46
Bush, Frank 74
Caballero, Largo 191
Cable Street *see* Jewish East End
Camacho, Marcelino 123
Cambridge 27, 144-145
Cameron, Jim 122
Cardiff 34, 35, 95, 99
Carmody, Jim 39
Carr, Raymond 151, 193-194
Casado, Segismundo 168, 199
Casajuana, Carles 37
Catholic Church 38, 43, 161, 162
Caudwell, Christopher 46, 186-187
Centre for Civil War Studies 153
Centro Ibérico 181
Cerva, Alfons 149
Chamberlain, Neville 101, 109, 133
Chambers, Arthur 106
Cheetham 30, 31
Chicago 12, 79, 80, 81, 119
Chilvers, Thomas 55
Christie, Stuart 19, 181-182
Christodoulou, Christos 48
Clarke, Joe 61
Clarkson, Adrienne 28
Clive, Lewis 69, 70
CNT-FAI 105, 109, 181
Cockburn, Claud 57
Cohen, Nat 18, 57-60, 135-136, 201
Coles, Bill 35
Comintern *see* Communist International
Communist International 14, 24
Communist Party of Cyprus 47
Communist Party of France 176
Communist Party of Germany 24
Communist Party of Great Britain 15, 23, 30, 35, 41, 47, 60, 82, 101, 104, 107, 111, 114, 115, 132, 133, 135, 138 146, 147, 176, 177, 189
Communist Party of Ireland 39, 163
Communist Party of Spain 46, 57, 106, 181
Communist Party of the USA 79
Companys, Lluís 206
Condon, Bob 35
Condor Legion 125, 141
Connolly, James 40
Cooney, Bob 15, 16, 43, 69, 70, 74, 76, 140
Copeman, Fred 36
Cornford, John 57, 60, 61
Courtenay, Tom 132
Criddle, Edgar 115
Crome, Dr Len 28, 29, 44, 145
Crossey, Ciarán 39
Crowdy, Rachel 102
Crowe, Victoria 112-113
Cunningham, Jock 27, 43, 61, 62, 65
Cyprus 23, 28, 47-49
Dąbrowski, Jarosław 186
Daily Worker 21, 25, 41, 57, 100, 127, 132-133, 135, 179
Darton, Patience 133
Davies, Tom 35
Davies, W.J. 35
Day Lewis, Cecil 186
de la Cierva, Ricardo 153
del Castillo Sáez de Tejada, José 33
Derry 38-39, 157
Dickenson, Ted 65
Dickson, Archibald 98
Digges, Alec 122, 123, 146
Dimitrov Battalion 24, 65-66
Donnelly, Charles 41, 66, 162
Doyle, Bob 40, 159
Droescher, Werner 59
Dublin 39, 40, 164
Duchess of Atholl 101
Dunbar, Malcolm 69-70
Durán Jordà, Frederic 112
Ebro 15, 16, 17, 39, 41, 44, 68, 72, 75-76, 78, 83, 84, 85, 105, 121, 122, 125, 168, 172-173, 177, 183
Economides, Michael 15, 48, 75
Éditions Ruedo Ibérico 18, 149-154
Edwards, Bob 105
Edwards, Frank 40
Elliott, Lon 21, 121, 122
Ellis, Richard 96, 112
Estruch, Pepe 129, 130
Ethiopia 12, 176
Farr, Frank 90-92
Feiwel, Penny 186
Fernández, Aurora 82
Ferriter, Diarmuid 161
Figueras 175, 177, 202
Fimmen, Edo 99

Fitton, James 107
Fleming, Diarmaid 39
Flynn, Thomas 203
Foulkes, William 35
Fox, Ralph 61
Fox, Tony 69
Fraga Iribarne, Manuel 123
Francis, Hywel 33, 36
Franco, Francisco 12, 13, 14-19, 33-34, 75, 95, 102, 121-124, 149-154, 190-200
Frieze, J.S. 115
Fry, Harold 65, 115
Fry, Roger 107
Fullarton, Steve 16, 27, 77-78
Gálicz, Jânos 66
Gallagher, Willie 59
Gallego, Antonio 141-145
Gallego, José 141-145
Gallie, Donald 43
Gambon, Michael 132
Gandesa 16, 40, 44, 74, 75, 77, 78, 79, 92, 173, 203
García Lorca, Federico 115, 129, 130, 149, 151-153, 201
García Montero, Luis 152-153
García, Miguel 181
Garrett, Molly 129
Gellhorn, Martha 173-174
General Gal *see* Gálicz, Jânos
General Walter *see* Świerczewski, Karol
Georgakas, Dan 48
Georgiou, Yiacoumis 47
Germany 11-13, 14, 35, 51, 57, 80, 103, 108, 109, 129, 138, 161, 176, 178, 183, 187, 196
Gibson, Ian 149, 152-153
Gilchrist, Alan 122
Gill, Tom 186
Gillies, William 102
Gilmour, William 139
Glasgow 43-45, 98, 139, 181-182, 203
Gollancz, Victor 114
González, Bene 142
González, Felipe 189
Gore, Neil 186, 187
Göring, Hermann 194
Gourlay, David 111

Graham, Helen 19, 23, 165-166, 167-169
Grant, Donald 82
Gray, Dan 18, 43, 141-145
Green, George 172
Green, Martin 172
Green, Nan 83, 121, 122, 130
Gregory, Walter 12-13, 69
Grimau, Julián 123
Gross, Harry 67
Guernica 17, 33, 96, 102, 115, 132, 141, 144, 173, 177, 203
Guerricabeitia Martínez, José *see* Éditions Ruedo Ibérico
Haden-Guest, Carmel 115
Halifax, Lord 200
Hansen, Thorkild 128
Harris, Sydney 79-81
Haughey, James Patrick 41-42
Hemingway, Ernest 14, 133
Heywood, David 186-188
Hiddlestone, Reg 105
Hilliard, Robert 39-41, 159
Hinks, Joe 61
Hitler, Adolf 11-13, 14, 18, 31, 35, 62, 109, 122, 132, 141, 161, 166, 176, 190, 193, 196, 203
Holland, James 109
Holst, Wilhelm 127-128
Home Guard 17, 132-134, 139
Horton, Percy 107
Howson, Gerald 125
Huddar, Gopal Mohan 23
Hunter, Hughie 39
IBA *see* International Brigade Association
Ibárruri, Dolores 37, 45
IBMT *see* International Brigade Memorial Trust
ILP *see* Independent Labour Party
Imperial War Museum 48, 111, 125-126
Independent Labour Party 15, 40, 59, 104-106, 128
International Brigade Association 112, 121-124, 146, 147-148, 171, 176
International Brigade Committee for Children 117

International Brigade Memorial Trust 13, 14, 18, 20, 28, 29, 38, 84, 159, 170, 172, 174, 187, 191
International Transport Workers' Federation 99
Ioannou, Toula 47
IRA. *See* Irish Republican Army
Ireland 14-15, 23-27, 39-42, 159-164
Ireland, John 67
Irish Republican Army 40
Italy 14, 17, 80, 84, 103, 161, 176, 178, 196, 203
Jackson, Angela 18, 127-128, 159, 166, 191
Jackson, George 183
Japan 165, 176, 196
Jarama 16, 25, 27, 34, 35, 39, 40, 44, 45, 46, 63, 64-66, 68, 76, 106, 112-113, 115, 122, 133, 156, 162, 170, 173-174, 177, 186-188, 203
Jewish East End 15, 23, 61, 104, 186
Jirku, Gusti 83
Joannou, Jimis 48
Johnson, Judith 186
Jolly, Douglas 16, 17, 82-85
Jones, Brinley 35
Jones, David Joseph 35
Jones, Jack 27, 98, 100, 172, 186
Jones, Toby 132
Jones, Tom 122
Jordá, Octavio 151
Julius, Emmanuel 60
Jump, Jimmy 183
Kahle, Hans 122
Katsaronas, Panayiotis 48
Katz, Otto 101, 102
Kenton, Lou 186
Kerrigan, Peter 148
Killoran, John 186
Kinder Scout 15-16, 30-32, 187
Kipling, Rudyard 79
Kirkpatrick, David 187
Kisch, Richard 57-59
Klugmann, James 140
Kobani 204
Koumoullos, Jacovos 48
Kriegel, Frantisek 83-84
Ku Klux Klan 12
La Marseillaise Battalion 24, 62
La Rioja 16, 88-89

Labour Party 15, 17, 59, 60, 61, 96, 98, 99, 101-102, 104, 122, 133, 183, 196
Ladyman, Phyllis 109
Laufer, Eva 59
Lawson, Alan 21
Lazareno, Manolo 130
League of Nations 11, 12, 176
Lee, Laurie 14, 19, 201
Leeson, George 115
Left Book Club 114
Lesser, Sam 16, 21, 61-63, 87, 186
Levine, Walter 25, 30-32
Levitas, Maurice 40
Lewkowicz, Karl 185, 186
Lezama, Raimundo Pérez 141, 143, 144
Lichfield, Alfred 203
Lincoln Battalion 15, 23, 26, 47, 66, 79-81, 119, 121
Lincoln, Abraham 183
Lindsay, Jack 115, 187
Liverpool 98-100, 115, 175, 191, 203
Lloyd Jones, Sydney 34
Lloyd, Will 35
Loach, Ken 18, 104, 176, 177, 178-180, 195
Lomon, David 18, 155, 170, 171
London 15, 23, 24, 28, 33, 37, 47-48, 82, 92, 96, 111-112, 115, 122, 123, 129-131, 132, 133, 135-136, 138, 146, 147-148, 151, 155, 161, 166, 170-171, 172, 181, 184, 186, 194, 195, 200, 203
Longo, Luigi 26, 117, 122
Longstaff, Johnny 17, 84
Lopera 16, 24-25, 61-63
López Raimundo, Gregorio 146, 147
Lopoff, Aaron 81
Lozano Díaz, Cayetana 183
Lucas, Jim 109
Luftwaffe 125-126
Mac-Paps *see* Mackenzie-Papineau Battalion
Macartney, Wilf 24
MacDougall, Ian 43
MacFarquhar, Roderick 138
Mackenzie-Papineau Battalion 23, 79
Macmurray, John 82
Madrid 16, 33, 34, 38, 44, 49, 61-62, 65-66, 67, 82, 83, 102, 118, 127, 130,

144, 150, 162, 168, 172, 177, 193, 198, 199
Madrigueras 24, 25, 46, 65
Mallorca 16, 57, 135, 136, 201
Manchester 30, 127, 128, 185
Mann, Tom 183
Manning, Leah 95-97, 112
Marshall, David 60, 136, 173, 191
Martín-Artajo, Pepe 181
Martin, William 59-60
Martínez Guerricabeitia, José 149
Marx Memorial Library 111, 170-171
Masters, Sam 57, 60
Matthews, Charlie 172
Maura, Antonio 193
Maxton, James 104
McCartan, Eugene 162
McColl, Ewan 44
McCusker, Frank 65, 140
McDade, Alex 44, 170
McGovern, John 106
McGrath, Harry 39
McGregor, Liam 38
McGrotty, Éamon 39
McGuinness, Charlie 38-39
McGuire, Tommy 138
McNair, John 104
Meadows, Mark 186
Menai Williams, Alun 36, 186
Mendel, Harry 31
MI5 139-140, 147-148
MI6 34
MI9 128
Middleton, Robert 139
Midgley, Harry 38
Mola, Emilio 33
Monks, Joe 62
Moon, Jimmy 50-53
Moore, Aileen 96
Moore, Christy 39-40
Moore, Henry 109
Morgan, Morien 35
Morocco 33-34, 101
Morris, Sam 35
Morris, William 107
Mosley, Oswald *see* Blackshirts
Murphy, Pat 35
Murray, Annie 21, 43
Murray, David 106

Mussolini, Benito 11-13, 14, 18, 31, 35, 62, 95, 109, 122, 161, 166, 176, 193, 194, 196, 203
Nalty, Jack 38
Nathan, George 24-25, 61
National Clarion Cycle Club 16
National Union of Seamen 98, 100
Negrín, Juan 48, 129-131, 190-191, 195, 199, 200
New York 47-49, 79, 99
New Zealand 23, 82, 84
Newsome, Arthur 31
Nickson, Esta 97
Nicolaides, Evanthis 49
Nicolaou, Maria 47
Nighy, Bill 132
Nikiphorou, Eleni 47
Nin, Andreu 57, 179
O'Brien, Rebecca 178
O'Daire, Paddy 163
O'Donoghue, Michael 35
O'Duffy, Eoin 15, 34, 161-163
O'Flanagan, Michael 38
O'Neill, Dick 39
O'Riordan, Michael 15, 39-42, 77, 78, 159-162
O'Shannon, Cathal 162
O'Sullivan, Paddy 77
Orchard, Robert 115
Orwell, George 14, 18-19, 104-106, 159, 165-166, 177, 193-195
Ottawa 28
Oxford 27, 112, 132, 192-193
Palestine 28, 173
Palfreeman, Linda 191
Pantazis, Georgis 48
Papaioannou, Ezekias 48
Paris 18, 23, 24, 33, 49, 99, 128, 129, 135, 149-150, 161, 166, 183, 194, 198, 203
Pasionaria *see* Ibárruri, Dolores
Paterson, Bill 132
Patten, Tommy 38
Pattikis, Vasilis 48
Paynter, Will 35-36, 123
Peake, Maxine 89
Peel, Bill 59-60
Peel, Robert 59
Peral Vega, Emilio 114
Pérez Galdós, Benito 198

Perí, Peter 109
Philippou, Paul 15, 28, 47
Philipps, Wogan 121
Pitcairn, Frank *see* Cockburn, Claud
Polanyi, Karl 82
Pollard, Hugh 34
Pollitt, Harry 82, 187
POUM 57-59, 104-106, 159, 165-166, 175-177, 178-179, 190, 192, 195, 196
Prendergast, Jim 25
Preston, Paul 19, 125, 131, 153, 181-182, 189, 190-200
Priestley, J.B. 111
Prieto, Indalecio 190-191
Pritt, D.N. 100
Queipo de Llano, Gonzalo 61
Radosh, Ronald 26, 168
Rajoy, Mariano 197
Ramona *see* Siles García, Ramona
Rathbone, Eleanor 101, 103
Rea, Betty 107-110
Ridruejo, Dionisio 125
Roberts, Florence 95
Roberts, William 95
Robeson, Paul 81
Robinson, James 98, 100
Robson, Spike 98-100
Rocabert, Juan 179
Rojo, Vicente 167
Romero Maura, Joaquín 189
Rothman, Bernard 30-31
Rowe, Cliff 107
Ruedo Ibérico 18, 149-154
Ruskin, Jim 122
Russell, Audrey 96, 112
Russell, Sam 172
Ryan, Frank 36, 66, 122, 162
Saklatvala, Shapurji 24
Saxton, Reginald 53, 112
Scotland 23, 27, 43-44, 139
Scott, Bill 40, 60
Segal, Harry 61
Sexton, Cyril 16, 67-68, 173
Shalloo, Jack 186
Shammah, Victor 4, 184
Shaw, Liz 39
Sheffield 30, 31, 140
Sheller, Alec 57
Siles García, Ramona 18, 60, 135-137, 201

Silverman, Sydney 98
Sinclair-Loutit, Kenneth 59
Sinn Féin 25, 38
Slater, Jim 100
Smillie, Bob 106
Smith, John *see* Huddar, Gopal Mohan
Smith, Mark 186
Socialist Medical Assocation 111
Sotelo, José Calvo 33
Southampton 97, 131, 141-145
Southworth, Herbert 149-154
Soviet Union 17, 36, 71, 98, 101, 107, 117, 139, 161, 165, 182, 196, 203
Spanish Medical Aid Committee 17, 53, 87, 109, 111-112, 127-128
Spender, Stephen 111
Sproston, Walter 106
Stalin, Joseph 161, 179, 186, 196
Steinbeck, John 192
Stevenson, Daniel 43
Stewart, James 106
Strachey, Amabel 111
Strachey, John 111
Stradling, Rob 33
Sugarman, Martin 28
Świerczewski, Karol 26, 61
Swingler, Randall 115
Tapsell, Walter 16, 26, 69-71, 105
Taylor, Jack 35
Tebbutt, Laura 186
Teruel 16, 44, 63, 79, 124, 167, 177
Texidor, Greville 59-60
Thälmann Battalion 24, 57
Thälmann Ernst 183
Theodoulou, Antonis 48
Thomas, Antonis 48
Thomas, Frank 34
Thomas, Hugh 149-152, 192, 193
Thornycroft, Priscilla 108, 109
Tom Mann Centuria 57-59, 60, 135, 136, 201
Tomalin, Miles 36
Townsend, Louise 187-188
Toynbee, Philip 92
Trades Union Congress 99, 101, 122
Transport & General Workers' Union 99
Trevelyan, Julian 109
Tribune 133, 183-184

Trioli, Giorgio 136
Union of Spanish Intellectuals 150
Unity Theatre 17, 114-116
Vasiliou, Nicholas 48
Vaughan, Janet 17, 111-113
Wainman, Alec 129
Wales 23, 33-35, 203
Walsh, James 203
Watters, Thomas 43
Wattis, George 27
Wesker, Arnold 201
West, Rebecca 111
Wild, Sam 21, 32, 121
Wilkinson, Ellen 17, 101-103
Williams, John 35
Willis, Ted 115
Winnick, Wilfred 30-31
Wintringham, Tom 17, 57-60, 60, 66, 82, 132-134, 136
Woolf, Virginia 111
Working Class Movement Library 135, 136
Yates, James 12-13
Youngman, Fran 109
Youth Aid for Spain 122
Zeta-Jones, Catherine 132

Ingram Content Group UK Ltd.
Milton Keynes UK
UKHW050519280423
420892UK00004B/21